CHELF(

AND

ITS NEIGHBOURS

BY

MAVIS AND KEITH PLANT
ASSISTED BY
ROGER J ROYCROFT
&
JULIA SLATER

LOWER WITHINGTON, SNELSON, NETHER ALDERLEY, OLD WITHINGTON AND LITTLE WARFORD

THIS BOOK IS DEDICATED TO ALL MEMBERS OF CHELFORD AND DISTRICT, PAST AND PRESENT.

Published by Mavis & Keith Plant at 22 Chapel Croft, Chelford, Cheshire.
Tel/Fax: - 01625-860074
E-mail: - Wkeith@Plant30.freeserve.co.uk

ISBN   0 9536123 1 7

All rights reserved. No part of this publication may be reproduced, stored in a retrieval system or transmitted, in any form or by any means, electronic, mechanical, photocopying, recording or otherwise without the prior permission of the authors and publishers in writing.

Typesetting and Design by: Mavis Plant

Printed in England by:
MFP Design & Print, Longford Trading Estate, Thomas Street, Stretford, Manchester, M30 0JT

Date of issue – December 2001

Mavis and Keith Plant moved to Chelford thirteen years ago. Mavis was a Pensions Officer before she retired and Keith was Director of a Multi National Engineering Company before retiring. He is now a volunteer guide at Quarry Bank Mill and a duty volunteer at the Alderley Edge Research Centre of the Family History Society of Cheshire.

Julia Slater has lived in the Chelford area all her life and is the daughter of Alan Barber who has been a member of Chelford Parish Council for 50 years, many as Chairman. Julia works as Practice Manager at Chelford Surgery and is also a member of the Parish Council and the Parochial Church Council.

Roger J Roycroft has been one of the village doctors for 39 years. He is a member of Chelford Parish Council, the Parochial Church Council and on the governing bodies of the church. Seven years ago he published Reflections upon the Chelford Railway Disaster of 22nd December 1894. He is also a warden at Chelford Parish Church.

ACKNOWLEDGEMENTS

The authors would like to express their thanks for the assistance given and photographs loaned by various members of the village. Without their help this book would not have been possible.

Certain information contained in this book has been extracted from the records deposited in the Cheshire County Record Office, Duke Street, Chester and is reproduced with the permission of Cheshire County Council. Where applicable, a description of the records, together with their reference is given.

Thanks are also expressed to the John Rylands Library of Manchester University for permission to use information extracted from the Astle Estate documents deposited in the Library archives.

The picture on the front cover of the book has been reproduced from a painting by Frances Crompton, a former resident.

The authors would like to express thanks to the committee of the Family History Society of Cheshire for the use of their facilities at the Society's Research Centre at Alderley Edge.

Reference is made throughout this book where connections and/or further information is available in the authors previous publication 'Chelford - A Cheshire Village'.

Thanks are also due to Anne Ellis for proof reading the draft of this book.

Extracts from all original documents are reproduced with spelling as shown on the original document.

This book is the second in the series and in addition to further information on Chelford, includes selective details relating to the surrounding areas. Special thanks are given to members of Lower Withington, Old Withington, Snelson, Nether Alderley and Little Warford who have provided information for this book.

INTRODUCTION

When we produced our first volume on the history of Chelford some two years ago we little thought of producing a second. Often it is a comfort not to know what future tasks lie before one. However we were approached by so many readers, some to correct our errors or omissions (fortunately few), and many others who simply wanted more – a compliment which we received gracefully.

This then is the outcome of our efforts. Driven and largely undertaken by Keith and Mavis with a very much smaller input from Julia and I who had to admit that the demands of work simply did not grant us the time needed. As a book it has a different feel about it which, in part, is due to it encompassing Withington and other surrounding parishes and again in part that it has more raw data, the fuel of all historical research. To fully understand our history the reader needs to have one book in each hand and either cross-refer or have an excellent memory.

Gifted writers have, over the years, held different views on the value of history. Most recently Henry Ford was widely quoted as observing that *'History is bunk'* (1916) which fits well with his pragmatic, production line, approach to life. Further back one may quote GWF Hegel (1797-1856) who wrote in his Philosophy of History – *'What experience and history teach is this - that people and governments never have learned anything from history, or acted on the principles deduced from it'*. Yet I think the view I like best is that of Dionysius (30-7 BC) who wrote *'History is philosophy from examples'*.

Nostalgia can be a dangerous drug for bending ones perception of what life really was like in years gone by, indeed by today's standards it was often brutal, hard, and painful. Yet as you read these pages we hope you will find that fellowship that welded our predecessors together to face their difficulties on a communal front, and employ the same strategies in organising their entertainment's and looking after the older members of their community. Lessons that today's social groupings seem to have singularly neglected.

Within these covers are to be found the various stages of life that we all pass through. The fashions change; social structures change, but the individuals then as now face the same basic problems – of a journey through life. Take a few minutes to read again, and savour, the lines from Shakespeare, reproduced below, which are as apt now as when they were penned. And as you read them, and the rest of the book, we hope it will help you to define your own personal philosophy drawn from our localised pages of history.

All the world's a stage, and all the men and women merely players: they have their exits and their entrances; and one man in his time plays many parts, his acts being seven ages.
The first the infant, mewling and puking in his nurse's arms.

And then the whining schoolboy, with his satchel, and shining morning face, creeping like a snail unwittingly to school.
And then the lover, sighing like furnace, with a woeful ballad made to his mistress' eyebrow.
Then a soldier, full of strange oaths, and bearded like the pard, jealous in honour, sudden and quick in quarrel, seeking the bubble reputation even in the canon's mouth.
And then the justice, in fair round belly with good capon lin'd, with eyes severe, and beard of formal cut, full of wise saws and modern instances; and so he plays his part.
The sixth age shifts into lean and slipper'd pantaloon, with spectacles on nose and pouch on side, his youthful hose well sav'd a world too wide for his shrunk shank; and his big manly voice, turning again towards childish treble, pipes and whistles in his sound.
Last scene of all, that ends this strange eventful history, is second childishness, and mere oblivion, sans teeth, sans eyes, sans taste, sans everything.

RJR

Life in Chelford – Mid 1990's

Each day begins with the post and the news,
From the G.P.O. and the charming Sues.
On Mondays the farmers all come to town.
David Russell and team, then knock 'em down.

The early bird faithfully starts her day
It's Dolly helping someone, or going to pray
The shops are opening all their doors
The milkman's been and finished his chores.

Eileen and Paul have put out their stock
Anything from a pea to a wok.
Across the road   groceries galore
With wines and spirits   who'd want more?

If you want a grotto full of surprise
Then just look in at Farm Supplies.
At the butchers there's quality with a smile
Near by your hair is cut with style.

Should you choose to wine and dine
The Dixons or Egerton will suit you fine.
There's Irlams for transport, a Builders yard,
A railway station   but no clerk or guard.

The doctor's surgery in Elmstead Road
Offers services which are varied and broad.
Reception, nurse and doctors have but one goal.
To help with your problems whenever you call.

The roundabout garage fill up or wash down
Next door a car service without going to town
Perhaps you'd prefer to please an old flame
By having your portrait put into a frame.

Near by at the Post Office pensions are drawn,
And they offer you turkey   yes off the bone!!
Amongst our community a good happy band
Caring for cattle and tilling the land.

It's not all just work, there's time for pleasure
The Village Hall caters for everyone's leisure
Scouts, Guides and Play Group, jumble and wares,
Badminton, bridge and antique fairs.

W.I., Thursday Club, discussion and tales,
A new weekend pleasure   car boot sales.
The village school always achieves many a first.
Crime is controlled by Mick Swindlehurst.

We have drama and fun with Chelford Players
A church to attend for your hymns and prayers.
A Vicar who leads all through pleasure and strife.
Good people of Chelford   "This Is Your Life".

R Link

CONTENTS

	Page No.
Origins of Lower Withington, Old Withington and Snelson	3
Memories:	
Chelford by Richard Boddington (former resident of Mere Court)	11
Lower Withington by Mabel Sheppard	14
Amy Dorothy Worthington	15
Eleanor Dingle/Barber by Desmond Ford	16
Street/Ward Family by Silvia Baguette	19
Chelford by Beryl Callwood and Jean Pearce	32
Chelford Girl Guides	40
Chelford Boy Scouts	51
Dixon Arms Bowling Club	65
Chelford School Children 1923, 1926 & 1963 (Pictures)	73
School that made its own history – Chelford School	76
Church Banner 1991 (Picture)	78
Chelford Parish Church Sunday School Party 1974	79
Chelford Village Queen 1991 (Picture)	80
Garden Party – Astle Cottage 1950's (Pictures)	81
Lower Withington School History	84
Lower Withington School Log Book 1878 to 1883	86
Lower Withington School Children 1921 (Picture)	104
St Peter's Church - Lower Withington	105
Early Methodism in Lower Withington	111
Band of Hope – 1883 - Lower Withington	120
Early Methodism in Over Peover and Snelson	124
Lower Withington Walkers 1969	139
Lower Withington Children (Picture)	140

Lower Withington Women's Institute – Winning entry of Produce Competition 1970	141
Arthur Burgess	142
Lower Withington Rose Queen Festival	143
Slater Family 1916 (Picture)	152
Black Swan – Lower Withington 1980 (Picture)	153
Norfolk Farm (Picture)	154
Lapwing Cottage (Picture)	154
Trap Street, Lower Withington 1918 (Picture)	155
Holmes Chapel & Lower Withington 'worthies' visiting Northwich 1902 (Picture)	155
Holly Tree Farm – Lower Withington (Picture)	156
Daisy Bank Farm – Lower Withington (Picture)	157
Frances Eliza Crompton 1866 – 1952	159
Chelford Ministers/Local Preachers 1648 to 1678	169
Oath of Allegiance 1723 Chelford, Lower Withington, Old Withington And Snelson	174
Astle Estate 1784	176
Chelford & District – Early 18th Century	180
Station Road – Chelford 1920 (Picture)	192
Larchwood – Pepper St., Snelson 1921 (Picture)	193
Chelford Corner Shop and Post Office (Picture)	194
Old Vicarage Chelford (Picture)	195
Jessie Slaters Cottage – Chelford (Picture)	196
Astle Hall (Picture)	196
Excerpts from the Wilmslow and Alderley Advertiser 1874/5 & 1890	197
Cricket – Over Peover v Chelford 1955	204
Chelford Evacuees	206

The Diamond Jubilee of Queen Victoria 1897	214
Over 60's party at Chelford 1971 (Picture)	218
Chelford Seniors Football Team c 1895 (Picture)	219
Chelford Fellowship dines at the Angel 1971	220
Mother and Toddlers at Chelford 1976	221
Christmas 1973 – Chelford Dance	222
Christmas Fair – Chelford (Picture)	223
Confirmation at Chelford 1975 (Picture)	224
Garden Party – Chelford 1970	225
New Year's Eve 1973 – Chelford Dance	227
Open Day at Chelford School 1975 (Picture)	228
Santa at Chelford 1979 (Picture)	229
Santa at Chelford 1975 (Picture)	230
Chelford Sunday School (Picture)	231
Women Bowling at Dixon Arms (Picture)	232
Commercial Directories	233
Fallows Hall – Nether Alderley	240
Monks Heath	249
Sketch Map – Nether Alderley (drawn by Audrey Walsh)	258
Soss Moss Hall – Nether Alderley	260
Little Warford	267
Peck Mill Farm – Little Warford	277
Fir Tree Farm – Little Warford	286
Register of Gamekeepers 1711-1868	289
Tithe Award – Lower Withington and Snelson	291
Tithe Award – Chelford	319
Soldiers who died in The Great War – Chelford, Snelson Lower Withington and Old Withington	324

Population Study	331
The Mysterious Tunnel	341
Further Reading	343
Dovecote – Withington Hall (Picture)	348

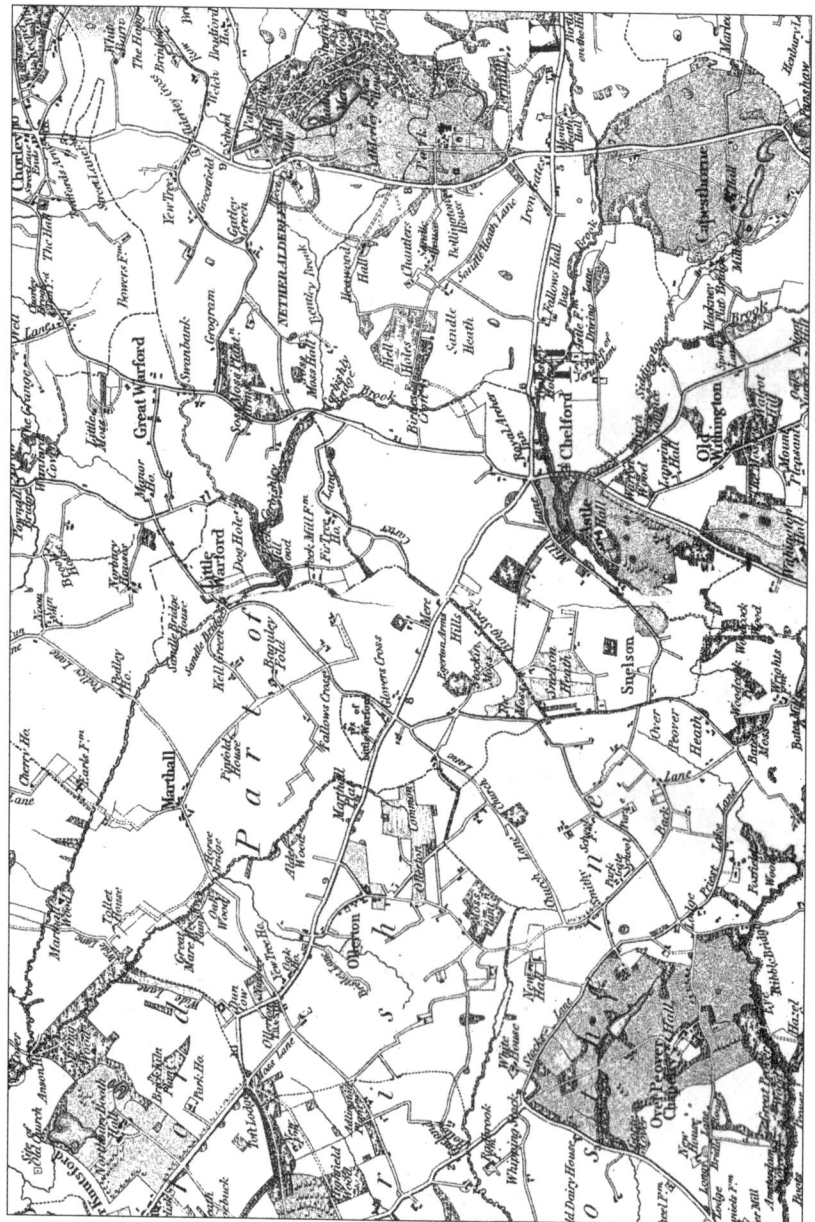

Extract from Bryants 1831 Map of Cheshire – Cheshire County Record Office

CHELFORD AS SHOWN ON 1909 OS MAP

ORIGINS OF LOWER WITHINGTON, OLD WITHINGTON AND SNELSON

It has been established in the previous publication, 'Chelford – A Cheshire Village' that, at the time of the Norman Conquest in 1066, Chelford was inhabited by Anglo Saxons, the name of Chelford being derived from the Old English person, Ceola, or Ceolla and ford.

Even though there is no specific evidence of Anglo Saxon activity in Withington or Snelson it is probable that people of Scandinavian or North German (Danish Viking) origin were active in these areas. Dr Ormerod, in his History of Cheshire states: -

> "In this township (Lower Withington) is a singular hill called Tunsted which, precisely resembles in form an enormous tumulus, and is the first commencement of the natural undulations of surface which distinguish Macclesfield hundred, and gradually increase in size and number of hills ranged along the Staffordshire frontier. If the obvious etymology (original site) and Tunsted may be trusted, it would seem probable that before the Saxon period the houses of a village of some importance had been grouped upon its summit."

The name Tunsted occurs in early deeds and charters of the 12th and 13th centuries as 'a croft called Tuncroft', 'the ditch of an old curtilage [v.tun,croft]' which could suggest an old habitation site.

It is therefore probable that Tunsted is now known as Broad Hill, which can be identified as in the same area near Welltrough – see later.

Lower Withington is not specifically named in The Domesday Survey of 1086. However, it is now widely accepted that the reference to 'Hungrewenitune' in the Survey is in fact Lower Withington. The prefix 'Hungre' probably refers to wasteland and the remaining, 'wenitune', to either the Old English person, Wine and ingtun, or an outlying farm or village settlement.

The settlement is described as Widington in 1186 and alternatively the name could have derived from the Old English Withing, meaning willow, with the name meaning atun (settlements) among willows.

The entry for HUNGREWENITUNE in The Domesday Survey is as follows: -

> *The earl himself holds 'Hungrewenitune' Godwine held it.*

There is half a hide[1] paying geld. It was and is waste.

According to the Survey, Godwine also held: -

Eddisbury	Lea(near Aldford)
Mollington	Shavington (jointly with Dot)
Byley (jointly with Godric	Nether Alderley
Amketil)	Congleton
Kinderton	Davenport
Blakenhall	Croxton

A total of 12 manors were in 1086 held by Godwine, though it must be said that this represented different men with the same name. The records for Mollington, Shavington, Byley, Nether Alderley, Kinderton, Blakenhall and Croxton refer to Godwine as a freeman, the others do not. Therefore it is probable that there were three people named Godwine, one holding the manors of Mollington, Shavington, Byley, Nether Alderley, Kinderton, Blakenhall and Croxton, one holding Eddisbury and Lea and a third holding Lower Withington (Hungrewenitine) and also holding Congleton and Davenport.

In Anglo Saxon times the term Freeman or Free Peasant described a tenant who held his land from the Lord at the fixed rate as opposed to a villein who had to give labour and produce for his holding. His position in the village community varied throughout the country. It was possible for a poor freeman to be employed by a villein.

At the time of the Domesday Survey the levels of the working society were as follows: =

Radman	=	Upper Peasant
Frenchman	=	Upper Peasant
Villein	=	Larger Peasant
Border	=	Smaller Peasant
Oxman	=	Lower Peasant

Early in the 13th Century the village of Lower Withington was exchanged by Randle Blundiville, Earl of Chester with Robert, son of Saleman, for land which the latter held in Normandy. The township with its appurtenances and liberties was given by Randle, together with rent from the mills of Macclesfield and the land held by his

---

1   One hide equates to approximately 120 acres.

father or grandfather in Golgisley or Lindsey. In return Robert passed over all the land his father held in Normandy.

In the latter part of that century Robert Saleman granted to Roger de Davenport, son of Vivian de Davenport, in free marriage with Mary, his daughter, a part of Withington together with 'the services, reliefs and ward of John de Withington and Richard, son of Lawrence, and Roger de Toft'. Included in the settlement was a part of Tunsted and all the wood of Hewode, with aviaries of hawkes, bees, etc.

Thus began the connection with the Davenport family, a branch of the Davenports seating themselves at Welltrough Hall early in the 14th century, the Hall remaining in the family until the end of the 17th century when it passed into the possession of the Hollinsheads of Macclesfield.

Wheltrough Hall is sometimes referred to in ancient documents as Tunsted. Certainly it was in the same area, being positioned, according to the records, on the northern side of Tunsted Hill; the site of the original Anglo Saxon village.

Old Withington is not mentioned in The Domesday Survey and appears to have been included in the villages of Chelford and Lower Withington from very early times. What is known is that at an early period it formed part of the estates of the Ardernes of Aldford, to whom it had probably been granted by the Earls of Chester and under whom it was held by the Camvilles of Clifton Camville, i.e., Stafford. In the 13th century Walkelyn de Arderne granted to Robert de Camville 'a release of all homeages or rents due to him in Old Withington in recompense for the great services he had rendered him in the wars of Gascony'. This Robert gave one half of the manor to Oliver Fitton and the other half, around the year 1266, to John de Baskervyle.

The Baskervyle family have long been associated with Old Withington, living in Old Withington Hall, an ancient mansion completely rebuilt by John Glegg in 1819.

The name **Snelson** possibly derives from the Old English personal name of Snell and tun (Anglo Saxon settlement) i.e. Snells settlement.

Snelson was referred to in the Domesday Survey when it was part of the possession of Ranulph the ancestor of the Mainwaring family, as follows: -

> The same Ranulph holds Senelestune. Leofnoth [or Leofrath] held it. There is one virgate of land rateable to the gelt tax. The land is half a carvcate. It was, and is, waste.

There appear to be 18 manors previously held by Leofrath, in twelve of which he is shown as a Freeman, and six, including Snelson, without reference to his position as a Freeman. It is therefore possible that there were two Leofraths, the one holding Snelson also holding Meols, (two manors), Over Leigh, Handbridge and Bartington.

Sometime between 1209 and 1229 Snelson and the adjacent lands were granted by Ralph de Mainwaring to Henry de Aldithelegh in free marriage with Bertrea, his daughter.

Little is known, however, of the history of Snelson in succeeding years. A family by the name of Snelson, possibly descended from the original settler, subsequently held a large portion of the lands of Snelson. An Adam de Snelestun is mentioned in documents early in the reign of Edward the First (1239-1307) and in 1270-4 William, Lord of Snelleston, was in dispute with the abbot of St Werburgh relative to lands in Chelford.

In 1369, Alice, the widow of William son of William de Snelleston, was involved in an action against John, son of William de Snelleston, and the name occurs regularly in early records.

It is not known where the original settlement was. However, it is reasonable to argue that the original site may have been in the area of Snelson's Farm (called Snells Farm in some documents) on the south side of Chelford Heath and not far from Ceolla's site of Chelford.

So what was it like in the Chelford area before the Norman invasion? There is no doubt that a number of settlements were already established in the 9th century, with the descendants of Ceola's settlement in the area at present covered by the lake in Astle Park (See Chelford – A Cheshire Village) with other settlements in Lower Withington, near Welltrough (Tunsted) and Snelson occupied by descendants of Wine and Snell respectively.

At the beginning of the 9th century Cheshire enjoyed a period of peace where, after a period of bitter fighting, the Anglo Saxon families settled down to farm. However, that all changed in 833 AD when the Norwegian Vikings landed on Deeside, making an alliance with the Welsh to attack Cheshire territory. King Egbert was predictably infuriated with the Norwegian invaders of his territory and their Welsh associates. He consequently brought a great force of warriors from Wessex and cleared the Norwegian Vikings and the Welsh from Cheshire, the Welsh returning to North Wales and the Norwegian Vikings moving on, and settling, in Ireland.

Whilst the Norwegian Vikings were settling in Ireland, the Danish Vikings were raiding eastern England (Angle-Land), eventually reaching Cheshire, where they settled in East and Mid Cheshire, including the area around Chelford. However, constant skirmishes were still taking place between the Norwegian Vikings and the Danish Vikings and, for a spell later in the century, North and Mid Cheshire including Croxton, Holmes Chapel, Hulme Walfield? Toft, Rostherne, Kettleshulme, and presumably the Chelford area, were ruled from Danish York.

Throughout the 10th century the eastern areas of Cheshire became gradually more settled and, if it is possible to state when the mainly Anglo-Saxon but also the Anglo-Danish, people of Cheshire started to think of themselves as Danish English, it was during this time. This same basic stock formed the backbone of the Mid/East Cheshire population for the next nine hundred years. An examination of the Cheshire dialect in the eighteenth century confirms that the majority of the population continued to use the root language of their Anglo-Saxon and Viking ancestors.

During the early part of the 11th century King Canute becomes involved in Cheshire's history. Canute was the younger son of a Danish warlord, Swein Forkbeard, who, at eighteen years of age proclaimed himself King on the death of his father. However, there was an immediate reaction from other warlords and Canute was forced to flee to Denmark where his elder brother was the king.

It wasn't until 1015 that Canute returned, landing on the South Coast before building up a force of fighting men and forcing Edmund, King Ethelred's son, to retreat northwards through Cheshire into South Yorkshire. Canute followed him with a fast-moving strike force, intent on taking York, leaving many slower moving bands encamped in Cheshire and Staffordshire. It was during this march that Canute passed through what is now Knutsford, the town being named after him. If in fact Canute travelled north through Staffordshire to Knutsford it is possible that he passed through the Chelford area and the number of small Danish settlements that had become established in the area.

Eventually, following a number of battles in various parts of the country, Canute the Dane became King in 1017. His reign saw many changes relative to the administration of Cheshire. Canute died in 1026 being succeeded by one of his sons, King Harold Harefoot who died in 1040. Harold Harefoot was succeeded by his despotic half brother, Harthacnut. A period of bitter fighting amongst the warlords then followed and when King Edward died childless in 1066, Earl Harold, seized the throne of England, much to anguish of William, Duke of Normandy, who had earlier been promised the Kingdom. Later that year the battle of Hastings took place and William became King.

During the early period of his reign William had many problems with Cheshire. Swein of Denmark, who also claimed the English throne, landed in England in 1069 in a belated attempt to take the crown. His Vikings massacred five hundred Norman Knights at Durham, captured York and burnt the Minster down. Ever the opportunists, this landing acted as a signal for Cheshire men to join forces with the Welsh and attack Shrewsbury and Hereford.

When he heard the news, the new King swore death to those who had crossed him. He bribed the Danes to leave England before marching into Cheshire. Any resistance was put down by William's army with unparalleled ferocity, all the land and every settlement, devastated by the torch and the sword, until the countryside was said to resemble a field in winter.

According to the Domesday Survey taken some seventeen years later, the area around Chelford was described as waste and must have been subject to the ravages of William's army. As a result weeds grew out of the ruins and fields became wildernesses. Famine followed the sword and the fire of King William right across the Cheshire Plain. The displaced poor begged for bread at any door they could, including church or monastery, and it was recorded that many died as they begged.

It must have taken many years for this area to recover, and it was well into the 12th century before the people returned in sufficient numbers to repair the damage caused by William the First and his army.

At the time of the Domesday Survey (1086), the size of both Chelford and Lower Withington was 60 acres and Snelson 40 acres, based on the amount of land subject to payment of geld. This would equate to about 6 households for Chelford and 4 for Snelson. If it were assumed that there would be four people per household, the population of Chelford and Lower Withington would each be in the region of 24 and Snelson 16 to 20.

The settlements would have been wattle and daub timber framed single storey buildings with the family habitating one end and the domestic animals, the other. There would have been no chimney, the smoke from the fire finding its own way out through a thatched roof.

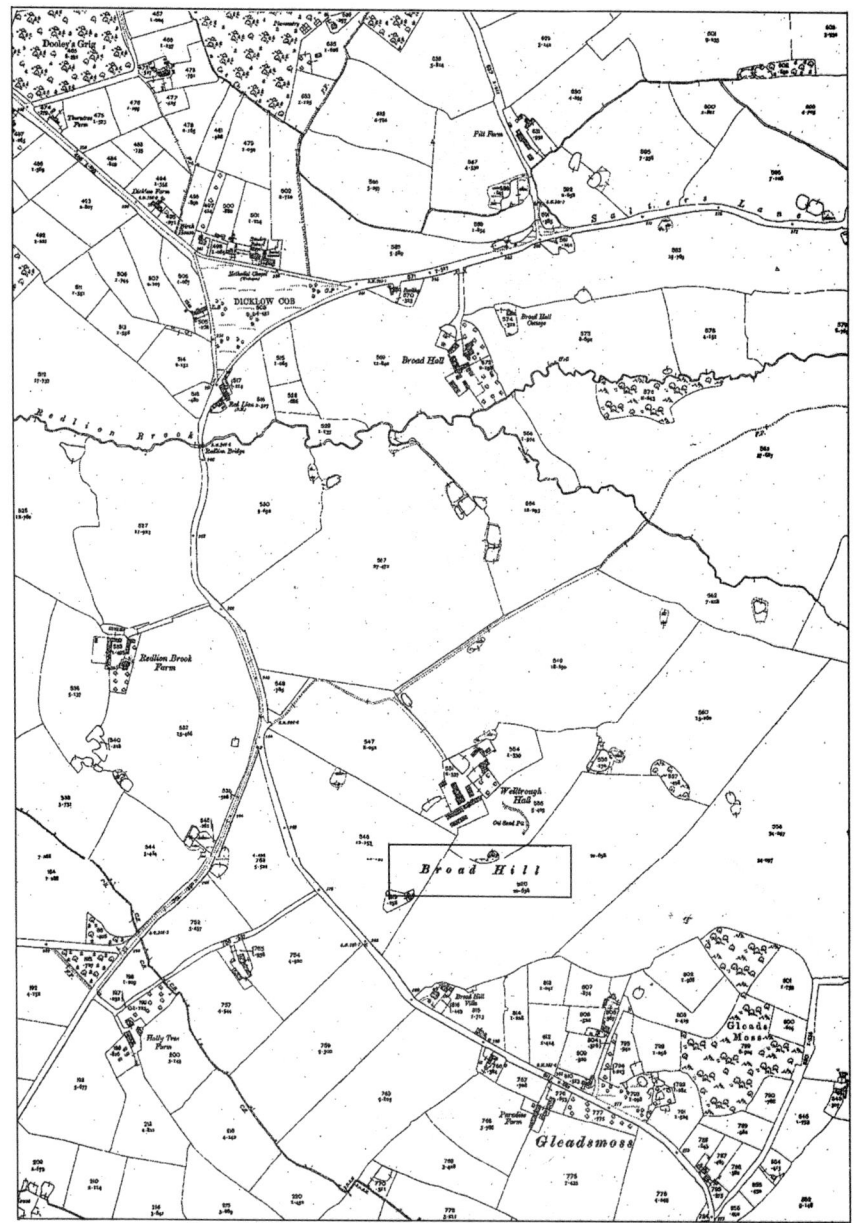

Broad Hill – Lower Withington – 1909 OS Map
Possible site of original Anglo Saxon Village

1909 ORDNANCE MAP

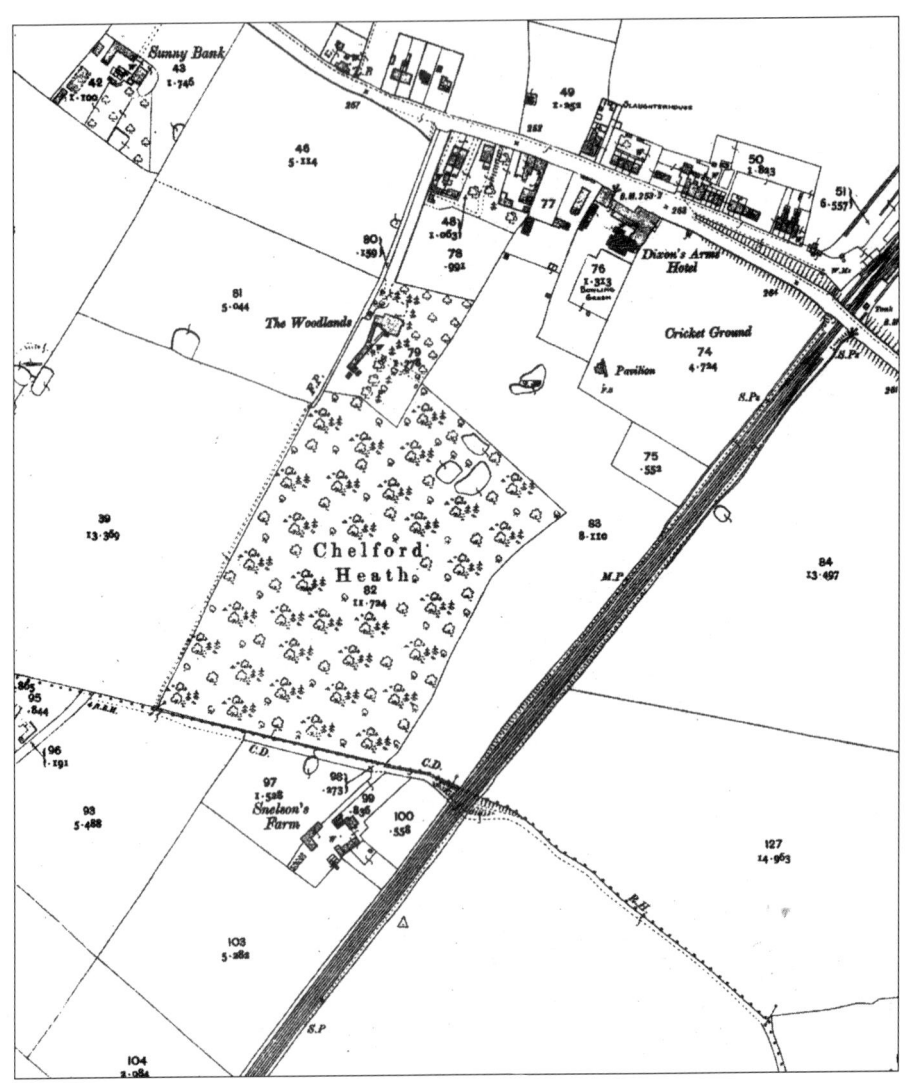

Snelson Farm, possible site of Snells Anglo Saxon Settlement

MEMORIES OF CHELFORD
By Richard Boddington (formerly resident at Mere Court)

Authors note: *The Boddington family lived at Mere Court from 1928 to 1953 – for further information see Chelford – A Cheshire Village, published in 1999.*

MERE COURT

I well remember in September 1939, Jack Burgess (brother of George, Frank and Harry) coming to brand Aviator (my brother's horse) with the War Office arrow and numerous 'Chargers' being loaded at Chelford station for service with the Cheshire Yeomanry – most ended up in Palestine via Crewe, Worksop and Marseilles. The horses had labels attached to all the collars giving notes as to the merits etc., of each horse and considerations as to which trooper or officer might have him/her as their charger.

This memory, together with lying in bed at Mere Court listening to the sound of the hounds kennelled overnight at the 'Dixon', symbolise to me the end of an age at Chelford – I am not defending what society was like in the twenties, and doubtless others can remember the poverty and drudgery of service as farm labourers, domestics, small self employed (Thomason, Knowles, Drew, Burgess, Blackhurst etc.). The village, even in 1946, was nevertheless very different from what it was in 1939, as in most other places.

I suppose the loading of cavalry horses at Chelford station (together with a few other contemporaneous like situations) was the last time such happenings were ever to take place and merits some interest as an event and as a historically significant occasion.

L to R: - Richard's elder brother on Aviator, Younger sister on Flash, Elder sister on Monkey and Myself (Richard) on Rag & Bones.

Taken 1938 on the drive at Mere Court.

**Philip Boddington (Richard's father)
1953**

MEMORIES OF LOWER WITHINGTON

The following information has been submitted by Mabel Sheppard.

Jessie Dale, my great aunt and sister of Minnie Dale from Astle Farm, married Charles Dakin. They lived at the "Home Farm" at Lower Withington and had 8 children, 4 girls and 4 boys, in that order. The youngest son, Jimmy, had the well known Traction Engine.

In 1931 or 32 Uncle Charlie's cows succumbed to the dreaded foot and mouth disease and the complete herd of 26 cows had to be destroyed.

The cows were buried in the field below Lower Withington Hall, opposite the drive to the Home Farm.

Where each cow was buried Uncle Charlie planted a sycamore tree. As you pass along that stretch of the Holmes Chapel Road on the left you can see the 26 mature sycamore trees.

Poor Uncle Charlie, he never really recovered from this loss – no compensation in those days.

The Sycamore trees as they are now

AMY DOROTHY WORTHINGTON

Dolly, as she was known, was a feature around Chelford for many years, and is still remembered with affection by many of the present villagers.

She arrived in the village as Dolly Clay from Frankton, Shropshire in 1922 at the age of 15 to work for the Dixon family at Astle Hall. It was whilst in service at the Hall that she met her husband to be, Charles Worthington.

Following their marriage they lived in Station Road, Chelford where their daughter, Nesta, who sadly predeceased Dolly, was born.

Dolly had a huge character and capacity for helping others. There was never an event raised in the village that Dolly was not involved in. She was a tireless worker both before, during and well after the event.

Her life included a considerable amount of work for St. John's Church, Chelford and she was actively engaged in many other local causes and organisations.

She arranged sponsored events, raising thousands of pounds for just causes. In fact she participated, even into her eighties, in these events.

In 1992 she was presented with the Maundy money by the Queen at Chester Cathedral. An honour she was particularly proud of.

Dolly died in hospital on 9 November 1998, aged 91, and following a service at St. John's Church, Chelford, officiated by the Rev. John Ellis, committal followed at Macclesfield Crematorium.

Her capacity to enjoy life and at the same time put something back into the village was quite unique. The village is a poorer place without her.

MEMORIES OF ELEANOR DINGLE/BARBER

The information below has been submitted by Desmond Ford from details compiled by Keith Ford in 1980.

Eleanor Dingle was born in Siddington in 1832 and married a Hugh Barber, also of Siddington, some time around 1854.

I am not sure where they lived when they first married but do know that in later years they lived at a place named 'Harbour', a part of Siddington that at one time had been a brick yard. The foreman at the yard was nicknamed Windy.

Eleanor and Hugh lived at Windy Harbour next to the brickyard in a little farm comprising 3 or 4 fields, the farm being part of the Capesthorne Estate of the Bromley Davenport family. I know that Eleanor was born of farming stock and Hugh, I am almost certain, was also of a farming background. His downfall was drink and I will come to that later on.

A total of eleven children were born to Eleanor and Hugh, Annie, Dora, Fred, Jane, Hugh, Arthur, Reg., John, Thomas, Robert and Emma.

As mentioned before, Hugh Barber liked to have a drink and was a frequent visitor to the local pub called the Trap (now known as the Black Swan, Lower Withington). There was a footpath to the Trap from the Harbour across the fields, the regular route for Hugh to take. One night Eleanor was at home and Hugh had gone for a drink. As time went by, she kept looking at the grandfather clock and thinking, "Now I wonder where is my husband?" Some of the children may have been downstairs with her. After a while she decided to go out and look for him walking along his normal path. Eventually she came to a bridge over a little stream and, with the aid of an old lantern, she noticed a shape by the side of the stream. The shape was that of her husband, Hugh, and he was dead. On his way back from the pub he must, due to his drunken state, have fallen off the bridge into the ditch and drowned.

WKP note   *The death certificate for Hugh Barber dated 7 January 1881 shows Hugh's age as 54, his occupation as Market Gardener and the cause of death as 'Found drowned in a ditch in Lower Withington.*

Eleanor would have been about 48 at the time with some of her children still at home plus a grandson, Walter Barber, born 1876, illegitimate. Hugh was buried in Siddington churchyard.

Without a husband Eleanor was soon in financial difficulties and sought help from an old lady who lived at the back of the Harbour. This lady helped Eleanor out financially and she started a little business-selling hens, ducks, chickens and geese using the money given by the old lady to purchase a pony and trap.

Using this pony and trap she travelled to the markets at Macclesfield and Altrincham. On occasion she would take the pony and trap to Chelford station and then transport her produce by train to Stockport for sale at the Stockport markets.

Walter Barber, the grandson, was the illegitimate son of Eleanor's daughter, Jane, who was born in 1856. Jane went to Siddington School leaving school when she was 13 years of age and working as a domestic servant at the Dairy House, Capesthorne, the head of the Dairy House being a Mary Waltley. The Dairy House was situated where the Capesthorne Estate Office now stands. Eventually Jane became a pastry cook at Capesthorne Hall but in 1875 found herself pregnant and moved to the Stockdove Hotel at Romiley near Stockport working as a barmaid until Walter was born. Jane never divulged the name of the father but, soon after the birth, Jane was given enough money to buy Tithe Barn, Siddington. In 1881 Jane married a Joseph Barber, had a further nine children and died in 1932.

Walter Barber married my grandmother's sister, Annie Walley in 1898 at Siddington Church and they lived in a cottage near Hodgill Farm, Siddington. They had seven children and in 1913 moved to Watford near London. Walter died in 1937.

WKP note   The 1881 Census shows the following information relative to Eleanor Barber.

NAME	RELATIONSHIP	CONDITION	AGE	OCCUPATION	BORN
Eleanor Barber	Head	Widow	48	Market Gardener of 6 acres	Siddington
Jane Barber	Dau	U	25	General Servant Domestic	Siddington
Hugh Barber	Son	U	21	Agricultural labourer	Siddington
Annie Barber	Dau	U	17	General Servant Domestic	Siddington
Dora K Barber	Dau	U	15	General Servant Domestic	Siddington
Frederick Barber	Son		11	Scholar	Siddington
John R Barber	Son		5	Scholar	Siddington
Walter Barber	Grandson		5	Scholar	Siddington

From the above we can establish that Eleanor had taken over her husband's Market Garden business. Also Walter is shown as being born at Siddington, whereas according to Keith Ford he had been born at Romiley.

Thanks are due to Desmond Ford for the above article, the original containing considerably more information relative to later members of the family.

MEMORIES OF THE STREET/WARD FAMILY OF CHELFORD

By Sylvia Baguette, great grand daughter of William Street (Ward) and Emma Dunn.

Phoebe Street was baptised in Goostrey on 3 April 1836. Her parents were Thomas and Phoebe Street, Thomas being a bricksetter. **Phoebe Street** had an illegitimate son she called William on 16 November 1854. On June 22 1856 she married Peter Ward. All his life William Street was known as Ward. Phoebe told him Peter Ward was his true father and he was proud of the name. He called his first son Peter and all the family used the surname Ward. William Street became a postman at Chelford and was known as 'Billy Ward the postman' for the next 40 years. His eldest son, Peter, always signed his name 'Ward' and it came as a shock to his fiancée, Annie Murphy, when he told her shortly before the wedding in 1911, that she would be called Street. She told her daughter years later, "I didn't want to be Mrs Street, Mrs Ward sounded much better."

When Frederick Street died in 1973 his brother, William Henry, had Ward put on the gravestone as well as Street. The two brothers, sons of William Street, had never married and still lived in the house where they were born at Church Cottages[1], Chelford. It was William Henry who found the body of William Reeves in the yard at Knowsley Farm when he was murdered in 1914[2]. He had followed in his father's footsteps and become a postman. He also died in 1973. Recently family members had his name put on the gravestone and made sure it said Street and Ward.

My grandfather, Peter Street, worked for the Venables family at Piggott Hills Farm (always pronounced Pickertills) until his marriage at 32 years of age. He spoke fondly of his time there. He worked with the horses and used to describe how he plaited and dressed the manes and tails for shows. He also painted signs on carts etc. He had the loveliest handwriting in daily life, which is a tribute to the teaching at Chelford school.

He used to tell my mother stories of his life on the farm and the seasonal work. The workers slept up in the attics (house or stable?) and in the winter it got so cold that the chamber pots under the beds froze over.

He was a God fearing man and tried to go to church as often as he could. Sometimes work at the farm prevented this, and that is why my grandmother had met all the rest of the Street/Ward family but not Peter until the commemoration

---

[1] Church Cottages were not numbered until the 1960's. Frances Street followed by Geoff Street lived at 5 Church Cottages. Cottages 6 + 7 (the ones adjacent to the church) were originally called Curfew Cottages.

[2] Chelford A Cheshire Village p 296.

service for King Edward VII in 1911. On that day everyone was given time off to go to the service[3].

The day before my grandfather married, Mr John Venables gave him 2 copies of a reference, which we still have. The family gave him photos and some large framed ones of John and his sisters, Lucy and Jessie. We still have the small ones but the larger ones went astray in a removal. Mr Venables and his son, John, wrote to my father with news and always welcomed him when he visited. When John was killed in the First World War grandfather was very upset and he said it broke Mr Venables heart. Amongst my grandfather's papers I found an obituary for Mr Venables cut from the local paper.

Peter Street played the violin, (we still have it), and I often wonder who taught him. It is only an ordinary violin but it said on it Stradivarius (they were copies) and during the First World War he scratched the name out to be patriotic. He went to work on the railway at London Road Station, Manchester after his marriage and was deafened in a shunting accident at work but, he could still play by the vibration of the violin. He loved singing and, luckily, we recorded him singing 6 months before he died at the age of 82 in 1960. He sang a semi-religious song 'The Flowers in The Garden' and a secular one, 'The Woman You Should Marry'. Not bad for a man who had been deaf for nearly 50 years.

When Peter went for his medical in the First World War and said he was deaf, the doctors said that it didn't matter because everyone was deaf after 2 weeks. Then they saw his foot with 3 toes missing and dismissed him "he could never march 20 miles a day on those". (Account of his farm accident in Chelford – A Cheshire Village, page 285.) So Peter went back to the railway and worked with horses.

One family puzzle centres around William Davies. Annie met Peter Street at Chelford because she used to visit the Street/Ward family with her aunt and uncle, William and Hannah Davies. Annie's mother died when she was only 3 years old and her mother's sister brought her up (her father having 4 more young children to raise.) Hannah had been a nanny for a family at Liverpool and then moved to Manchester. How she met her future husband remains a mystery. He first appears when he writes a letter from Gatley Green Farm, Nether Alderley in August 1885 and writes about the harvest. They married on 25th April 1886. It appears they went regularly to Chelford to visit his family and one of his relations was a tenant at Chorley Old Hall. His father had been born at Siddington.

---

[3] Chelford - A Cheshire Village p 284.

THE WARD/STREET FAMILY OF CHELFORD

Peter Ward – bt 14 July 1826- d 24.6.1875
m Phoebe Street[4]

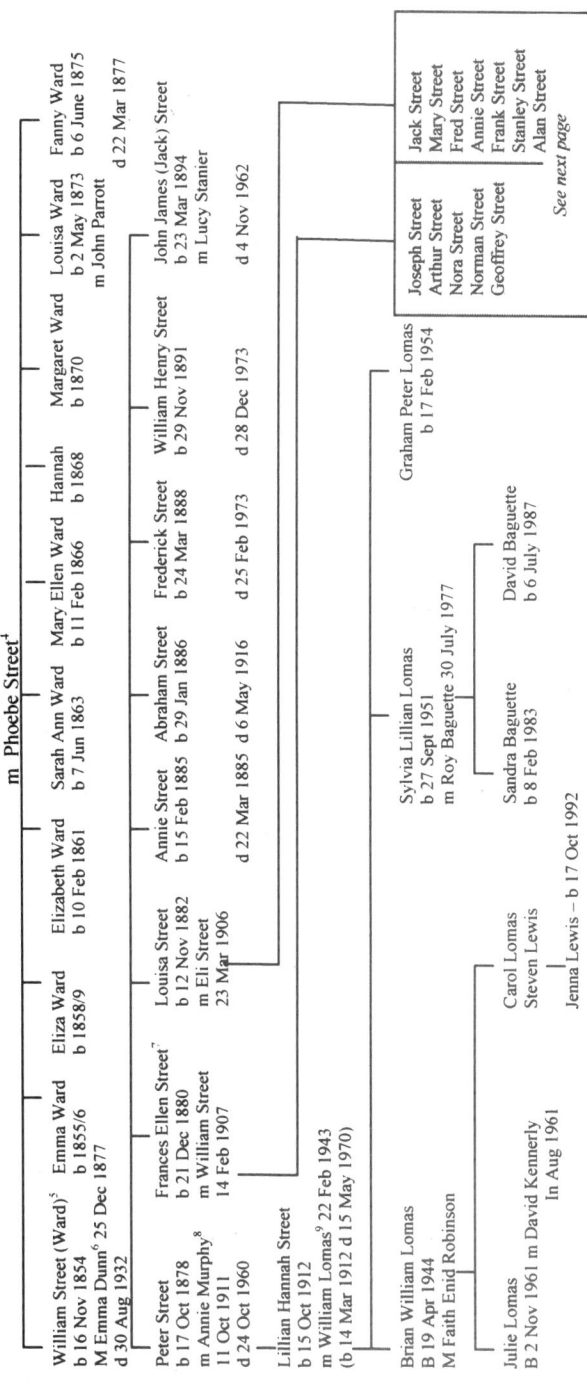

[4] Phoebe Street re-married Samuel Tomlinson – d 10.1.1900.
[5] William Street was illegitimate and took mother's name. Street. and Ward name later.
[6] Emma Dunn b 12 Aug 1855 d 17 July 1919
[7] Known as Cissie
[8] Annie Murphy b 16 June 1892 d 17 Dec 1977.
[9] Wm Lomas b 14 Mar 1912 d 15 May 1970

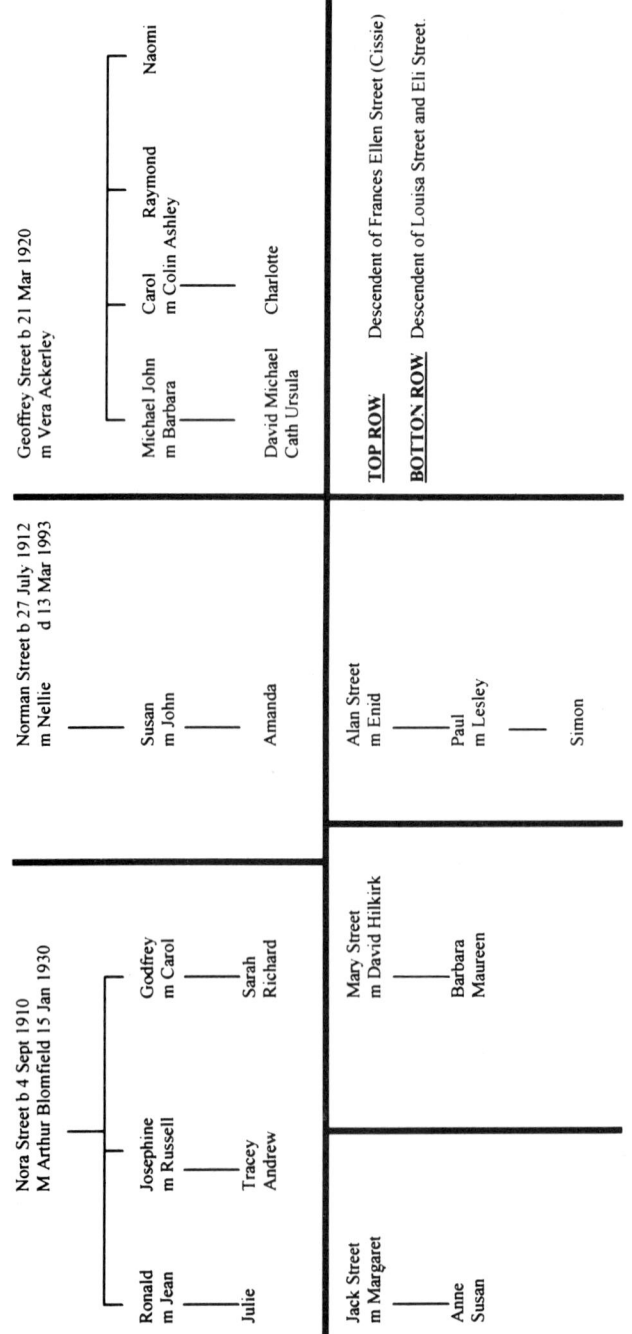

John James Street (always known as Jack), the youngest son of William Street/Ward, was born on 23 March 1894 and died on 4 November 1962. He fought in Salonika in the First World War in the 12th Cheshire Regiment and wrote letters home from Malta where he convalesced from wounds. He was a marvellous storyteller and told my parents many tales of his escapades when he came to stay. One day in the First World War he and other soldiers were on a slope in Salonika and were desperately thirsty. As the day wore on they had to move around the base of a hill in the heat and the dust until they suddenly saw a stream trickling down the hill. The men were overjoyed and drank eagerly until an officer screamed at them to stop. It was then that they discovered that the stream was the discharge from a hospital on the hill! However, Jack said it was the best water he ever tasted.

Uncle Jack always came to stay with us at Christmas when he was a widower. He was my younger brother's godfather. I was only a little girl but I remember one night when we sat round the blazing fire with the lights turned off and Uncle Jack told us about a dark night when he was a young man. He'd stopped a little later in the pub than he'd intended and had a few pints more. Finally he set out to walk home along a narrow lane on that moonless night. He started off quite briskly but gradually became aware of footsteps behind him. He stopped and the footsteps stopped too. He set off again and the footsteps commenced once more. Jack now felt quite scared and he began to do a slow trot down the pitch-black lane. The footsteps did a slow trot behind him. Plucking up courage Jack looked round and saw a great white shape bearing down on him. He cried out in terror and froze to the spot. The great "Mooooo" that came from the cow showed the same level of terror!

Jack married Lucy Stanier in the 1920's. He was a postman at Siddington most of his life and lived in Mill Lane. After having pneumonia the doctor advised retirement. Jack retired as a postman but went to work as a builder/repairer on cottages on the Capesthorne Estate. Finally, when he officially retired, he worked in the Car Park. My elder brother went to stay with him in the early 1950's and remembers the pig in the back garden and the gooseberry bushes. Jack took him down the lane to collect eggs and gave him rudimentary fishing lessons with a stick and a piece of string. No fish caught!

One tragedy in his life was the death of his mother-in-law. She had come to live with them and my mother said she was a lovely old lady. Jack's letter describes what happened. Lucy had gone out to feed the chickens and suddenly her mother came out all ablaze. He dress must have caught on the open fire in the kitchen. Lucy managed to get the flames out but her mother was terribly burned and they said it was a blessing when she died that afternoon.

Uncle Jack loved to sing and used to entertain us at Christmas. We have a recording of him singing two of his favourites; "The Volunteer Organist", and "The Little Shirt my Mother made for Me". My great uncle Jack was a special part of my life as a child."

The Street/Ward family has a special connection with Chelford as postmen.

William Street/Ward died at Church Cottages in 1932, his obituary saying that he had been a postman at Chelford for 41 years. He was always known as "Billy Ward the Postman". He only had one arm and had to walk 18 miles a day to deliver the mail.

William Henry Street, (son of William Street/Ward) was also a postman as was his brother, John James (Jack) Street who delivered the mail in the adjoining village of Siddington.

The Street/Stanier family at the wedding of Jack Street to Lucy Stanier.

Left to Right: Annie Street, Frances Street, Peter Street, Lillian Street, A Stanier, Wm. Street/Ward, Louisa Street, (not known man in cap behind Louisa), Jack Street, (sat), Jack Stanier, not known, Lucy Stanier (sat), Harriet Stanier, Arthur Street, Mrs Stanier, Mary Stanier, Billy Street (Wm. Henry), Bert Stanier and family. Children's names not known.

Peter Street/Ward and Annie Murphy taken on their wedding day 11 Oct 1911

Norman Street, the son of Frances Ellen Street who married a William Street, (gets a bit complicated doesn't it), and was therefore a grandson of William Street/Ward, was also (yes you guessed it) a postman. He lived in Robin Lane before moving to Broken Cross and working at Macclesfield Post Office. He was a postman for 44 years.

So there were 'Street' postmen in Chelford for over 100 years.

The Street Family at the 80th birthday of Peter Street 1958

Back row left to right: - Geoff Street, Jack Street, Jessie Morris, Frances Street and Eli Street
Front row left to right: - Wm Henry Street, Peter Street, Annie Street and Louisa Street.

Peter Street with John Venables at Piggott Hill Farm

Fred and Peter Street c 1910

Peter Street at Piggott Hill Farm c 1905

Taken c 1920 outside Church Cottages – adjacent to Church
Jack Street William Street/Ward William Henry Street
(Postman at Siddington) (Postman at Chelford 41 yrs.) (Postman at Chelford

Abraham Street c 1910
For the strange story of Abraham Street see Chelford – A Cheshire Village p 275.

MEMORIES OF CHELFORD

By Beryl Callwood (nee Taylor) and Jean Pearce (nee Bloor)

Beryl Callwood is the daughter of Harry Taylor who came to Chelford after the First World War, took over the management of the General grocers shop (now Williams) when Mid Cheshire Farmers acquired the adjacent corn mill (previously Bolderstones) and ran the shop until he retired in 1956.

Beryl and her two sisters, Marjorie and Joan, were born at the shop, the family eventually moving to a new house on the opposite side of the road when this new property was built in 1925.

Jean was born in Station Road, the daughter of Wm. Thomas Bloor who lived all his life in Chelford. Wm. Thomas Bloor worked on the railway as a platelayer, moving into Station Road when he married.

We have many happy memories of Chelford, as young girls before the Second World War. The village was then one happy family with everybody joining in the activities; no distractions like television and computers in those days – you had to make your own entertainment.

As girls, we were both in 1st Chelford Brownies and Guides and we remember Mrs Audrey Bythell of the Grange, who was the Captain and Jean Wilson of Sunny Bank, who was the Lieutenant. There were three patrols, Nightingale with Peggy Cash as the leader, Kingfisher with Muriel Barber as the leader and Blue Tit with Mary Gould as the leader.

On Tuesday 25 February 1936, 1st Chelford Guides, Brownies and Scouts put on a production at the Village Hall, the Guides presenting 'Toad of Toad Hall', the Brownies 'The King's Highway' by Freda Collins and 'Camp Fire', a joint presentation by the Guides and Scouts.

Those taking part in the production are shown on the programme.

The presentation of Camp Fire consisted of:

A Camp (song)	by the Guides
Do you ken John Peel (song)	by the Scouts
My mother-in-law (recitation)	by Harry Bloor
Three Pirates (song)	by the Guides
Alay and the Bear	by the Scouts
Oh! No John (song)	by the Guides
Maresfield Road (song)	by the Guides
Limericks'	by Richard Boon
Orleans (song)	by the Guides
Breton Fisher (song)	by the Guides
1½d a foot (recitation)	by Stanley Potts
Oh how lovely (song)	by the Guides
The White Roadway	by the Guides
National Anthem	

1st Chelford Guides production of 'Toad of Toad Hall'

1st Chelford Brownies' production of 'The Kings Highway'

The rehearsals for the show took place at the Grange and also the Guide Hut: the wooden hut as we used to call it, situated adjacent to the Parish Room[10]

Also as Guides we remember in 1936, planting cherry trees in the pouring rain on the slope (as we used to call it), the Station Road side of the bridge of the railway. Ten trees each costing 4½d were planted, one for each selected Guide. Jean's was the second going up the slope and the last one was planted by Eileen Snead who, unfortunately died when she was 16. The funny thing was that the year after she died the tree also died. The trees are still there, a memory of a past long ago.

In my very early days, we used to play in the pathway (which is still there) between the Corn Mill, (now the saddle shop,) and where Dr Roycroft now lives.

---

10 Authors note – This is the same hut now known as the 'old' Scout hut. The Guides claim that they used the hut first and the Scouts followed, after being given permission by the Guides.

COPY OF PROGRAMME – 25 FEBRUARY 1936

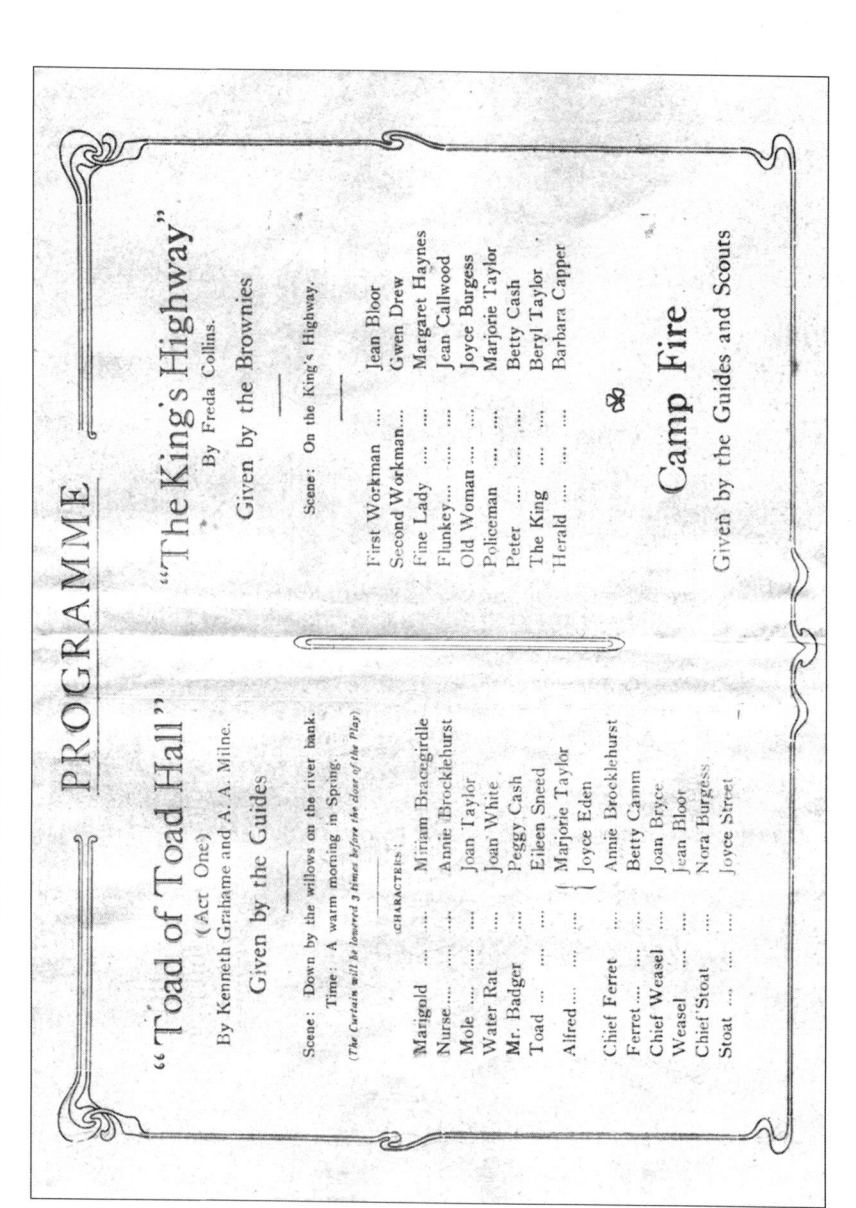

PROGRAMME

"Toad of Toad Hall"
(Act One)
By Kenneth Grahame and A. A. Milne.

Given by the Guides

Scene: Down by the willows on the river bank.
Time: A warm morning in Spring.
(The Curtain will be lowered 3 times before the close of the Play)

CHARACTERS:

Marigold	....	Miriam Bracegirdle
Nurse	....	Annie Brocklehurst
Mole	....	Joan Taylor
Water Rat	....	Joan White
Mr. Badger	....	Peggy Cash
Toad	....	Eileen Sneed
Alfred	....	{ Marjorie Taylor
		{ Joyce Eden
Chief Ferret	....	Annie Brocklehurst
Ferret	....	Betty Camm
Chief Weasel	....	Joan Bryce
Weasel	....	Jean Bloor
Chief Stoat	....	Nora Burgess
Stoat	....	Joyce Street

"The King's Highway"
By Freda Collins.

Given by the Brownies

Scene: On the King's Highway.

First Workman	....	Jean Bloor
Second Workman	....	Gwen Drew
Fine Lady	....	Margaret Haynes
Flunkey	....	Jean Callwood
Old Woman	....	Joyce Burgess
Policeman	....	Marjorie Taylor
Peter	....	Betty Cash
The King	....	Beryl Taylor
Herald	....	Barbara Capper

Camp Fire

Given by the Guides and Scouts

35

Marjorie Taylor c 1924
In pathway, side of Corn Mill

Marjorie Taylor c 1924 –
with dog Flora
Showing storage vats of Corn Mill

The big event, as far as we girls were concerned, was the Village Rose Day, which took place right up to 1934. A few years ago an effort to restart it was tried but somehow it wasn't the same. Maybe our memories were too strong but the later event didn't seem to have the 'magic' of the pre-war event, which involved, in some capacity, the whole of the village. Everybody participating in the procession used to meet at the school (the old school in Alderley Road) where we mounted the various decorated floats. The procession moved down to the village crossroads, then up through the village along Knutsford Road to Jessie Slater's cottage, (now the corner of Dixon Drive) where it turned round and came back through the village, to the crossroads where it turned right, into Astle Lane (now called Peover Lane) to Astle Cottage, the home of Sir John and Lady Dixon. Lady Dixon provided tea and cakes and we all took part in various competitions, maypole dancing and games. Rose Queens that we remember from this period were in 1928 Elsie Baskerville, 1930 Marjorie Dale, 1932 Eva Williamson, 1933 Marjorie Taylor and the last Queen of that era in 1934, Joan Norbury – now Joan Sutcliffe. What memories – we can still 'taste' the excitement that that day created.

Chelford Rose Day 1930 – Marjorie Dale Rose Queen

Rose Day c⁴1933

Left to right:
Gwen Drew, Marjorie Taylor and Beryl Taylor.

Another thing that I can remember of pre-war days was the Christmas Parties given by Lady Dixon for all the children of the village. The parties were held in the Village Hall. We played games followed by tea and on leaving were given a present and an orange.

However it was not all play. We had to help in the house. It was the job of the children to collect water from the pump in Station Road. Two buckets in the morning and two at night. Sunday was worst because we had to make numerous trips in order to fill the boiler so that mother could do the washing on Monday. The pump was at the end of Station Road, near the railway and to the side of the last house. Quite a walk for some of us small girls. I remember the water as lovely drinking water.

From memory, there were two other pumps in the same area, one at the back between Hornby's and the Paper Shop and the other, also at the back, between the butchers and the Bank. The pumps in Station Road were supposed to be for the residents of Station Road only.

The Knowles family were the butchers at that time and they had a van to deliver their produce. Charles, son of Edward? and Maria Knowles, later moved to Merehills Farm.

Charlie Knowles and his van pre-war

We have so many memories of Chelford, which have been the single major influence of our lives. Thank you Chelford.

View from Cheshire Farm shop (now William's shop) down Knutsford Road.

Note – Beech tree on corner of what is now Dixon Drive.

View looking towards Station Bridge,.Dixon Arms on right hand side.

CHELFORD GIRL GUIDES

Chelford Girl Guides was founded in 1929 with the first meeting held on March 9th[1].

The following extracts, written and drawn by the Guides themselves, are taken from the Log Book of the 1st Chelford Guides 1929 – 1933 and have been reproduced by permission of the present Guide Leader, Mrs Christine Sullivan.

14 June 1929 - Knutsford May Day

This May Day will always be remembered because Princess Mary was present. It was held on Friday June 14th. All the schools round about Knutsford were given a holiday to celebrate it. The May Queen was a Knutsford Guide.

It was a terrible day, it rained in bucketsful and thundered and lightened but it was not cold so we did not take much harm although we all got soaked. About six of our Guides went. Captain took us in the car.

The Guides all met at the Headquarters Hut in Knutsford about 2 p.m. and from there we marched to the Heath by Canute Square to join the procession. We followed the men of the British Legion and formed a double Guard of Honour with them in front of the Royal Box. Miss Royden the County Commissioner met Princess Mary at the top of the Guard of Honour and they walked down it into the Royal Box. Princess Mary was not in uniform as it was not a Guide Ceremony. The Guides formed fours and turned right and marched passed with colours. Afterwards we sat on benches in the pouring rain but we had to smile and make the most of it to follow out the Guide Law. We watched the procession and Dancing and crowning of the Queen who presented Princess Mary with a beautiful bouquet.

Evelyn Wright

The Princess in the Sleeping Wood

Acted by the 1st Chelford Girl Guides 13th January 1930

A good many people are very superstitious about number 13 but, seemingly the 1st Chelford Girl Guides are not when they gave their first big entertainment on the 13th January. There were 14 of us in this play. Three months before the day we had rehearsals at our Guide meetings and also Green curtains were made to hang round

---

[1] See 'Chelford - A Cheshire Village' published in 1999 by the authors.

the stage, which we hoped the entertainment would help to pay for. The week before the entertainment, Captain invited the Mobberley Girl Guides to our dress rehearsal. On the 13th Jan. Captain and Lieutenant went to prepare the stage for us (in the morning). It was a very wet night and we all wondered if we should have a very big audience. The doors opened at 7 o'clock and the entertainment started at 7.30, in the Parish Room. Mr Brodie Hoare had very kindly offered to paint us all and we looked very queer with our green eyebrows and red faces. Oh dear it was 25 mins past 7 and Annie Stephenson had not come and she was one of the first to go on the stage. Of course we all got rather anxious when suddenly some of the Guides shouted, "Here she comes now." What a relief it was to us. Whilst we were waiting for 7.30 we all kept running on to the stage and peeping through the curtains at the audience, which was not very big at first, but the room was quite full at the last moment. Everything was quite ready by 7.30. The play was taken from the Sleeping Beauty. It will take up too much space to give the full details of the play so I am making if very brief. The King of Merry-land is R Drew and the Queen, A. E. Bythell, and their daughter, M Dale, the princess Celandine.

M Brodie Hoare was the Wicked Fairy, Malicia, who said the princess would prick her finger on a spinning wheel and sleep for a hundred years. Evelyn Wright was Prince Charming who found the Princess asleep and kissed her, which broke the spell and she awoke and all the royal Household with her. Everyone acted splendidly, especially M. Brodie Hoare, R Drew, and J Thompson.

We then had another play given by Captain, Lieutenant, A.E. Bythell, M Brodie Hoare, and E Wright. It was called Alice in Wonderland. The first scene was The Duchess's Kitchen, the second scene was, Outside the March Hares House. Here came the interval for about 15 mins. After this we gave a campfire scene and sang songs and acted 2 sea shanties. Billy Boy and Sherandoah in which two Guides, J Thompson and J. Brodie Hoare dressed up as Red Indians. Jean sat in a little wigwam cutting a stick while Joyce sang the Indian love song. In the middle of this something went wrong with the curtain and the audience were requested to close their eyes until it reached the top. We then ended with Taps and God Save the King - everything having gone off satisfactorily.

Altogether we made:

£10 in tickets and as we had about £2.5.0 expenses we made £7.15.0. We gave £3.0.0 for the new Imperial Headquarters in London, 10/- to the S.P.G. for Girl Guides in India, £1.5.0 towards the new stage curtains for the Parish Room. We then had enough left to buy our own Union Jack of which we are very proud of and then we had £1.11.0 over to put in the Company Funds.

                           May Peatfield

January 13th 1930

PROGRAMME

1ST CHELFORD GUIDES

"THE PRINCESS IN THE SLEEPING WOOD"

The King of Merryland...	R Drew
The Queen...	A E Bythell
Princess Celadine, their daughter....................................	M Dale
Prince Charming...	E Wright
Tricot, the Jester...	J Thompson
Fairy Marigold..	J Brodie Hoare
Fairy Heatherbell..	H Ford
Wicked Fairy Malicia..	M Brodie Hoare
An imp servant of Malicia...	B Dixon
Trusty John servant of Prince..	H Ford
Meg, the kitchen maid...	M Gibbon
A Courtier...	A Stevenson
A Herald..	M Peatfield

SCENES

1. A room in the King's Palace 2. 16 years later
3. A wood near the Palace, 100 years later
4. The same as scene to.

The wicked Fairy Malicia, trying to make Princes Celandine
prick her finger on the magic spinning wheel.

1st Chelford Company 1930

Back row – Maisie Peatfield, (Nightingale P.L.), J Thompson, M Brodie Hoare, (Kingfisher P.L.) R Drew, J B Hoare (Blue Tit P.L.)
2nd row - Muriel Gibbon, Muriel Barber, Annie Barber, Mary Gould.
3rd row - Margaret Drew, M Baskerville, Mildred Gibbon, M Taylor.

1st Chelford Guides – June 1931

Back row L to R: E Smith, A Slater, E Houldsworth, J Thompson, M Gould, M Fisher. Front row L to R: M Barber, M Baskerville, M Taylor, M Drew & W Bloor.

Camp at Gayton in the Wirral 26 July – 3 August 1932

Rest Hour at Camp
Nora Cullaton, Evelyn Wright, Dorothy Stringer, Evelyn Houldsworth,
Mary Gould & Amy Slater

Outside the tent
E Houldsworth, E Wright,
A Slater & M Gould,
M Barber, Captain &
M Cheetham

1st Chelford Company
Empire Day – 24 May 1933

Mary Gould, (Blue Tit P.L.), Dorothy Warburton, (Blue Tit P.S.), Lieutenant, Marjorie Taylor, Evelyn Wright, (Packleader.)

Doris Walken, M Baskerville, M Barber, (Kingfisher P.L.), M Drew, (Kingfisher P.S.), Bertha Thomas & W Bloor.

Jean Bloor, (Brownie), J Lawton, J Taylor, J White, (Brownie) B Worthington, B Cash & G Drew (Brownie).

<u>1st Chelford and 1st Utkinton Camp – 9th – 16th August 1933 – Caldy Manor</u>

<u>Friday August 11th</u>

On Friday August 11th we got up at 8 o'clock and had a wash. Then we got ourselves dressed. We then went to prepare for breakfast and after everything was ready we then had breakfast. After breakfast we had certain tasks to do then we had inspection. We had half an hour stalking then it was dinner time. We had five visitors for dinner. There was the Utkinton Captain, and four others. We had our dinner then we cleared away after dinner and the things were washed up. Then the visitors went home. We then went to Hoylake baths for the afternoon. Then we came back for tea, we got the tea ready then after we had had our tea we washed up. When all was ready we had the camp fire, there was the Utkinton Guides and the Knutsford. They sang songs and told a story then it was time to go to bed. Captain said now all the baby's must go to bed first so we all had a wash and went to bed when we were in bed we had taps and Captain sent a kiss.

Drawings by E Snead and M Drew

Drawing by Bertha Thomas – Nightingales and Mildred

Chelford Guides at Tatton Park August 1931

Left to right: Back row: Mary Gould, Alison Bythell, Amy Slater, Evelyn Wright and Joyce Thompson. Front row: Evelyn Houldsworth and Margaret Drew.

1ST CHELFORD BOY SCOUTS

The information and photographs in this chapter have been taken from the archives of Roger Crompton Walsh of Snelson House who was, for many years, group scoutmaster. The archives are now in the possession of the 'District Commissioner', Chris Slater.

The first meeting of the 1st Chelford Boy Scouts took place on Saturday 20 January 1934[2], the group commencing with ten members, formed into two patrols.

Fox Patrol	**Hounds Patrol**
Stanley Potts	James Camm
Harry Drew	Wilfred Massey
Kenneth Kirk	David Harradine
Harry Bloor	Norman Woodall
Geoffrey Street	Richard Boon

The hut, known by the Guides and Scouts as, 'the old hut' was in use until 1977 when the new Scout Hut at the rear of the Village Hall was opened

1st Chelford Scouts are still in operation and meet in the Scout Hut. The present leader is Richard Pickering, who can be contacted on www.Chelfordscouts.org.uk.

---

[2] The girls had beaten them to it – 1st Chelford Girl Guides had been formed in 1929.

The first member of Chelford Scouts to become a King Scout was H Newton, who received the award in July 1944. Since then the following scouts achieved Kings/Queens Scout standard – Brian Harradine, Brian Ranson, David Peake and Anthony Harrison.

Bell ringing card containing details of a peal rung as a compliment to Brian Harradine when he was Made a Queen Scout.

Brian Harradine

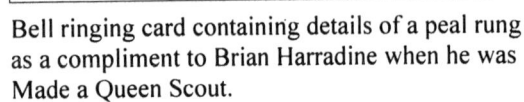

Anthony Harrison Receives Queen's Scout Certificate

February 1954

Parents and Friends joined the Chelford Boy Scouts in an enjoyable evening on Thursday last week.

There were about fifty people present, when Scoutmaster Walsh called upon District Commissioner, C Jaffrey, to present the Queen's Scout certificate to Anthony Harrison, who has been a member of the group for nearly five years.

The commissioner spoke of the value of scout training in the life of the individual, and paid tribute to the way in which Anthony had applied himself to his scouting. He congratulated him on his success in the severe tests.

Group Cups

Mr Jaffrey also presented two group cups, one for the best patrol to patrol Leader, G Warhurst, of the Hounds Patrol, the other to John Gresty, adjudged to be the best individual in the group. Gifts were also made to K Bromley and G Treweek, who tied for the best attendance during the year.

Refreshments were served and organised games were enjoyed by parents and boys.

The Ref. J S Gamon opened the meeting with prayer.

Anthony Harrison hopes to receive a warrant as A.S.M. in the near future.

Chelford Scouts through the 1950's

The Scouts Camp – Year not known

On Monday 5th August, the Chelford and Peover Troup set out from the two headquarters to go to camp at Wincle, on the other side of Macclesfield. It is about 14½ miles from our Scout hall. Those who had bicycles cycled, but the rest went in Mr Green's car. Mr Bailey took the kit in his waggon right to the field. Each patrol set out separately. The Patrol Leaders were provided with a map each and we were left to find our own way to the campsite.

As soon as we arrived we had our dinner. Then we pitched our tents. There were four Patrol tents and another Bell tent for the cookhouse. Then there was a smaller tent for the two scoutmasters. After we had pitched our tents we had a bathe in the brook. The water was lovely and warm but it was not very deep, so after we had changed we built a dam with some big stones that were a bit further up the brook. Each patrol had a day on duty and they were responsible for keeping the fire in and helping to do the cooking of the meals.

On Wednesday we took tea with us and went to the top of Shuttlings Low, about 1,600 feet high. Thursday we cycled to Dane Bridge where the three shires meet (Cheshire, Derbyshire and Staffordshire). The camp, in spite of the weather, being rather wet and cold was a very jolly camp, and we were always ready for our meals.

We returned home on Saturday, a dreadful morning and by the time we reached home we were all soaked through.

KC

The Chelford Scouts -Year not known

This year the camp was held at North Rode, near Congleton. The site was a particularly nice spot by the River Dane, with no road or habitation in sight. Again we were unfortunate with the weather, very wet and rather on the cold side, but it did improve a little by Friday. The conditions were too bad to permit us to climb the Cloud as we had intended. One afternoon we explored the canal, which is nearby. There are a few barges on it, though we were not so lucky as to see one pass through one of the locks. Probably the most surprising thing was the number of locks so close together. In spite of the moist time, we managed to keep reasonably dry (though Skip did fall in the river one afternoon), and no one appeared to be the worse for it, certainly appetites were as good as ever. The Hounds (P L G Burgess) won the camp competition. We all wish to join in thanking Mr and Mrs Brown for permitting us to camp and for their kindness and generosity.

We should like to take this opportunity of congratulating Troup Leader, P Green and Patrol Leader, K Clarke on gaining the First Class Badge. The Badge was presented to them at a weekend camp at Altrincham in July by the Chief Scout, Lord Rowallan. A further point with regard to the camp was the great improvement in gadgets.

R C W

Chelford Scouts 1951

The Summer Camp for 1951 was held at Allgreave near Wincle. There is little to be said for the weather, except that it was probably not quite as bad as last year. The seniors had a weekend camp on their own; the rest of us joined them on the Monday (when all the work had been done!) An attempt on Shuttlings Low was a failure, as we only reached about halfway when a thunderstorm started. It was astonishing that we did not get very wet, but we had a friendly lift back to camp in a lorry. Another afternoon we visited the baths at Macclesfield. We have to congratulate one Scout on passing his First-class swimming test there. Another troop from Ilkeston, camping near by, played us at cricket, and defeated us. We also had two joint campfires.

In spite of the weather, all appeared to enjoy themselves, and appetites were well up to standard.

We cannot close without expressing our grateful thanks to the father of one of the boys, who transported the equipment to and from the site, as well as the troop; also the Troup Leader. was a great asset to the success of the camp.

It is understood that this is the Skip's last camp, though the troops have other views and are already talking about next year's camp, which is to be further afield.

R C W

1st Chelford Boy Scouts' Summer Camp, Llandrillo
19.7.52 – 28.7.52

The Scout Troop left Chelford on Saturday, 19th July, on the 7.59 train to Crewe, picking up three other members of the troop at Holmes Chapel. Travelling from Crewe, we changed at Chester and Ruabon, arriving at Llandrillo at 12.30 in glorious sunshine, and full of eagerness to set up our camp, which was within a short distance of the station and about one mile from the village. On Monday we all went to Bala, and spent an enjoyable afternoon swimming and boating on the lake. Tuesday was spent in camp. Wednesday we went to Llangollen, a small, very well known, holiday resort, where the annual Eisteddfod is held, some of us went boating on the canal. Thursday was spent in camp. Friday we travelled by train to Barmouth, a small Welsh seaside holiday resort, where we spent a grand afternoon in the sea. The River Dee, which flows past by the side of our camp, was perfect for bathing and quite a fair amount of time was spent in fishing. While fishing one Scout was fortunate enough to kill a very large pike, some three feet in length. Some members of the troop went mountaineering during the week.

We invited the farmer and his wife (Mr and Mrs Jones) along to our campfire singsong, on the last Saturday night of our stay.

By the time Monday morning came, everyone agreed that the ten days had passed too quickly.

Mr and Mrs Jones were exceedingly kind and generous for, after packing everything away and taking the kit to the station, the whole troop was invited to the farmhouse, where we were served with cups of tea and home made cake by Mrs Jones.

We all thanked them very much for having let us camp on their land. They said they would look forward to seeing us again next year. The troop arrived home on the 6.10 p.m. train from Crewe, on Monday 28th July.   AH

P.S. The patrol competition was won by the Foxes. I should like to take this opportunity of expressing my great thanks to Mr and Mrs Jones at Llandrillo for their kindness, not forgetting their two little girls. I must acknowledge the great assistance and helpful advice I had from Mr Jones, the stationmaster here, also the stationmaster at Llandrillo. The weather was wonderful; no coat was necessary from start to finish. As usual our Troup Leader was worth his weight in gold.
RCW

The Scout Camp, 1953

The camp was held at Llandrillo (Cilan), the same site as last year, from July 18th to 28th. The weather was not too warm, rather wet and a good deal of wind; unlike last year, when we had no rain till we were on our way back home. But in spite of the weather, we had a good time. The Sunday morning service was in English on both Sundays, which we attended. This time we had an Assistant Commissioner to visit the camp; this is the normal procedure, to check that the camp is conducted in a proper manner; he is the Vicar of Llanuwchllyn, and is leaving there this month to take a new living at Altrincham. There was a little bathing as the weather was not too good, which was perhaps as well, as the river was in flood most of the time.

One wet evening a visit to Bala, for the first house at the cinema.

On the Friday afternoon, we all went to Llangollen; most of the boys did some shopping; boating on the canal was enjoyed by all. One of the main causes of the success of the camp was the kindness of Mr and Mrs Jones and their two daughters; we are exceedingly grateful for their hospitality. We had only one real disaster, this was when the pigs raided the cookhouse and ate or spoiled the bread and cereals.

The Hound Patrol won the competition, P L G Warhurst.

I cannot close without adding a personal note. The standard of the camp was very good, mainly due to our Troop Leader, whose untiring assistance in every way was an example to all.

R.C.W.

Hound Patrol	Fox Patrol
P L G Warhurst	Wilfred Dykes
Kenneth Bromley	N Ryder
David Harrison.	D Schofield
Gordon Treweek	David Bromley
Robin Copnall	G Irlam

1st Chelford Scouts 1954

Two years ago a very fine flag was given to the Alderley, Wilmslow and District Boy Scouts' Association, as a Trophy, to be competed for annually. In 1953 it was won by the Wilmslow Group, this year the Chelford Group were the winners.

The competition open to all groups in the local association is in two parts, the first is a Patrol Camp, consisting of a Patrol Leader and about five scouts, they have to look after themselves for 24 hours. A Commissioner goes round the site during the camp and judges the best camp. Chelford were first, they were first last year. The second part of the competition was held at the Carnival field, Wilmslow, this consists of various tests, such as: Fire Lighting and Cooking, Mass Signalling, Semaphore Messages, Trestle Building, FlagPole Erecting, Tenderfoot Knots and First Aid. The Chelford scouts are to be congratulated on their achievement.

The scouts cannot let the opportunity pass of acknowledging their gratitude to Miss Robertson for the time she gave in giving instruction on First Aid.

The 1955 Competition will be held at Chelford, June 11th.

SKIP

Chelford Scouts win Trophy - 1954

Members of Chelford Boy Scout Troop, with the Alderley Edge, Wilmslow and District Boy Scouts' Association Trophy, which they won at the annual field day at Wilmslow. Admiring the trophy are Pauline Bromley and Joy Kennerley. Chelford had 220 points, beating Wilmslow, the holders, by 30.

58

Jumble Sale aids Chelford Scouts 1956

Included in picture are Michael Brown, David Harrison, John Bradley, Raymond Pattley and Miss Gwen Bradley.

1st Chelford Scouts Parade – St. George's Day 1955

Chelford Briefs 24 February 1957

Special services were held at Chelford Church on Sunday in connection with the 100th Centenary of the birth of Lord Baden-Powell. At night the Scouts paraded to church led by their Scoutmaster, Mr R Walsh, and Assistant Scoutmaster, Mr A Harrison.

The flag bearer was Gordon Treweek and escorts were David Harrison and Robin Cotmall.

The flag was presented to the Vicar of Chelford, the Rev. C H Lee, who was the preacher, basing his sermon on the life and work of Baden-Powell. Lessons were read by Mr C Jaffrey (District Commissioner) and Mr R Wilkins.

New guides were guests at Chelford party.

Guides from the 1st Chelford Company, officially re-formed a few days before, were guests at Chelford Scouts annual party, in the Hut on Friday.

About 50 attended the party, among them the Rev. M J B Henry, the Vicar of Chelford, the Rev. P Truswell, Vicar of Over Peover and the new guide captain, Mrs N Hulme.

After refreshments, provided by the scouts and guides and their parents, the annual awards were presented to the scouts, by Mr R Walsh, the group scoutmaster.

They were received by: R Burgess and G Beeby (attendance record), Hound Patrol, leader G H Beeby (patrol cup), K Ashbrooke (individual cup), B Ransom (venturer cup), E Hughes, R and I Burgess and G H Beeby (ambulance and public service badges), R Burgess and E Hughes (1st class badges).

During the year D Peake became a Queen's Scout and the troop won a certificate in the county commissioner's challenge competition.

Tonight the scoutmaster, Mr A Harrison, will receive the wood badge from the district commissioner.

Authors note: - 1st Chelford Guides were re-formed 10 January 1966.

Diary of Scouts Camp – Llanddulas 1938   by R C Walsh

Party: - From Chelford, S Potts, R Boon, K Kirk, A Barber, W Baskerville, H Newton and J Norbury. From Holmes Chapel, J Benson, N Burt and G Scovell.

Saturday 13 August 1938

We caught the 7.59 to Crewe, the Holmes Chapel party joining us at the latter place. From Crewe we went on the 9.46 to Abergele, it was nearly an hour late. On arrival at Abergele I found the camp equipment had been delivered at Plas Newydd, by the Railway Co. I had sent a box and screen in advance the previous day, I had addressed it to Abergele to be called for but it was not there, I told the carrier to call at Llanddulas station to see if it had been sent on there, fortunately it had. I sent Dick and Ken with the kit with John Norbury, the rest of us went on by bus to Llanddulas, walking from there to the camp site at Plas Newydd. We had been here in 1935 and 1936.

After some lunch we pitched the tents etc., by the time we had finished, it was time for tea. Stan arrived about 18.00, he could not get the morning off from the office in Manchester. A good many bathed after tea. Supper then bed.

Sunday 14 August

Very wet in the night, but fine when we got up. Dick, Ken and J Benson acted as cooks for the day. After breakfast I took the boys for a walk, we returned for dinner. We had a bathe in the afternoon and again after tea.

Monday 15 August

Fox lost 1 point for being late up and the others lost 1 for bits at inspection. Fine and sunny, after breakfast we had Flag raiding. Defenders led by Norman were J Benson, G Scovell, A Barber and J Norbury, the attackers led by K Kirk were S Potts, J Baskerville, H Newton and self. Result was 2 Flags and 3 Dead of the attackers, while the defenders lost 2 men. Bathing in the afternoon, after tea all of them went to Colwyn Bay.

Tuesday 16 August

Wet in the morning, bathing in the afternoon. No points lost, still level at 24 each, started with 25 each.

Wednesday 17 August

Foxes 24 (late up) others 23 bits at inspection. Fine and warm during the day, though cool when the sun had gone down. After breakfast we had a return match of flag raiding, the only difference was, Dick took the place of Ken (who was on cook duty.) Norman's side got 4 flags (all) and killed, whilst they lost. In the afternoon I went to Colwyn Bay to the Bank. Boys bathed etc.

Thursday 18 August.

Fine and similar to yesterday. After breakfast we had Dispatch riding, Ken and George went down to Llanddulas, from there they had to try to return to camp, one of them carrying a message, which the others had to try and get, by stopping them and examining them, 3 minutes being allowed to examine them, it not found they were allowed to proceed, anyone else could stop them and do likewise. They also carried false messages, though the real message was known. They got through, Ken having the note.

After an early tea, they all went to Colwyn Bay for the evening. Rather rough in the evening. Points – Foxes 24, Others 23.

Friday 19 August

Showery in the morning. Foxes lost a point for paper found. After it had cleared, we had rounders. Dinner was not till 14.00, as they wanted to go to Colwyn Bay before tea, though only the 3 youngest left before tea, the others did not get themselves ready till too late.

As this was the last day in camp, we had what is known as a spree up in the evening, followed by a good camp fire, which was very successful. The box of chocolates awarded to the winning patrol was awarded to both as they each finished up with 23 points. The boys very kindly gave me a pipe and tobacco.

Saturday 20 August

We returned home today, nothing of note occurred, except we were held up outside Crewe for about 15 minutes. When we did get in, the train was so long that we were off the platform and could not get through to the next coach. This resulted in our missing the 16.15, we had to wait for the 17.48, and we arrived at Chelford about 10 minutes. No reserved compartment could be found at Abergele, nor was the Stationmaster polite or helpful. But coaches on the rear, reserved for a large party of girls, were not all required we had the last compartment.

Special Notes

As only 10 came to camp, I arranged 2 each day on cook duty (Monday – Friday) inclusive. The first and second Saturday I relied on voluntary assistance as well as Sunday. Sunday, J Benson and R Boon volunteered. 1st Saturday, N Burt and G Scovell. Best kept cook house -- N Burt and G Scovell.

R C Walsh

SCOUTS AUTUMN FAIR
(The Advertiser 5 October 1974)

This massive marrow, grown by a 1st Chelford Scout Group instructor, earned its keep on Saturday when it became the subject of a guess-the-weight competition at the group's annual Autumn Sale in Chelford Parish Hall. Anne Baskerville (9), of Chelford, who organised the competition, helps Janice Brown (14), of Chelford to try her luck. Looking on are Cubs and Scouts who helped during the afternoon to raise a record £96 for the group's new hall building fund.

DIXON ARMS BOWLING CLUB, CHELFORD
By Harold Bradley – President

It was a few years after the Second World War that two men in Chelford thought it was time to revive the Chelford Bowling Club as there was two vacant greens at the Dixon Arms Hotel but, both had gone wild. These two men – Geof Woodward, the Landlord and Jim Camm decided to notify the patrons of the hotel that a meeting would take place to find if there was any interest in starting a Bowling Club. Consequently in 1957 the Dixon Arms Bowling Club was formed and has since been led by a very active group of officers and committee members. The club has always been well supported by the Chelford National Farmers Union Bowling Club who have their green at Siddington and many of them are members of both clubs.

County Express 9 May 1957

Mr R H Wood of Alderley Edge and Knutsford, President of the newly formed Dixon Arms Bowling Club, Chelford, starts the opening match on Monday.

The new Dixon Arms Bowling Club of Chelford played the inaugural game on Monday evening on the green behind the hotel.

This is the club's first year, but already they have 56 members enrolled and hope to join a league next season. Mr R H Wood, who is president of the Club, "christened" the green on Monday, when he bowled the first jack.

There has been a great response from local people since the formation of the club and they have already had four trophies promised.

The idea of a bowling club at the Dixon Arms had been in the air since last year, and a meeting is to be held soon to decide which league the club will enter for its first "proper" season."

The main green was in need of a lot of hard work to bring it into bowling condition but the other distant green was so much in need of renovation that it was ignored. Both greens had been used for the production of eggs and poultry – a wartime necessity. As town and country clubs were forming leagues the club was soon able to gather quite a large number of members and over the years have had good support from the surrounding districts.

The aim was to make available pairs of bowls (crown green bowls are in pairs) for new members and to play friendly matches for practice to enable the Club to join a league.

The Club has four teams in the Knutsford League the 1st Team was entered in 1961, the 2nd team 1964, the 3rd team 1968 and the 4th 1978. Each team has eight members bowling on Tuesday, Wednesday or Thursday evenings for nineteen games throughout the summer season. The Green is also used by the Chelford and District Ladies Bowling Club, Monday evenings, Tuesday and Thursday afternoons and by the Knutsford and Cheshire Leagues for special events. Private parties can hire the green by arrangements with the hotel proprietor. The Club was fortunate to have Cups and Trophies presented by members and friends to compete for and each year a competition away from Chelford. These have been very good sources of enjoyment along with the Annual Dinner and Prize Presentation.

The functioning of the club was disturbed in 1967 by the severe outbreak of Foot and Mouth disease in cattle throughout the country especially in Cheshire. It was a very uncertain time for the Club members as farms were being affected daily.

The club maintains the green, the hedge and path surround and pavilion, and pays rent to the hotel; helped in this by the Ladies Club who also pay rent. The pavilion was erected by the Greenall Brewery in 1959, the old one on the south side was destroyed some time later and lighting was installed along with side windows in 1962. The green was drained by the Brewery in 1967 and again by club members in 1988. Four floodlights were erected and wired up in 1978 by the club, strongly led by the NFU Club, financed by Whist Drives held in the Hotel. Chairs have been purchased over the years for use around the green by both the ladies and gentlemen's clubs. Tom Perratt, President donated a long bench seat and a seat was presented in memory of George Barber by his family. George had mowed the green for many years and Peter Kitching has now taken on the greensman's duties, mowing and cutting hedges. Recently the pavilion roof was renewed by Alan Norbury and other club members.

Bushes and shrubs were cleared off the west side of the green with the help of Alan Read and his agricultural machinery and in 1985 leylandii bushes were planted as a screen between the green and the haulage company next door. The whole green has been recently surrounded by a flagstone path by Sam Shemilt on behalf of the Club and the board surround had been renewed.

Presidents	Chairmen	Vice Chairmen
1957 R H Wood	1957 H Burgess	1957 J Wilkins
1963 L S Dunning	1961 J W Bowers	1961 J E Camm
1975 J H Bowers	1975 T Perratt	1975 T W Massey
1980 T Perratt	1980 S Harding	1977 S Harding
2000 H Bradley	1992 D Lowe	1980 E Plant
		1985 E Wain
		1990 D Lowe
		1992 B Johnson

Secretary	Treasurer	Club Captain
1957 H Bradley	1957 W Boyd	1957 J W Bowers
1968 J Baskerville	1958 J Wilkins	1959 A R Rowbotham
1972 R Blain	1961 W Lowe	1965 T Perratt
1973 H Bradley	1973 G Broadbent	1982 A Fletcher
1977 D Couling	1977 T W Massey	1984 C Ball
1978 R Blain	1984 A Thomas	1985 S Massey
1979 G Burgess		1988 J Bloor
1983 H Bradley		1995 S Massey
1988 J T Venables		1999 P Newton

Life Members	Honorary Members	
1972 W Lowe	1968 C Wright	1974 W Crimes
1975 L S Dunning	1968 G White	1974 J Davies
1979 H Bradley	1968 T Hughes	1974 F Marshall
1979 J E Camm	1969 N Brown	1976 G Stanier
1985 T Perratt	1970 F Hatch	1976 J Acton
1985 J W Bowers	1971 E Bailey	1976 A Turnock

1988 L Kellet	1971 C Atkinson	1978 H Bradley
1988 E Dale	1972 G Woodward	1984 K Ford
1992 S Harding	1973 R Rigby	1984 G Barber
1992 J Wilkins	1973 T Newton	1984 D Crump
1994 J L Venables	1974 F Bancroft	1984 T W Baskerville
1994 R Holt		

Friendly Games Played   Cups and Trophies

Playing Fields	Alderley Edge	Broadbent Cup – N W Broadbent
Private Club	Knutsford	Highfield Cup – R Holt
Cross Town Club	Knutsford	Woodward Rose Bowl – M Woodward
Swettenham Club	Swettenham	Cowley Cup – Mrs Cowley
Bears Head	Brereton	Wilkinson Trophy
Cranage Hall Hospital		President's Trophy – L S Dunning
Drovers Arms	Allostock	Hoyle Smith Trophy – T Hoyle Smith
Victoria Club	Holmes Chapel	Duckworth Prize – R Duckworth
Pack Horse	Macclesfield	Stanier Trophy – G Stanier
Mere Club	Mere	Lowe Shield – D Lowe
Calderfield	Liverpool	

Membership		Subscriptions	
1974	77	1958	10s 0d
1983	52	1968	17s 6d
1987	62	1978	£3.00
1998	45	1988	£5.00
2000	47	1998	£12.00

Annual Midsummer Tournament Venues

Bowling Green Hotel, Chester	1959
Calderfield, Liverpool	1962,63,64
Ave & Cleaver, Timperley	1965
Greenall Whitley, Warrington	1966,67,68,69,70
Railway Hotel, Acton Bridge	1971
The Jolly Thrasher, Lymm	1972
Hazel Pear, Acton Bridge	1973
Corbett Arms, Market Drayton	1974,75,76
Swettenham Club	1977,78,79,80,81
Golden Pheasant, Plumley	1982,83
Red Lion, Little Budworth	1984,85,86
British Aerospace, Woodford	1987,88,89,90

GREENALL'S SOCIAL CLUB 10TH AUGUST '1967

Roll of Membership 1957 – 2000 – Past and Present (Year 200 membership underlined)

C Atkinson	J Acton	W Aymes	
W Baskerville	J Baskerville	T Baskerville	F Baskerville
A Baskerville	H Burgess	G Burgess	F Burgess
R Burgess	C Ball	C Ball	N Brown
F Bell	W Bailey	E Bailey	S Barber
G Barber	J A Barber	A J Barber	A Barber
D Barber	D Bloor	D Bloor	J Bloor
E Bloor	H Bradley	A Bradley	R Blain
R Blain	W Boyd	J Breen	G Broadbent
J Bowers	S Bowers	F Bancroft	K Bagnall
N Butler	D Barratt	P Brookes	T Bullock
P Bass	N Broadbent		
H Callwood	D Crump	W Crimes	A Crimes
J Camm	F Cowley	J Coppack	H Clarke
A Clarke	G Clarke	D Campbell	D Craven
J Collins	J Chesters	R Currie	J Coates

69

Lt Col Dickinson	N Dennett	E Dingle	L Dunning
H Dakin	L Davenport	B Dingle	J Driver
J Davies	K Dawson	M Dennison	M Dalton
R Duckworth	C Duckworth		
B Evans	J Egerton	A Eyres	R Eades
E Evans	A Ellison		
Capt L Foers	A Fitzsimons	G Fernie	A Fletcher
K Ford	K Fisher	A Ford	
L Gosling	F Gledhill	K Grimes	J Gregory
G Greenwood	G Grasse	D Godsmark	A Gibson
G Glover			
R Holt	G Holt	F Hatch	R Holal
J Harrison	P Hackney	H Horsley	I Hewitt
F Hampson	S Harding	H Hammerlsey	R Hooley
C Hadfield	T Hughes	L Hankey	D Halman
B Johnson	J Jonson	J Jackson	H Jackson
C Jones	D Jones	K James	R Jefferies
P Jung			
P Kitching	K Kavanagh	J Kelly	W Kerrigan
L Kellett			
W Lowe	D Lowe	C Lowe	A Longworth
W Longworth	H Lobell	A Large	B Leech
B Mottram	F Marshall	I Morrell	P Morrell
W Mottram	R Mattinson	J Morris	S Massey
T Moulton	W Massey	R Massey	J Massey
A Massey	E Massey	A Moston	D Morris
R Millington	R Mumford	R Mayer	R McFall
T Norbury	A Norbury	P Newton	A Newton
R Neil	G Nuttall	C Newton	
T Perratt	S Pratt	J Potts	E Plant
I Pearson	M Pimlott	E Pimlott	E Trunier
A Prestley	D Parfitt	A Pollitt	A Parker
J Parry	K Powrie		
H Ryder	A Read	P Read	D Read
P Ross	F Read	G Read	R Rigby
R Rigby	R Roycroft	A Rowbotham	D Rooney
K Russon	T Roy	J Rishworth	B Ridehalgh
R Roberts	F Roebuck	D Rhodes	
W Stanier	J Skerry	S Sutcliffe	H Swain
S Shuttleworth	S Shemilt	K Shemilt	M Shemilt
C Skelton	T Sutton	F Sharpley	J Stanier
G Stanier	A Stubbs	A Smith	S Smith

S Stone			
W Tomkinson	A Turnock	J Turner	M Trevor
A Thomas	A Tatton		
C Venables	L Venables	W Venables	J T Venables
J Venables	A Venables		
G Woodward	R H Wood	J Wilkins	R Wain
E Wain	D Wain	C Whittaker	M Walker
D Whitehurst	K Whitehurst	A Wood	F Worthington
G Wallis	M Wallis	R Wakefield	R Wynn
C Wright	H Wright	J Warhurst	G White
F Williamson	J Walsh	M Wardell	A Woodward
D White	L Warhurst	E Winters	G Worsley
Lt Col Wilkinson			

Landlords

G Woodward	1957
Mrs M Woodward	1972
Manager	1974
A Large	1976
Manager	1981
G Waters	1982
S Oshaughnessy	1998

Dixon Arms Bowling Club - AGM 2000
Mr H Bradley (President) and Mr D Lowe (Chairman)

NFU members at Dixon Arms Bowling Green

Members of Dixon Arms Bowling Club at the AGM 2000

CHELFORD SCHOOL 1923
Head Teacher – Mr J W Naylor

Back row L to R: Sam Hopkins, Philip Wright, George Abrahams, Ernest Houldsworth, Harold Rowlands, ?.

Second back row L to R: Alice Callwood, Harold Wright, Arthur Jackson, Dennis Houldsworth, Norman Street, ? , Geoffrey Thorley.

Third back row L to R: Rene White, Muriel Gibbons, Annie Barber, Peggy Green, Elsie Baskerville, Evelyn Massey, Rene Drew, Betty Rowlands.

Fourth back row L to R: Louis Jones, Helen Heathcote, May Walker, Evelyn Wright, Phyllis Sneyd, Winnie Taylor, May Massey, Nora Potts.

Front row L to R: Wilfred Rowlands, Ernest Barber, Charles Callwood, Alan Barber, Thomas Adderley.

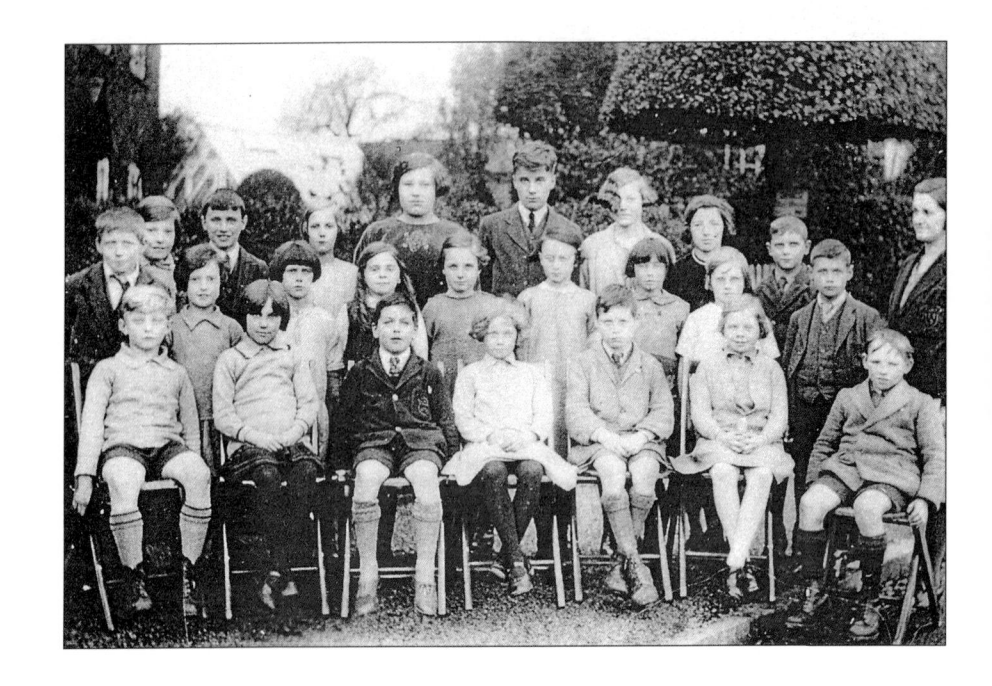

CHELFORD SCHOOL 1926
Head Teacher – Miss H Mollart

Back row L to R: Norman Griffiths, Marjorie Taylor, Walter Green, Evelyn Houldsworth, Betty Dakin, Geoffrey Thorley, Marjorie Dale, Annie Barber, Stanley Potts.

Middle row L to R: Joan Taylor, Jean Bloor, Marion Naeds, Edith Outram, Elsie Broughton, Winnie Bloor, Ethel Heathcote, James Camm.

Front row L to R: Geoffrey Blackhurst, Margaret Drew, Harry Drew, Edna Dale, Arthur Baddiley, Muriel Barber, Joseph Heathcote.

Picture taken in front of The Cottage, Alderley Road.

CHELFORD SCHOOL 1963

Back row left to right: Kathleen Bloor, John Camm, Mrs Styman, Leslie Boon and Sheena Burgess.

Middle Row left to right: Carol Bradley, Peter Lofthouse, David Williamson, Alan Oliver, Philip Hall and Andrea Kitching.

Front Row left to right: Judith Pimlott, Shirley Callwood, ? Millward, Nigel Kerrigan, Gail Burgess and Helen Okill.

Sitting at front: Richard Okill.

SCHOOL THAT MADE ITS OWN HISTORY
Manchester Evening News – 9 April 1984

Recipe for success ... Mrs Hornby – with her cake – and Mr Bailey celebrate with the pupils. At the back are teachers Elaine Walker (left) and Emily Wilson.

When it comes to history lessons the 33 pupils at Chelford primary school are in a class of their own.

Their tiny Cheshire Church of England school is 230 years old this month! And they decided to celebrate the occasion in style.

Cook, Mrs Anne Hornby, baked a cake – and decorated it with a picture of the school. The headmaster, Mr David Bailey, and his staff masterminded a pictorial display of the school and its scholars through the ages.

But it is the children who are the main attraction. They have turned the clock back to 1754 when the board of trustees was founded and dressed in the styles of the period.

The girls wore frilly dresses and the boys tricorn hats, toppers and breeches for a special concert. Mr Bailey said, "We have uncovered many interesting items from the old records. The frustrating thing is that we cannot find an exact date when it was founded. The documents only go back to the day in April when the trustees first signed."

In the 18th century a charge of three shillings for reading and writing and six shillings for full lessons was made. The school originally catered for 117 pupils of all ages and offered 13 free places to the poor.

The records show that it was closed many times by measles epidemics and for a time lessons were held in a tithe barn while building work was underway.

"We decided to make it a special occasion," added Mr Bailey, who has been at the school for 11 years. "There is talk of a new school being built and it might be the last full decade here."

CHELFORD NEW SCHOOL – OPENED SEPTEMBER 1999

Mrs Ruth Taylor (Headmistress) with group of pupils Back row L to R: Emily Eastaugh, Liam Sullivan, Mrs Taylor and Michael Norbury

Front row L to R: Aisling Robinson, Laura Jarrold, Stuart Gresham, Ben Barron, Laura Strudley, Katy Michell, Megan Duncalf and Tom Mount.

CHURCH BANNER

The Church Banner shown below was prepared for the 450th anniversary of the Chester Diocese 1541-1991. It was designed by Annwen Nicholas and worked by Muriel Kellett, Annwen Nicholas, Phillis Madgen, Hilda Lowe and Hilda Reed.

Pictured L to R: Muriel Kellett, Annwen Nicholas, Phillis Madgen, Hilda Lowe and Hilda Read.

The cross was made by the late Peter Hale of Alderley Edge and the pole was presented by Alan Barber.

CHELFORD PARISH CHURCH SUNDAY SCHOOL PARTY
AND PRIZEGIVING JANUARY 1974

The occasion was reported by The Advertiser in their issue of 10 January 1974.

"Children who attend Chelford Parish Church celebrated two occasions on Saturday when their Sunday school party and prize-giving ceremony were held at the parish hall. About 36 children were entertained with games at the party and a comedy film show was presented by Mr Chadwick. The refreshments were arranged and made by Mrs T Newton, Miss L Tickle, Mrs J Camm, Mrs P Kitching and Mrs H Bradley.

The party was organised by Mrs M Henry, who was assisted by Mrs E Karrigan, Miss C Street, Miss C Pimlott, Mrs S Barber, Miss S Moody and Miss J Brown. Afterwards, at the prizegiving ceremony, books were presented to the children by Mr R Forrester, who is at present training for the ministry at Chichester Theological College. In the absence of the vicar, Mrs M Henry, the Sunday school superintendent, congratulated the children on their excellent attendance throughout the year and thanked parents for their encouraging support."

VILLAGE QUEEN – MAY 1991

CHELFORD's new May Queen is Joanne Norbury, who was selected last Friday at Chelford Village Hall. She is pictured, left, with her ladies-in-waiting, who are, from the right, Lindsey Annikin, Rebecca Amos and Kathryn Davies.

GARDEN PARTY

Garden party – Astle Cottage 1950's

GARDEN PARTY

Garden party. Astle Cottage 1950's

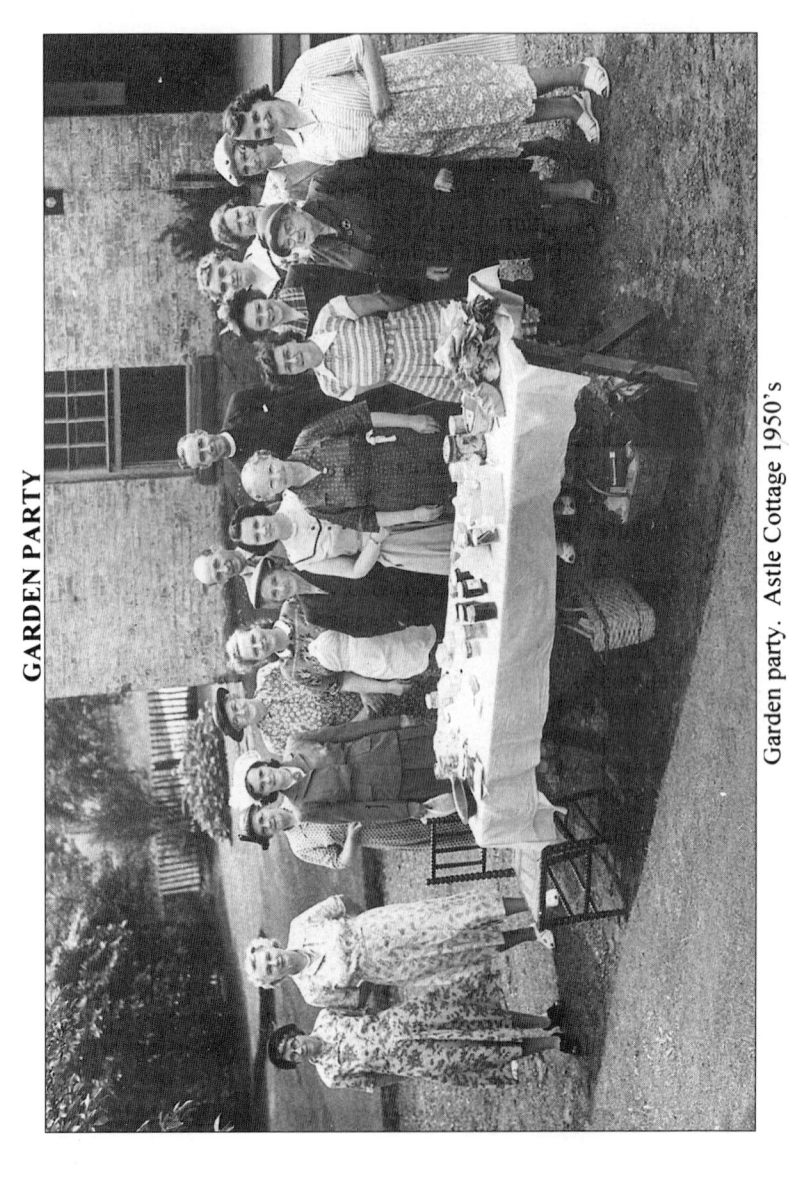

Included above are Dolly Wothington, (striped dress, front row,) Mrs Capper, (far right), Mrs Taylor, Mrs Harry Potts, Mrs Bill Bailey and Mrs Holt.

Ladies and children at Garden party having a cup of tea.

Left to right: -?-, Elsie Barber, Rev. Gamon, Charlotte Barber (with Julia Barber on her knee), Muriel Kellett, Philip Kellett (in pram), Dolly Worthington, Mrs Capper, children sat at front, Stuart Kellet and Andrew Barber.

LOWER WITHINGTON SCHOOL
HISTORY

The will of Thomas Boden dated 21 May 1834 included an indenture dated 8 February 1834 between himself on the one part and Edward Foden and Richard Benjamin Finney of the other part, whereby he conveyed to the last mentioned parties the interest in certain messuages and lands, for the benefit of two institutions for education established in Lower Withington, called the Township Charity School and the Sunday School, and if these schools cease to exist, for promoting generally the education of the poor children of the township of Lower Withington. In case the interest 'failed' he gave £480 to the parties named, on trust that they should invest the money in their names and use the interest raised for the purpose of the Indenture but not for the purchase of lands or buildings or the construction of the latter.

The trustees were required to pay the annual surplus of the rents to defray the expenses relative to the education of poor children who were scholars at the township charity school and Sunday school held in certain rooms belonging to the chapel or meeting house of the Wesleyan Methodists in Lower Withington, or in the event that both schools should cease to exist, to pay and apply the same for the education of the children of Lower Withington in such manner as they should see fit.

In a letter dated 22 June 1881, the Charity Commissioners were informed that the Township Charity School had ceased to exist but that a new voluntary school was being built[1]. The Commissioners made a judgement that the income be divided into three equal parts, two thirds for Wesleyan purposes and one third for the National School.

The National School was built in 1876 with Mr Stringer of Sandbach as contractor at a cost of £500 and the cost defrayed by a voluntary rate of 2s.6d, in the £. Mr Egerton Leigh paid all the rate levied on his tenants and Mr J B Glegg paid half his tenants' share with the tenants themselves paying the other half. Other landowners living on their own holdings paid their own rate. The land for the school was given by Mr Glegg of Withington Hall and all materials for the building were carted by local farmers free of cost. The playground and wall in front were paid for out of school funds after the school was opened.

At a public meeting held in the Wesleyan Sunday school, Mr G Glegg, Rev. W G Armitstead, Mr E Lea and Mr E Gilbert were appointed trustees of the school. At the same meeting Mr Edwin Gilbert was appointed Corresponding Manager.

---

[1] The school had in fact already opened.

The school was opened on the morning of 14 January 1878.

From the opening day the events at school were recorded in the school Log Book[2].

In 1881 a school house was built on land donated by Mr Glegg of Withington Hall, the majority of the building costs of £516.2s 11d being raised by public subscription. The original specification proposes the building of the new School House and Curates' Rooms.

By the late 1890's the need for an additional classroom for infants was being stressed in the annual reports and in September 1899 the school managers approved a tender quoting £191 for the necessary work. At the same time the widow of Edwin Gilbert, (the school's treasurer and correspondent) made an offer, in memory of her husband, to pay the school's final debt. The land for the new classroom was donated by Mr J Baskervyle Glegg, whose father had given the land for the school.

The Managers' Report of 1906 recommended further improvements – better cloakroom facilities and that a pail system should replace the existing closet system[3]. The cesspool had not been emptied for a considerable time.

---

[2] Cheshire Record Office – Ref SL 154/2

[3] As stated in the records – it may however have been incorrectly recorded – possibly the closet system replaced the pail system.

After 42 years as headmaster, Mr Cheetham retired in 1919 and was succeeded by Mr G Newport.

According to the Log Book entry for 9 May 1918, hardly any children returned to school for the afternoon lessons – in fact there were so few that the school did not re-open. The reason was that three aeroplanes had come down in the neighbourhood and the children had all gone to look at them.

In the late summer of the same year the school was closed on a number of occasions so that the children could go blackberrying. Due to the food shortage towards the end of the Great War the children were allowed time off for potato picking and harvesting.

Mr Newport was head of the school until 1929 when Miss I Moore was appointed. Miss Gladys Jackson, later Mrs Brocklehurst, was the next headmistress from 1943 until she retired in 1966. Mr J E Taylor then completed the final years until the school closed in 1969 and all the pupils transferred to a new, purpose built school at Marton.

Following closure the school was converted into a house.

LOWER WITHINGTON SCHOOL
LOG BOOK 1878 TO 1883

The contents below are an edited version covering the years 1878 to 1883 inclusive and Inspectors Reports from 1884 to 1888. (Cheshire CRO Ref: SL 154/2.)

1878

This new school was opened in January on 14th for the first time this morning by H Cheetham of the training college, Chester, having been appointed Master on 15 December 1877. The morning went very well, 46 children admitted.

During the month Messrs Gilbert (one of the Managers) and Duckworth (Master at Goostrey) called. On 15th it was stormy and 12 children admitted. Miss Callwood was appointed as Sewing Mistress and to assist generally in the school and commenced her duties on 16th. 2 more children were admitted and Mr Lee called in the afternoon. On the 18th Miss Foden of Goostrey made a visit. Mr Heathcote, the Attendance Officer for Macclesfield called on 21st and left a number of "Child's School Books". Had occasion to punish a boy and a girl on 25th for misconduct during prayers. The Rev. W G Armitstead, vicar of Goostrey called in the afternoon of 31st.

In February a meeting of the Managers was held in the morning of the 5th to sign the papers sent by the Department respecting the managers application for the school to be placed upon the list for inspection. Lessons on maps and the noun were given to classes one and two. Miss Callwood left school early on 12th to go to Manchester. Mr Rostron of Blackburn came on 22nd, children sent home earlier than usual.

On March 4th the scripture syllabus was received from Rev. J F Buckler and the examination fixed for November. Gave children half-holiday – Shrove Tuesday. Miss Callwood was away from school – not well. Heywoods parcel came on 13th, a new harmonium from Highams, Manchester. The attendance officer called in the afternoon, gave him the names of two children who attend very irregularly. Word came down on 22nd that the examination of scholars will not be held as previously arranged (5th March) but in April 1879. Miss Callwood was away on 28th.

During April Mr Gilbert (Manager) called. Had occasion to punish a girl for absenting herself from school for 10 days without knowledge of parents! Closed school on 18th for Easter Holidays (Thursday). School opened on 24th – great many children away.

May brought with it some rain which was an excellent subject lesson for classes one and two. On 6th a girl, (J Bloor), left this school for Swettenham because she could not be allowed to work the whole of the day. Her mother came and informed managers. A boy was punished for gross misconduct in the playground. Owing to the interference of his father, he was afterwards dismissed from the school. Examined Standards 1, 2 and 3 during the month in arithmetic and dictation, did fairly in arithmetic – dictation weakest point. Miss Callwood was away on 30th and on 31st.

Closed school in afternoon of 7th June for Whitsuntide holiday on Monday only. Opened school on 11th, many children were away. Miss Callwood not well and away on 21st.

Rev. W G Armitstead called on 1st July in afternoon and heard children sing and read prayers. Mrs Reiss and Miss Reiss of Jodrell Hall called this morning, 9th, and promised to give children a treat in the Jodrell grounds on 19th July. Miss Callwood away from school on 15th, not well. Holiday on 19th for children's treat in Jodrell grounds. Examined children on 18th in arithmetic and dictation for prizes. Messrs Gilbert and Lea promised to provide prizes. Captain Egerton Leigh called on 29th. Mrs Carter of Goostrey called in afternoon of the 30th, stopped to see girls sew. With the consent of the Managers the Master left school early on 31st and left Miss Callwood in charge of the school for the remainder of the week.

Mrs Gilbert and Mrs Lea came to school in the afternoon of 5th August and the School closed on the afternoon of 8th for holidays. Gave out the prizes.

In September School opened on 9th, morning very fine, moderate attendance. Miss Wood commenced duties as Sewing Mistress in the afternoon. Miss Callwood left on 8th, her services being required at home which was against the wishes of the Managers that she could not continue teaching here. During her stay she gave satisfaction to all connected with the school. Holiday on 12th in afternoon, Goostrey Harvest. Timothy Wood commenced teaching with the intention of his settling as a candidate for Pupil Teacher. Miss Callwood called in afternoon of 17th and took a class. Very wet and stormy on 30th – great many children away. Sent a list of those who attend irregularly to the Attendance Officer.

Rev. W G Armitstead called on the morning of 2nd October and wrote to the Diocesan Inspector asking what day we must expect him in November to examine children in scripture. Miss Callwood came to school on 11th in afternoon. On 18th examined classes one and two in geography (on paper) – not so good as could have been expected. Very wet on 24th – great many children away. Gave classes one and two a lesson on a river. Heard from Rev. J F Buckler, Diocesan Inspector, on 28th – exam in scripture fixed for 11th November. Two cart loads of tiles for paving footpath in yard arrived on 31st, altogether 900 at 6s.6d, per hundred.

In November Mr Gilbert called on 6th. On 11th examination in scripture, the Rev. J F Buckler the examiner – half holiday. Miss Callwood came to school on 12th early afternoon and took a class. Mr Gilbert called on 13th and holiday on 14th, - Master away from home. It was very wet and stormy on 15th. Rev. Armitstead and A Leigh Esq., called on 19th and brought scripture report. Great many children away on 22nd, (40) some of them supposed to have some kind of fever. One girl, Hannah Parrott, died on the 20th inst., from the illness, which the others are supposed to be suffering. Had no medical warning as to the closing of the school. School closed on 25th for a fortnight on account of a large number of children being away sick.

The following is a copy of the report made by Rev. J F Buckler, and copied by Mr Gilbert, one of the Managers.

<u>First Scripture Report</u>

This new school was inspected for the first time on 11th November 1878. Mr Cheetham has made very good use of the few months the school has been open. The children were found in excellent order and had (especially the higher group) a very good knowledge of the subjects prepared. They answered well in the scripture and accurately in the Catechism. Their repetition was very well said and the hymns were carefully read. A creditable knowledge of the order of the Christian seasons was shown. Some papers were satisfactorily written by some of Group I. The rest wrote accurately from memory on their slates. Mary E Davis and Joseph Potts answered with most credit. Amy Slater, S Summerfield, Emily Roylance, Hannah Bradley, Ann Newton and Annie Foden are also honourably mentioned. Present 82.

Signed by Albert Gilbert, Manager

On 16th December school opened after being closed for three weeks, very poor attendance. On 26th very wet and cold all week, great many children away. Timothy Wood away from school on 27th. The Rev. W G Armitstead and Mr Hutchinson called several times during the year and also the Attendance Officer called on a regular basis.

1879

In January Rev. Armitstead gave out prizes for scripture. Timothy Wood was away on 24th and later in the month a parcel containing reading books and Royal Readers was received from Heywoods. During February there were a great many children absent due to the very stormy weather with snow and many children away suffering from severe colds. A half holiday was given for Shrove Tuesday, 25th.

In March attendance forms were returned with names of scholars to the Local Authority. Singing lessons and Catechism were held on 21st. Heard from T. L. Gleadowe Esq., HMI, on 24th that the exam would take place on 1st April at 10 o'clock. Exam of PT's on Saturday 29th March, Crewe NS.

The examination took place on 1st April as scheduled and Mr Nicholl, HMI, was the examiner. A half holiday was granted in the afternoon. School closed on 10th for Easter holidays and opened again on 16th with moderate attendance. The Master was away on 25th and Miss Wood came and took sewing with the girls and the boys worked according to the timetable.

Mrs Slack commenced her duties as school cleaner with a wage of £4 per year on 7th May. Sewing was the last lesson on 13th and had occasion to speak to Timothy Wood about lessons not being properly prepared. The children in classes two, three and four continue to do very well in arithmetic but poorly in dictation. Timothy Wood asked permission to be absent from school on 23rd and the school closed on 30th for Whitsuntide holidays.

There were a great many children away on 4th July, Withington Club Day. Miss Wood was late in the afternoon and two boys, Chas Heath and Geo. Dakin had to be punished on 26th for running about during the dinner hour and breaking two easel pegs. The report on 24th June was as follows: -

"This school has made a good start and promises to do well under Mr Cheetham, arithmetic has been very successfully taught. I shall look for improvement in singing and infant instruction another year. The order is very good.

An Assistant Teacher (Article 79) should be engaged at once, or one Pupil Teacher transferred from some other school (Article 32). T Wood is disqualified on 24th for admission by Article 70. Mr Cheetham will shortly receive his certificate, Henry Cheetham, Certificated Teacher of the 2nd class."

In July Miss Wood sent word that she could not come to school on 1st. Girls took sewing on 4th, took lessons as for Tuesday. Several children were punished for writing their names in school reading books. Master received his Parchment from Education Department. During the hay harvest season there were a great many children absent because they were helping at home.

Many children were away in August because of very wet and stormy conditions. Miss Wood was away one afternoon. Mrs Reiss and Miss Reiss called on 13th in the afternoon and promised to give the children a treat in the Jodrell Hall grounds on 22nd. A treat which they all enjoyed.

School opened after the summer break on 22nd September – it was very wet and only moderate attendance, this was also the case in October. A great many of the older boys were away working in the harvest and parents had sent word that they would be required at home to assist with the corn. The yard gate, the door and boards over the windows had been painted in September. A new lamp came during the month from Heywoods.

Science class commenced on 10th November, taking principles of agriculture. Rev. D Shaw examined the children on religious knowledge on 13th and sent in his report later in the month. There was a meeting of the Managers and the Master was requested to obtain applicants for the post of Assistant Mistress in this school.

In December the school opens for afternoon period at 1 p.m. instead of 1.25, dismissal at 3.35 p.m., this will continue for the next few weeks owing to the fact that most children have a long way to go to their homes and especially for the comfort of the younger ones. Many children were away during the month due to heavy falls of snow. Spoke to T Wood again about home lessons not being prepared, no excuse, no work books brought to school even. Mr Gilbert, School

Manager, and Mr Heathcote, the Attendance Officer called frequently throughout the year, sometimes to pay the school fees allowed by the Guardians for two children. Sometimes Mrs Gilbert accompanied Mr Gilbert when he visited the school. Rev. Armitstead also called regularly throughout the year and gave out prizes in December provided by Mr Armitstead himself. School closed on 24th for Christmas holidays.

1880

During January and February the attendance was low due to very cold weather and several children were ill. Names of irregular attendees were sent to the Attendance Officer. The children had a half holiday for Shrove Tuesday, 10th February. The Inspectors visited the school on 12th. March was wet and stormy with many children away for various reasons. Mr Nicholl, the Examiner of the school came on 5th April to examine the school. The Master was away on 9th and later in the month a boy was punished for misconduct in the playground. Mr Nicholl reported that *"This new school has been well worked up by Mr Cheetham"*. The following is Mr Shaw's report signed by Rev. Wm. G Armitstead.

"This school has passed on the whole a very creditable examination. The first group was well prepared in Scripture and repeated the Catechism very correctly, answering questions on the meaning of it intelligently. Hymns, chants, collects and passages of Scripture were also nicely given and the children showed a good knowledge of the Order of Morning and Evening Prayer. The Scripture abstracts on paper were nicely done.

The lower group were fairly acquainted with the facts of the Scripture prepared and correctly repeated a part of the Catechism – the other repetition was good and the order of the Christian year fairly known. N.B. The school is in want of <u>Bibles.</u> The following deserve special mention, Group 1 – Thos Foden, Charles Staley, Richard Davies, Elizabeth A Bower, Ann Newton and Joseph Potts, Group 2 – Wm. Norbury, John Rathbone, Joseph Warburton, Mary Staley, Elizabeth Capper, Elizabeth Holden. Present 78 – on books 88 – average 63."

In May school fees were received from Guardians of the Woods children, 3/- the amount due up to 25th March. Fees were still owing from that date to present.

The Report by Henry Cheetham, Certificated teacher, 2nd class, Jane Graham, Assistant (Art. 79) as follows: -

"The discipline is very creditable and the instruction is given with decided care and success. Arithmetic continues good and the singing and infant instruction have improved. The class subjects and the writing need rather more attention."

The Guardians' children presented the Master with a reading lamp during May. A note was received from Mr Cullum, clerk to the Guardians, asking for the amount of school fees owing to date and an account was sent by return for fees due from 25th March to 28th May. Withington Club Day was in June and in July a form was sent by the Guardians', which was required to be filled to enable them to make out their yearly report. The form asked for the amount of grant earned at the two last examinations, number of children presented, number of passes, number on books for past two years (separately) and average attendance. Also a space on the form was to be filled up with any particulars to which the Master wished to draw the Attendance Officer's attention. His attention was called to the irregularity of certain scholars. Sent him the number of attendances made for a certain length of time. Also informed him that a visit from him might do something towards raising the attendance, but up to the 6th July have not heard from him, neither have the irregular ones been warned by him. This is not the first time he has neglected to apply force to irregular ones after he has sent a form to be specially filled up and returned to him for that purpose. He has only visited this school once this year.

School closed on 15th for holiday and 3 prizes for regular attendance provided by Messrs Gilbert and Lea were given to each standard. When school reopened on 9th August there was only moderate attendance. Orders were received on 8th September for school fees for Woods and Capper from the Attendance Officer. Goostrey Harvest on 16th was a very wet morning when the children had a holiday for the occasion. The name of a scholar who was attending very irregularly was sent to the Attendance Officer, informing him that the parent should be warned according to the law.

In October many children were away at the start of the month due to very wet weather. Night school met a couple of times in the month. A boy was punished on 11th for writing indecent and vile language on his slate during the arithmetic lesson. Having been given a set number of sums and having finished before some of the others, he employed his time in the manner above stated. His written language was such that common decency forbids quote. Kept the boy's slate with the writing on and showed it to Mr Gilbert. Rev. F R Preston was appointed curate. A little girl (Emily Street) caught fire in school on 23rd November, shortly before master arrived.

In December Miss Graham was away from school on 21st. Master away on 20th, leaving Miss Graham in charge. When returned found school in a very disorderly condition, children doing as they wished, Miss Graham sitting at the table writing letters. The children were given a treat in the afternoon of the 23rd when school closed for holiday and in the evening entertainment by children singing and reading.

Rev. Armitstead called regularly throughout the year and also Mr and Mrs Gilbert, but the Attendance Officer, Mr Pyatt, called on only two occasions during the year.

1881

School opened on 3rd and Miss Graham came on 10th after a fortnight's absence. Clothing club started on 17th for children attending Day and Sunday school. Closed the school in afternoon of the 18th on account of fire smoking, room almost full of smoke all morning. In February many children were absent early in month and the children were dismissed at 3.30 to prepare for entertainment at night on 15th. March brought with it snow and the 1st was half holiday for Shrove Tuesday. Heywoods' parcel came with registers and foolscaps. Note to Chairman of Attendance Committee on 9th complaining of neglect by the Officer, with respect to children attending irregularly and payment of school fees – which have been granted by Guardians. Rev. F R Preston came to question generally on work prepared for inspection and thought the children answered very well. A Copy of bye-laws was received from Attendance Committee.

There was a meeting in April of the trustees of the school with Egerton Leigh Esq., and Mr Douglas, architect of Chester, to consider what was to be done towards building a school house. It was agreed that Mr Douglas should draw up plans and that Mr Lea, Mr Clarke and Mr Gilbert should be a committee to superintend the building. Rev. Armitstead called throughout the year

In May Mrs Reiss and Miss Reiss of Jodrell Hall called at the school. The school closed from 3rd June to 10th for Whitsuntide Holidays.

Report

"The order continues very good and the school generally is doing well. The infant need attention especially as regards writing and the third standard might show more intelligence (their grammar is a failure and arithmetic and geography are hardly as good as usual) but the other classes have been carefully and successfully taught. The arithmetic of the fourth standard deserves praise and the papers are creditably neat though the writing is only moderate. The first and second standards passed well in all subjects. Geography pretty fair, grammar, owing to sickness in the third standard, fails to reach the required standard of proficiency."
Signed Henry Cheetham, Certificated 2nd class, Jane Graham, Article 79.

On 25th July building commenced on the new school house. Mr J Massey of Alderley was the builder, and its construction was superintended by the committee. School closed in August for holidays and re-opened on 5th September with only moderate attendance. The weather was very wet and stormy on 14th resulting in several children being away. The school was closed on 16th in the afternoon to allow painter to paint inside the school, windows and doors etc. Punished a boy (J Norbury) who was found breaking through a fence and throwing stones and also refusing to come out of the field when requested and otherwise being impertinent. November was also very stormy with snow resulting in poor attendance. School closed on 23rd December for the Christmas holidays. There was a tea party in afternoon, articles of food, butter, tea, sugar and cream given by Mrs Bower, Mrs Lea, Mrs Geo Snelson and Mrs Thos. Venables. At night children went through a programme consisting of songs, hymns and recitation. Admission of 6d each, proceeds went towards remaining expenses for the tea. Miss Reiss of Jodrell presided at the harmonium. Rev. Armitstead and Mr Downes, Attendance Officer called throughout the year.

1882

Scripture Report, 2 January

I consider this school efficiently and conscientiously taught. Group 1, lower, answered correctly and intelligently upon the Book of Genesis up to the death of Abraham and the outline of our Lord's life. I should like this class to present our Lords Parables or Miracles as a subject next year. The order of the Christian Seasons was well known and the scripture repetition very correctly said – Old Testament Scripture prints proved to be useful for this class I think.

Groups 2 and 4, written work. The lines here treated were remarkably well expressed, considering the writers' ages – distinguished, Wm. Slater, H Foden, and W Norbury. Standard 5 wrote very accurate scripture accounts, distinguished, H A Bradley, excellent Emily Phaler. The school has within it all the elements of excellence and should eventually reach a high degree of merit and usefulness. Signed by Edwin Gilbert.

On 4th January Master removed to new school house, from the house called Fithons in Lower Withington. T Callwood of Goostrey carted furniture etc., Mark Potts, Joiner assisted.

Many children were away on 9th January and when examined on 19th, irregular attendance pulled down the general work of the classes. In February a list of absentees was sent to the Attendance Officer. The classes were examined in March, Miss Simmonds of Jodrell being present part of the time. The Head Master questioned the children in Geography and took papers worked to J E Reiss Esq., of Jodrell Hall for him to see, for which he promised prizes to each Standard for each subject. One of the boys of this school (Henry Foden) died on 18th March, his complaint said to be diphtheria - not had any medical training to confirm this report.

There were great many children away during the month with parents afraid of this contagious illness being amongst the scholars. Rev. Canon Wilson called on 30th.

During April the prizes presented by E J Reiss Esq., of Jodrell were presented following examination in Arithmetic, Dictation, Geography and Grammar. Prizes given to Wm. Slater, Mary E Holden, Emily Phaler, Marjorie Parrott, Elizabeth Holden, John Rathbone, George Dakin and George Norbury. In June a girl was punished, (E A Warburton), for marking her sum right when she knew it was quite wrong. Dictation was very good, Emily Mee, Hannah Venables and Elizabeth Holden did very neat papers. Dr Smith of Chelford called at the school on 5th June, heard children sing. School closed in August for summer holidays.

Report for April 1882

Examiner T S Gleadowe Esq., HMI Lower Withington National School.

This school is going on very well. Reading will need attention (it is monotonous throughout the school) and the Geography and the Grammar of the third standard, though better than last year, are still capable of improvement, but with these exceptions, the work, both class and elementary, is good. Arithmetic is very accurately worked and the writing on slates deserves praise. Order very good.

Signed by Edwin Gilbert, Correspondent.

School opened on 14th September. The Master, with the sanction of Mr Gilbert, left school in charge of Assistant at 1.30. Attendance was very good on 15th and on 29th a half holiday for Goostrey Harvest Home. During October attendance was very poor, in fact every Friday afternoon attendance was bad sometimes with over 20 away; several of the children were away to go picking blackberries, at least that was the reason the parents gave.

A public tea party was held on 29th November when a half holiday was given in the afternoon, proceeds for the school fund. All provisions found by the farmers in the neighbourhood, 9 tea makers, Mrs Lea, Miss Jones (for Mrs Glegg), Miss Bowen, Mrs Newton, Mrs Venables, Miss Massey, Mrs Dakin, Mrs Gilbert and Mrs G Snelson. Little over 200 for tea – cleared close upon £12. On 30th school children's treat, tea at 4 in afternoon provided by the above. In the evening a programme consisting of songs-hymns, recitation and dialogues was gone through by children assisted by a few friends. Mrs Glegg of Withington Hall came in afternoon and stayed through part of programme at night. Admission to children's entertainment 6d, amount received at door for admission £2.13s.0d. Attendance fell during December – possibly due to heavy snow fall and school closed for Christmas on 21st.

Mr Gilbert and Mr Downes, Attendance Officer, called at the school throughout the year.

Scripture Report on examination held on 1st December 1882

The younger children answered very well and brightly upon their scripture subjects and said their repetition with freedom and accuracy. The course of the secular year should be taught before the Christian year is attempted, otherwise the little children become confused.

The elder children possessed a sound and accurate knowledge of Joshua and Judges and the Acts, this knowledge was shown as well by their written as their oral work. A large quantity of repetition including hymns, collects and Catechism was presented and well known. The school steadily and consistently maintains the excellent standard of religious knowledge, which I noticed last year.

Signed Edwin Gilbert.

1883

School opened on 8th January with only moderate attendance, a great many children were away ill with measles. School should have opened on 1st but was unable to because of the number of children ill with measles. During February a boy was punished on the 8th, (Wm. Pimlott,) for running girls out of the school during the dinner hour and otherwise being insolent when spoken to about it. When caned (one stroke on hand) attempted to walk out of school and when asked where he was going, said to his home - ordered him to take his place. Attendance on 12th was poor, rather wet, but probably owing to the meet of the hounds at Jodrell. Miss Graham went home on 14th because her mother was very ill. Entertainment held in school on 16th, programme consisted of songs, reading and dialogue. Received at door £6.3s.7d and nearly 200 were present. Proceeds after expenses for school funds. Miss Graham returned to school on 25th.

Mr Stanley called at school in the morning of the 5th March. Exam held on 14th and all papers worked were sent to Mr Gilbert who will judge which is neatest etc. When the best and neatest paper is selected a prize will be given. Miss Graham's mother died on 15th and she went home. Later in the month Emily Mee and James Venables each received a prize for the best, although the others had done fairly too. April and May passed without much incident although attendance was poor on 10th May, it was very wet. A great many away through Rent Day, left to take care of the house whilst parents away from home. Received from H L Reade, Solicitors, for completion, a form from the Charity Commissioners, relating to the application of the "Boden" Charity and the names of the present Trustees of that Charity. Asked by Mr Reade to place it along with the records of School – have placed it in school portfolio. Mr Ed Lea of Old Withington, Agent for the Withington Estate, a Manager of this school from its commencement, died on 22nd after about 9 days illness.

Report on examination taken 23rd April. 1883

"The children are in very good order and pass satisfactorily. Much of the reading is still painfully monotonous, and the geography of the first class and the spelling of a few scholars in the third and fourth standards are far from good, but in all other respects the results of the examinations are creditable." Signed by Edwin Gilbert. Correspondent.

Half holiday was taken on afternoon of 25th, Mr Lea's funeral at Goostrey church and on 30th, half holiday for tea party at Chapel Sunday School.

In June a holiday on 6th for Withington Club Day. Several boys were punished on 14th, F Bickerton, C Heath, F Capper, N Pimlott, J Pimlott, M Potts, Geo. Norbury and Jos Foden for throwing stones at railings in Gleggs wood. A half holiday on 20th for Confirmation at Chelford – first. On 12th July a treat at Withington Hall with games and prizes provided by Mrs Glegg. Summer holidays began on 26th and school opened on 20th August for the new term.

In September and October attendance was poor with very wet weather. On 3rd October only 12 children arrived at opening time, a few more came afterwards, but all so wet did not think it beneficial to their health to keep them sitting in their wet clothes, several who had come across the fields had wet feet. Did not open, sent word to Mr Gilbert. Attendance was again poor on 18th due to a tea party at the chapel.

November and December had little of interest apart from the Inspector's report.

Copy of Diocesan Inspector's Report of Examination in Religious Knowledge held on 10th December 1883 at 10 a.m.

"Lower Withington School – inspected 10th December 1883. Present 83, on books 90 at date of examination.

This school continues to be taught with great care and success. Group I, Standards II IV. V., answered very well and sensibly on the two books of Samuel, knew Paul's life and travels well, had a satisfactory knowledge of the Prayer Book subjects, understood and repeated the Catechism subject correctly, knew its Hymns and Canticles very nicely and said selected collects intelligently.

Group II, infants, Standards I and II. I was much pleased with the liveliness and attention of this class. Old Testament good, New Testament very intelligently and thoroughly known for such young children. The Christian year was well understood. The Catechism was very good, repetition both separate and simultaneous was excellent and all hymns presented were well said.

<u>Children distinguished</u>

<u>Group II,</u>

Rose Anna Norbury, Francis Warburton, Emily Foden, John Foden, Sarah Potts, Beatrice Casey, Emily Ward, Walter Capper and Oliver Mee.

<u>Written Work</u>

Group I – This work was very evenly and well done; and the knowledge of the text of the Bible which it shows is <u>excellent</u>. Charles Heath, William Pimlott, George Norbury, Henry Derbyshire, John Rathbone. <u>Very good</u>. Joseph Warburton, Sarah Staley, Annie Holden and Alice Davies.

Signed by H Plumpton Ramsden, Inspector.

The following are Inspectors' Reports up to 1888.

Report

The following is a copy of the Report of the Examination held on 7th April 1884, Lower Withington National School.

"The children are in good order and with a few exceptions, pass satisfactorily. The work is done in pretty good style, but writing admits of little improvement, and reading, though fluent, is monotonous. Grammar and Geography, creditable; needlework, fair. The infants are very fairly advanced. The writing might be rounder and more even".

Signed Edwin Gilbert, Correspondent.

Scripture Report – Chester 31ˢᵗ December 1884 – Lower Withington School Inspected 12ᵗʰ December 1884.

"The school has passed an excellent examination. The work of both groups was very good in all subjects. The children have evidently been taught most carefully and effectively. The work is well arranged and every advantage is taken of the opportunities offered to the Master. <u>Distinguished</u>, Harry Robinson, Miranda Casey, Wm. Pimlott, John Rathbone, Ellis Robinson, Frank Warburton, Alice Davies, Eliz., Venables and Emily Foden, in Group I. Olive Mee, Albert Dakin, Albert H Hadley, Walter Pimlott, Sarah A Heath, Sarah Pott, Beatrice Casey and Herbert Norbury, in Group II. Present 84, on books, 92, average 71%. Signed by Rev. H P Ramsden, Diocesan Inspector.

<u>Report 1885</u>

"This school is thoroughly well conducted and much of the standard and class work is very creditable. Reading shows much improvement, but writing is not yet good and needlework needs closer attention. Poetry was repeated without much regard to expression. The elder infants pass pretty well.

Henry Cheetham, Master Certificated 2ⁿᵈ Class
Eliz Whitehouse, Assistant Mistress – Ex 1. T
Signed by Edwin Gilbert.

Diocesan Inspection taken from the Inspector's General Report for the Diocese

According to the Diocesan Inspector's General Report on the Schools examined by him in Cheshire during the year 1884 it appears that he examined 477 schools in Religious Knowledge. Of these 27 are classed as "Excellent", 307 as "Good", 128 as "Fair", and 15 as "Indifferent". The following schools are classified by him as "Excellent", Aldford, Altrincham, St Margaret's Girls, Altrincham, St Margaret's Infants, Ashley, Birkenhead, St Anne's Girls, Birkenhead St John's, Infants, Bridgemere, Bunbury Boys, Cheadle Heath Infants, Cheshire Diocesan Boys, Chester St John's Girls, Chester St Mary's Infants, Christleton, Davenham, Eastham, Knutsford Boys, Lower Withington National, Macclesfield St George's Infants, Mere Mixed, Middlewich Boys, Partington Infants, Stockport St Thomas Mixed, Stockport St Thomas Infants, Utkinton, Walton, Warmingham, Stockport St Peter's Infants.

The above is copied from the Inspector's Report which was forwarded to the Correspondent by the Inspector.

Signed by Edwin Gilbert

Scripture report on examination held 10th December 1885 – Lower Withington School.

"The school continues to do excellently. It is taught with exemplary care and success. The scripture knowledge was decidedly good and the Prayer Book subject had evidently been taught very carefully. In explaining verbal difficulties in the Prayer Book and other repetition subjects, the words of explanation should be the simplest possible, otherwise the explanation defeats its object, viz., simplification or the knowledge becomes mechanical. The repetition subjects were excellent, <u>distinguished</u> Group I, Beatrice Casey, Jas Bellinger, Olive Snelson, Thos Venables, Agnes Foden, Frank Warburton and John Kennerley. Group II, Jane Saundry, Herbert Street, Albert Haidley, Eliz Parrott, Edwin Newton and Anna Platt."

Signed by Edwin Gilbert.

Report on examination held on 19th April 1886 received 14th May 1886

"The order is very good and the school is generally doing well. Writing should be much neater in the third standard, and the Geography and Recitation of the first class need more attention. There is also room for improvement in the Tables of the first standard, and the Arithmetic of the fourth, otherwise the class and standard work is satisfactory. A start has been made with Agriculture, but no grant can be recommended at present. The infants have evidently received careful attention.

H Cheetham, Certificated 2nd class
E Whitehouse, Assistant Mistress Ex. P.T.

Signed by Edwin Gilbert

Scripture Report on examination held on 9th December 1886

"The first (highest) group in the school passed a very satisfactory and creditable examination, in a full and varied syllabus of Religious Subjects. The answers were well distributed over the group and were given promptly, correctly and with intelligence. The repetition and Catechism, Collects etc., was good. The answering on the meaning of the Catechism and Prayer Book subject was particularly good and showed a full and intelligent acquaintance with the subject. The singing was hearty and good. A little more softness and sweetness together with distinction of enunciation would make it better still. The Scripture Abstracts on paper were generally very well done, though some were incomplete. Those written by Mary Wood, Emily Street and John Barber deserve special commendation. The slate work by Standard II – III was very fair but not particularly accurate or neat. The lower group, Standard I, II V, and infants are not up to the same standard of efficiency as the upper group. Some of the children answered readily in Scripture and had a very fair knowledge of the subject, but the bulk of the Standard I was silent and all the infants. The repetition of texts and Catechism was fairly good when said simultaneously but the children were not able to repeat the verses individually and the infants could say nothing. The lower part of the school needs attention to diminish the great contrast between the upper and lower division of the school. The following deserve special mention: Maud Casey, Albert Haidley, Harriet Pimlott, Annie Mottershead, John Barber and Eliz Bickerton.

Examiner – D Shaw

Signed by Edwin Gilbert

Diocesan Inspection 26th April 1887

The following is copied from the Rev. H P Ramsden. Report to the Bishop on schools examined by him during the year 1886. He examined 479 schools – of these 38 are classed as excellent, 299 as good, 130 as fair and 12 as indifferent or bad. The following schools classed as excellent for 1886' are arranged in alphabetical order.

Boys schools	Girls schools	Infant schools	Mixed schools
Birkenhead, S Annes	Birkenhead, S Annes	Altrincham, St Margarets	Altrincham, St Margarets
Birkenhead, S Peters	Birkenhead, S Johns	Birkenhead, S Johns	Ashley
Birkenhead, Trinity	Chester, Grosvenor	Castle, Northwich	Bosley
Bunbury	Claughton, Christ	Chester, Sealand Rd	Bridgemere
Chester, Blue Coat	Church	Claughton, Christ Church	Lower Withington
Chester Diocesan	Lymm	Crewe,-Wistaston Rd	Micklehurst
Chester, St Michael's		Macclesfield, St Peter	Macclesfield Sutton
Chester, St Pauls		Overton, Frodsham	Brassel
Christleton			Macclesfield, St ?
Hoylake			Rudheath
Knutsford			Stockport St Thomas
Lymm			Ulkinton, Tarporley
Middlewich			
Sandbach			

Report 28th April 1887

"The discipline is good and the teaching for the most part has been successful. Counting on fingers is a weak point in the first standard and in the third standard *writing and problems need more attention. In other respects the standard exercises are well done. Pretty good results are obtained in English and Geography, Needlework fair. The Elementary work of the infants' class is satisfactory but the Needlework falls far short of the required standard of proficiency."*

Signed Edwin Gilbert
H Cheetham – Certificated 2nd class
Elizabeth Cooper Ex P.T. Art. 50

Extract from Log book November 1887

Miss Cooper not at school on 3rd and on 4th the attendance was poor with a great many children ill. School closed earlier than usual on 11th owing to dark days (3.45). During evening Dr Macindoe of Chelford called and reported Scarlet Fever in Township and advised closing school. On 14th Dr Rushton, medical examiner of Macclesfield Sanitary Authority, called. Also Mr Sheldon of Macclesfield ordered closing till permission to open. On 18th Percy Lea at Walkleys died of Scarlet Fever and on 24th Harry Bradley died, also of Scarlet Fever.

Copy of Certificate for closing school

Macclesfield Rural Sanitary Authority
Medical Officers Department, Macclesfield, 11 November 1887.

To Mr Henry Cheetham – Schoolmaster

I hereby request you to close the national school in the Township of Lower Withington during the prevailing Epidemic of Scarlet Fever and to keep it closed until you receive permission from the above authority to re-open it.

John Latham Rushton MD.
Medical Officer of Health

Dated this 11th day of November 1887.

<u>Copy of Certificate for opening school</u>

Macclesfield Union Sanitary Authority
Medical Officers' Department
Macclesfield, 16 December 1887

To Mr Henry Cheetham – Schoolmaster

I hereby give you permission to re-open the school at Lower Withington closed by an Order from the above authority on the 11th day of November 1887 the district being now free from Scarlet Fever and the school in a good Sanitary condition.

John E Rushton ND
                        Medical Officer of Health
Dated this 16th Day of December 1887

School Log Book December 1887

School opened on 19th December with very poor attendance – fall of snow. Mr Rushton directed that children from houses where Fever had broken out should not be admitted to school for 3 or 4 weeks after date of opening. Mr Downs, the Attendance Officer, called on 21st and paid fees for Dale and Wood. Fever broke out on 31st at Samuel Slaters'.

Lower Withington Mixed School. Inspected 18th December 1888

Teachers Henry Cheetham and Miss Cooper.

It has been a real pleasure to inspect this school and to find such efficient and zealous teaching of a wide and varied syllabus, producing such excellent results. The younger group (St. I, II and Infants) had a good and ready knowledge of a large selection of Scripture subjects, and answered with intelligence and animation. They also repeated passages of scripture and the text of the Catechism distinctly and correctly. They had also a good knowledge of and meaning of the Christian year. The elder Group (St. III and VI) had a full and accurate knowledge of the Old and New Testament subjects and answered with great readiness, intelligence and accuracy of detail. The repetition of passages of scripture and Catechism was accurately given, and the creditable answering on the meaning of the second part of the Catechism showed how carefully they had been taught. The Prayer Book subject was also very well known by all the groups. The scripture abstracts on paper were very well done, especially those written by Maud Casey, Olive Snelson, Annie Mottershead, Anna Platt and Samuel Rathbone. The singing was very good. The following deserve special mention for good answering – Fred Heath, Jessie Dean, Eleanor Foden, Walter Martin, Mary Foden, Henry White, Eliza Bradley, Annie Yarwood, Annie Mottershead, Olive Snelson, Maud Casey and Violet Bickerton.

Present at examination 72.
                        Rev. D Shaw.

Lower Withington School Children 1921

Top row: - Oswold Ashley, Bob Foden, Colin Bell, Frank Snelson, George Tompkinson, Sidney Bailey and Robert Kennerley.

Second row: - Joe Bell, Fred Bell, Charlie Richardson, Norman Burgess, Leslie Shufflebothan, John Gregory and Ike Robinson. (Three boys extreme left not known).

Third row: - Arthur Grantham, Vera Venables, Margaret Crimes, Leann Massey, Doris Brooks, Silvia Atkinson, David Goodwin and Albert Derbyshire.

Fourth row: - --?--, --?--, Mary Heath, Dorothy Read, Mary Tompkinson, Emily Skellen, Kathleen Massey, Martha Bell and Nora Bell.

ST PETERS CHURCH – LOWER WITHINGTON
(Known as the Tin Tabernacle)

Opened in 1891 and built as a replica of St John's, Adlington, the building of the church was financed mainly by subscription.

The following is an extract from the Prestbury Parish Magazine of February 1894.

"The greater portion of our alloted space must be devoted this month to the somewhat dry, though necessary, details of figures and balance sheets. The subscription list to the Lower Withington Church Building Fund will speak for itself, and especial thanks are due to Mr Gilbert, who has spared neither money nor time in superintending the work. The district is now provided with a church, excellent school buildings, and master's house, but it is still without a parsonage house, and any kind of endowment for the support of a resident clergyman. If the first could be secured we should be glad enough to wait for the latter.

BALANCE SHEET OF LOWER WITHINGTON CHURCH BUILDING FUND

Subscriptions	£	s	d		£	s	d
Mr Reiss	70	0	0	Mr Nichols	1	0	0
Mr Gilbert	31	0	0	Mrs Barber	0	5	0
Withington Estate	25	0	0	Mr Reiss, for shrubs	6	0	0
Mr Bromley Davenport	20	0	0	Balance due to			
Mr Dixon	20	0	0	Treasurer	4	10	4 ½
Mr Egerton Leigh	10	0	0		314	0	7 ½
Miss Reiss	10	0	0				
Mr H Clarke (for Church furniture)	10	0	0				
Rev. W Armitstead	5	0	0				
Mr Edward Antrobus Foden	5	0	0				
Rev. E Royds	5	0	0				
Rev. A Royds	5	0	0				
Mr Seaman	5	0	0				
Mr A Ashton	5	0	0				
Mr Venables	5	0	0				
Rev. Franklin Roberts Preston	5	0	0				
Mr Snelson	5	0	0				
Colonel Cross	5	0	0				
Mrs Sarah Massey	3	0	0				
Mr Bowers	2	0	0				
Mr Cheetham	2	0	0				
Mr S Lea	2	0	0				
Mr Hope	2	0	0				
Chelford Church (collection)	3	12	3				
Collection at Opening Service	10	0	0				
Miss Reiss' Theatricals	18	0	0				
Collection, Easter Day, 1892	2	13	0				
Collection, Easter Day, 1893	10	0	0				
Mr Sutton	1	0	0				

Items Paid	£	s	d
Humphreys and Co	181	8	0 ½
" for carriage of goods	2	11	11 ½
" for Chancel	18	0	0
Font	6	10	0
Altar Cloth	15	0	0
Licence	1	11	6
Printing	0	6	0
Harmonium	25	10	0
Ashwin	10	18	6
Crossley (painting)	2	15	0
Foden	10	14	1
Arighi, Bianchi, & Co	1	13	0
" " "	1	3	6
Dakin	2	17	4
Holden	3	15	8 ½
"	1	9	11
Cooke	2	0	0
Jones and Willis	10	3	0
Rathbone	1	13	6
Buckley	3	12	6
Roylance	0	8	0
Day	1	9	9
Carriage	2	9	10
Quicks for fence	0	7	0
Shrubs for Churchyard	6	0	0
	314	0	7 ½

The Church was originally designated as a Mission Church and in 1927 discussion took place between Mr Cecil Egerton, The Ecclesiastical Commission and the Rev. W H Parkes, relative to the conveyance under which the Mission Church will be acquired by the Chelford Parochial Church Council. The Mission Church and site amounted to 19 perches or thereabouts and is shown on the plan on next page.

— **PLAN referred to** —

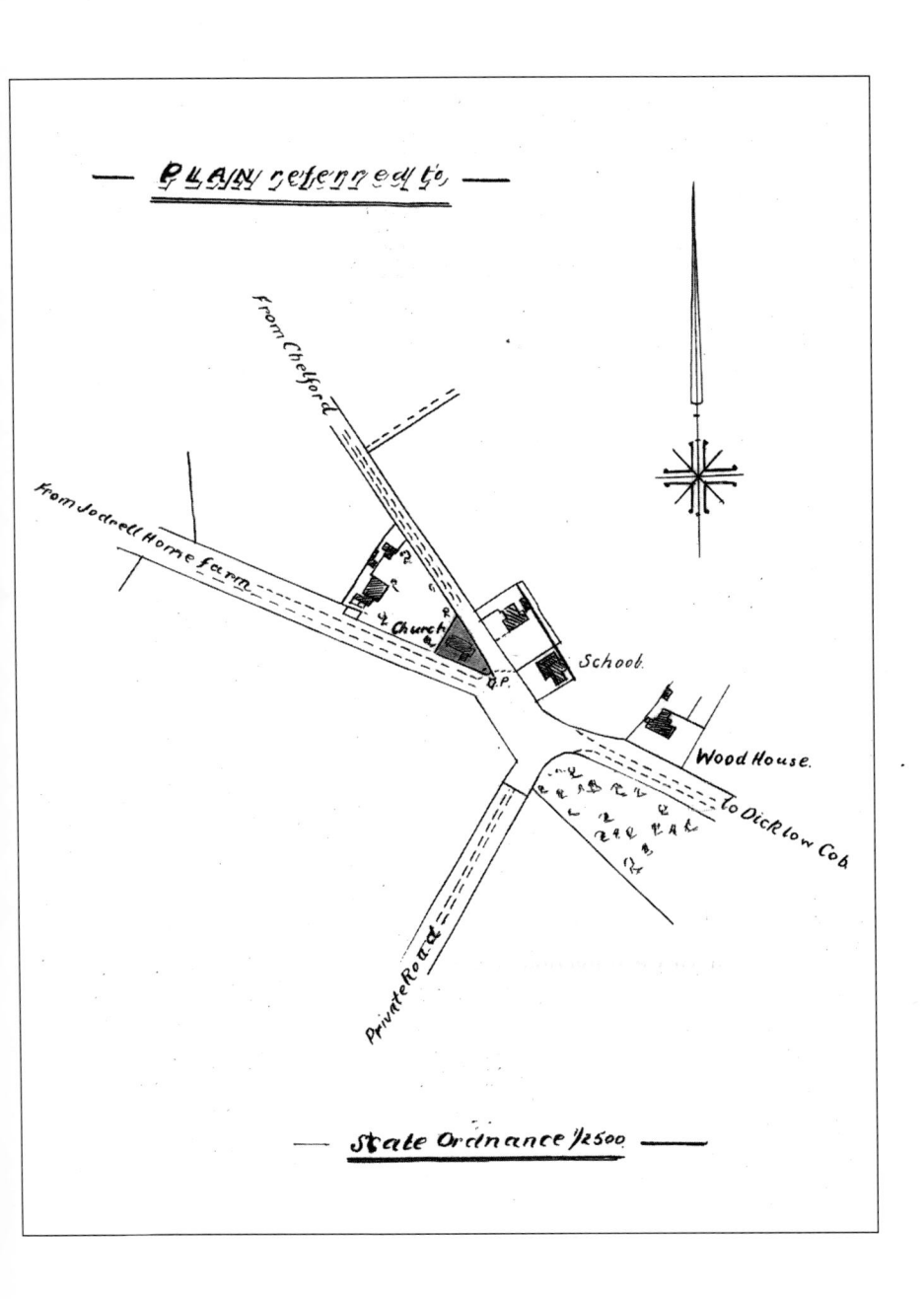

From Chelford

From Jodrell Home Farm

Church

School

Wood House

to Dicklow Cob

Private Road

— State Ordnance 1/2500 —

THE IRON CHURCH

Cheshire is the County I wish to name,
Lower Withington, a Township in the same;
Cathedrals one, and churches there are many,
But one I wish to name above any.
Down by the school house this iron church stands
Upon a peculiar piece of land,
For by a close inspection you will see
That it is in the shape of a letter V.
V stands for vicar, for virtue and for vice,
And that is quite obvious at first site.
The vicar how important his commands,
As he tells his congregation God's commands,
And if you look around you will see
That it is triangular as well as a V,
And is a splendid emblem of trinity combined
Which is of great importance to us and all mankind.
And just at the corner the post of wood it stands,
Points the road to travellers with it wooden hands;
But the vicar in the pulpit as you see
Has only two ways to point, not three.
He may not be a M.A. or bachelor of arts,
But one thing he must know that men have wicked hearts,
And that is why he's wanted to lead them on their way
That all whoever follow him may not go astray.
As V stands for vicar, for virtue and for vice, -
So C stands for church, for christian and for Christ;
And at this very corner is the place to make your choice
As there are only two ways and one leads to vice.
Narrow is the right way which to glory leads,
And oft we meet with difficulty which our path impedes:
But Jesus is our Captain who is to glory gone
And making intercession for us every one.
But all must be converted and have a change of heart
Before we can for heaven make a start.
This world truly is a wilderness and desert drear,
But trusting in our Captain we have nought to fear.

Anon

Loaned by Ann Venables

LOWER WITHINGTON CHURCH INTERIOR
Before new seating was installed from redundant church in Birkenhead c 1960

LOWER WITHINGTON CHURCH

Source of picture – Cheshire Churches Home Page on website www.moston.org/churches.html with thanks to Bill Moston

EARLY METHODISM IN LOWER WITHINGTON

As the 18th century drew to its close, Methodist preachers were known to be active in the area. It is believed that Acre-Nook, which at that time was a waste piece of ground, was the site on which the preachers spread the Gospel to the people of the village.

Methodism was becoming popular all over Cheshire, especially in the east, and chapels were built in the county from 1759. As Methodism developed, Methodist New Connection, Independent Methodists and The Wesleyan Methodist Association became established. It was quite common at that time for districts to have three circuits, each with ministers and lay preachers, one Wesleyan, one Primitive and perhaps one other. It wasn't until 1932 that all the strands of Methodism combined to form the Methodist Church.

Around the end of the 18th century Whitecroft Heath on Whitecroft Heath Road, then occupied by Thomas Braster, was opened for class meetings and became the first home of the little church.

The first class leader of the infant society was John Thorley who, because of his support for Methodism, was ejected from his house together with John Sommerfield, whose house was used for services, both being forced to leave the district. Following these set backs, meetings were held in the safe home of Samuel Wright of Withington Common.

During the early years persecution of Methodists was commonplace, as can be shown from the following extracts from 'The Methodist' of 25th November 1909: -

> "The Rev Miles Martindale was the second minister of the Macclesfield Circuit in 1796 and on one occasion, when nearing the house at Withington where he was due to preach, he was met by a man with a horsewhip who threateningly demanded his business. The minister quietly inquired whether there were no sinners in the neighbourhood who were in need of the salvation of the gospel. The remark proved to be the soft answer which turneth away wrath, and he was allowed to pass without further molestation".

> "Men of the baser sort joined in the persecution. The climax was reached when Mr Thomas Allen of Macclesfield, an influential and devoted local preacher, went to take an evening appointment at Dingle Smithy, at that time the home of the society. Riding a beautiful black mare he got quite near to his destination when

suddenly the horse struck her foot against an obstacle. Some dastards had drawn cart ropes across the road, designed to throw the preacher and were concealed in the hedge ready to gloat over his discomfiture. Happily the horse did not fall but as though comprehending the situation, dashed towards the men in the hedge, who were glad enough to drop the ropes and make their escape. Reaching the room where the service was to be held, Mr Allen found the congregation assembled and among them a grotesque figure with masked face and huge wig, whose body was clad with the ample folds of a cloak. This man sat motionless for a time but when the text was announced he rose and made a mocking bow to the preacher. Naturally, some confusion ensued, during which the preacher lost his text and while turning the pages to find it these words met his eye, 'Suffer me that I may speak and after that I have spoken, mock on'. This request of the patriarch was palpably appropriate and it was used as the basis of a dignified and severe rebuke, which evidently went home. But the end was nigh at hand. Mr Allen, securing the names of four of the chief offenders, procured a warrant for their apprehension. The men fled from the neighbourhood and the church had rest."

However, the society continued to grow and a chapel with day school attachment was erected at a cost of £700 in 1808 opposite the common, followed in 1816 by an extension for use as a Sunday school.

The original baptismal register shows that between May 1808 and September 1813 there were 55 baptisms:

Between 1814 and 1820 the following names are recorded in the register.

> Baskerville[2] – Worth[4] – Slack[6] – Johnson – Hackney – Frith[2] – Roylance[6] – Wood – Norbury – Taylor[2] – Almond 3 – Barber[4] – Booth – Cope – Boon[2] – Fisher – Smallwood – Dean – Ward – Tompkinson – Buckley.

From 1820 to 1837 a total of 61 baptisms took place

The Sunday school proved to be a success and 201 names were registered as attending during the first year including forty-two resident in Siddington. However, under the date 7th July 1816 an entry appears against several of these names as 'removed to Siddington school'.

It was common at this time for Sunday schools to teach reading and writing in addition to religious teaching though this practice began to decline particularly in town schools as day schools became more established. For many years the Sunday school at Withington continued to teach reading and writing as can be shown by an entry in the minute book dated 1st August 1816.

'At a meeting of the committee it is agreed that when the number of writers shall exceed forty, one half of them only shall be taught to write at once, the other half learning to read at the same time'.

Discipline appears to have been quite strict – an entry in the records dated 29th January 1817 stating,

'At a meeting of the committee it is resolved that no scholar shall be allowed to write with their hat or bonnet on. It is determined that each teacher shall take care of his class and that he suffer none to return home without permission.

The school records indicate the reason why scholars ceased to be attached to the school and against various names the following comments have been added:

'Left on account of bad attendance
Detained at home by parents.
Left – bad behaviour.
Left on their own accord.'

Financial matters were also recorded in the records, the accounts for 1820 containing the following:

'To John Roylance	s	d
7lb of cheese at 7d	4	1
Bread and cakes	4	6
10 quarts of ale at 7d	5	10

The records 12 months later make it clear that this expenditure was for Christmas Singers, a practice that appears to have continued in Withington throughout the 19th century. It was the practice of Withington residents to visit other members of the village at Christmas time. At first the group consisted only of singers but gradually, musical instruments were added until, by the end of the century, a brass band with something like fourteen instruments accompanied the singers. The event was taken very seriously and prior to the event, practices were held in Mr J B Kennerley's house. At six o'clock on Christmas Eve all the singers and bandsmen set out and for twenty-four hours toured the village. Various modes of transportation were used and meals provided at certain homes. It was said that a few would complete the full twenty-four hours but most would retire for a few hours' rest, others taking their place whilst they rested.

One of the most active villagers in the early days of the Chapel was Thomas Foden, whose name was the first among the trustees in the deed of October 1807 conveying the land on which the chapel was built. For thirty years he was choirmaster as well as holding many other positions within the organisation of the chapel. Other names active in the Chapel during the early years include Slack, Roylance, Garner, Slater, Snelson, Venables, Basford and Bloor.

By the mid 1840's the trustees of the Chapel were John Foden, Thomas Worth, John Darcey, Joseph Slack, Thomas Buckley and Richard Foden.

The grave yard came into being in 1813, early burials including:

> Ann Wood, wife of Thomas Wood of Siddington, 30th November 1813
> Martha Slack, wife of Peter Slack of Lower Withington, 20th March 1815
> Daniel Walkley, son of Jonathan and Sarah Walkley of Lower Withington, 20th March 1832

The burial ground was enlarged in 1870 and again in 1873, Richard Bloor donating a piece of land for the purpose.

A renovation scheme, incorporating a new heating system was carried out in 1878 and in 1893 further improvements were made to the Chapel. It was at about this time that new pews were fitted.

Prior to the centenary celebrations in 1908 further alterations were carried out and it is said that a new room was built for school purposes. However, any day scholars remaining would probably have left earlier when the village school opened in 1884.

The Methodist Currier reporting on the centenary states, after commenting on the history of the Chapel –

> "Similarly the spiritual side of the work is prosperous. Mr J B Kennerley, Missionary enthusiast, ever ready for every good work, has a most successful society class, and other good classes are led by Mrs Challinor and Mr Alfred Bloor. There are two flourishing junior classes. The Sunday school, which some thirty years ago had dwindled, gained ground under the guidance of Mr John Foden, its superintendent for twenty-eight years. Mr Foden has been chapel steward for a considerable period and at present is one of the circuit

stewards. Mr T Thorley is an admirable organist and society steward. There are many other capital helpers, such as Mr S Kennerley, Mr R Skellern, Mr R Kennerley and Mr Hudson."

REGISTER OF BAPTISMS IN THE PARISH OF PRESTBURY IN THE COUNTY OF CHESTER FOR THE USE OF THE WESLEYAN SOCIETY, WITHINGTON MAY 1808 TO SEPTEMBER 1813

Extracted from Cheshire Record Office Archives ref: MF1/7

DATE	NAME	SEX		PARENTS	OF	OCCUPATION	CEREMONY PERFORMED BY
6 May 1808	Sarah	D	Of	Joseph & Alice Slack	Withington	Wheelwright	Samuel Taylor
5 June 1808	Maria	D	Of	Wm. & Mary Parkes	Withington	Joiner	Theophilus Lessey
6 Oct 1808	William	S	Of	Ann Weatherby	Withington		John Hanwell
11 Dec 1808	Samuel	S	Of	Wm. & Sarah Roylance	Withington	Smith	Thomas Hutton
19 Mar 1809	Harriet	D	Of	John & Martha Hackney	Kermincham	Labourer	John Hanwell
20 Apr 1809	William	S	Of	John & Mary Roylance	Withington	Labourer	John Hanwell
30 Apr 1809	John	S	Of	John & Ellen Wood	Withington	Weaver	Thomas Hutton
5 May 1809	Mary	D	Of	Thomas & Elizabeth Slater	Somerford	Labourer	Thomas Hutton
29 Jun 1809	Samuel	S	Of	Peter & Jane Taylor	Withington	Labourer	John Hanwell
22 Nov 1809	John	S	Of	John & Mary Forster	Congleton	-	Theophilus Lessey
4 Dec 1809	Lydia	D	Of	Richard & Margt Slack	Withington	Cordwainer	Theophilus Lessey
8 Jan 1810	Lois	D	Of	Peter & Sarah Weatherby	Bradwell	-	Thomas Hutton
9 Feb 1810	Phebe	D	Of	Joseph & Hannah Ford	Withington	Labourer	Thomas Hutton
4 Mar 1810	Joseph	S	Of	Joseph & Alice Slack	Withington	Wheelwright	Thomas Hutton
18 Mar 1810	Elizabeth	D	Of	James & Ann Foden	Withington	Farmer	Theophilus Lessey
18 Mar 1810	Mary	D	Of	Joseph & Mary Weatherby	Macclesfield	-	Theophilus Lessey
22 Mar 1810	Jane	D	Of	William & Martha Norbury	Macclesfield	-	Theophilus Lessey

DATE	NAME	SEX		PARENTS	OF	OCCUPATION	CEREMONY PERFORMED BY
22 Mar 1810	Mary	D	Of	Ruth Mellor (bastard)	Withington	-	Theophilus Lessey
13 Apr 1810	Ann	D	Of	William & Mary Hadfield	Congleton	Druggist	Theophilus Lessey
?	?			James & Ann Lockett	Siddington	Labourer	Theophilus Lessey
1 May 1810	Henry	S	Of	William & Mary Smyths	Congleton	-	Theophilus Lessey
22 Jul 1810	Dinah (dead)	D	Of	Thomas & Dinah Worth	Siddington	Mason	Thos. Hutton
16 Sep 1810	Hannah	D	Of	Thos. & Lydia Booth	Congleton	-	Theophilus Lessey
28 Aug 1810	Rachael	D	Of	William & Rebecca Hathan	Congleton	-	Thos. Hutton
30 Sep 1810	George	S	Of	Ralph & Elizabeth Cartwright	Congleton	-	Zach. I Gurdall
18 Oct 1810	Samuel	S	Of	John & Theodicia Wood	Siddington	Weaver	Theophilus Lessey
28 Oct 1810	Thomas	S	Of	Thomas & Jane Barber	Withington	Labourer	Theophilus Lessey
28 Oct 1810	William	S	Of	Benjamin & Hannah Stafford	Congleton	-	Zach. I Gurdall
25 Nov 1810	Sarah	D	Of	William & Sarah Roylance	Withington	Smith	Theophilus Lessey
5 Nov 1810	Emma	D	Of	Wm. & Sarah Krinks	Congleton	-	Theophilus Lessey
23 Dec 1810	Hannah	D	Of	James & Mary Adshead	Siddington	Labourer	Theophilus Lessey
30 Dec 1810	Sarah	D	Of	Thomas & Elizabeth Boon	Somerford	Labourer	Theophilus Lessey
17 Jan 1811	George	S	Of	George & Martha Carter	Bosley	-	Theophilus Lessey
31 Mar 1811	Harriett	D	Of	Thomas & Ann Wood	Withington	Weaver	Tach[h] Gewdale
28 Apr 1811	Mary	D	Of	John & Mary Forster	Eaton	-	Theophilus Lessey
19 Sept 1811	John	S	Of	Peter & Jane Taylor	Withington	Labourer	Robert Hopkins
- Oct 1811	Elizabeth	D	Of	Thomas & Elizabeth Slater	Somerford	Labourer	Robert Hopkins
15 Apr 1812	Dinah	D	Of	Richard & Margaret Slack	Withington	Cordwainer	J Wheelhouse
10 May 1812	Joseph	S	Of	Wm & Martha Norbury	Macclesfield	-	J Wheelhouse
26 May 1812	Ann	D	Of	William & Sarah Krinks	Congleton	-	J Wheelhouse

116

DATE	NAME	SEX		PARENTS	OF	OCCUPATION	CEREMONY PERFORMED BY
7 Jun 1812	Elizabeth	D	Of	Thomas & Sarah Johnson	Marton	Joiner	J Wheelhouse
7 Jun 1812	William	S	Of	William & Hannah Weatherby	Withington	Farmer	J Wheelhouse
9 Jul 1812	Hannah	D	Of	James & Ann Lockett	Siddington	Labourer	Robert Hopkins
2 Sep 1812	Mary	D	Of	John & Lucy Bickerton	Withington	Labourer	William Ault
27 Sep 1812	Mary	D	Of	Edward & Ann Frith	Withington	Farmer	William Ault
8 Nov 1812	Mary	D	Of	Peter & Martha Slack	Withington	Wheelwright	Robert Hopkins
8 Nov 1812	William	S	Of	John & Ellen Wood	Withington	Weaver	Robert Hopkins
6 Dec 1812	Elizabeth	D	Of	William & Sarah Roylance	Withington	Smith	Robert Hopkins
12 Dec 1812	John	S	Of	John & Jane Oakes	Congleton	Cooper	William Ault
11 Feb 1813	Hannah	D	Of	Joseph & Mary Warmersley	Bosley	-	William Ault
6 Jun 1813	Jeremiah	S	Of	James & Ann Cope	Withington	Labourer	William Ault
10 Jun 1813	Silas	S	Of	George & Jane Worth	Withington	Weaver	William Ault
4 Jul 1813	Harriett	D	Of	John & Ann Booth	Kermincham	-	William Ault
4 Jul 1813	Peter	S	Of	Peter & Jane Taylor	Withington	Labourer	William Ault
12 Sep 1813	John	S	Of	Thomas & Jane Barber	Withington	Labourer	Robert Hopkins

LOWER WITHINGTON BAND AND VILLAGERS c 1908
Outside Methodist Chapel

Names of some of the people on the 1908 picture outside Lower Withington Methodist Chapel

Reading from left to right: -

The Band 1 ??, 2 Herbert Walker, 3 Samuel Bloor, 4 Frank Kennerley (Sandpit Farm, Marton), 5 Aaron Shuttleworth, 6 Ernest Bloor, 7 Robert Kennerley (Sandpit Farm, Marton), 8 Mr John Kennerley (Shellmore Farm), 9 Samuel Wood, 10 Timothy Wood.

Just behind the Band 1, 2, 3, 4, 5, 6 and 7 not known, 8 Mrs Massey, 9 Mrs Forden, 10 not known, 11 Robert Kennerley (Shellmore Farm), 12 Doris Kennerley.

Included in the second row are: - Mr William Slater, Mrs Anna Moss (nee Baskerville), Mr Hudson, Mr Ted Mee, Mrs Robert Kennerley (Shellmore Farm).

Included in third row are: - Mrs Snelson, Alfred Bloor, Peter mee, C Goodier, J Forden, J B Kennerley, Rev. T E Freeman, Rev. R H Higson, J Wood, C Roylance, T Garner and Samuel Kennerley (Sandpit Farm, Marton).

Included in fourth row are: - Mr George Moss, Mrs Reuben Skellern, Mrs Challoner, Mrs Samuel Kennerley (Sandpit Farm, Marton), Mrs Snelson, Mrs Oliver Mee, Mr Oliver Mee, Mrs Stephen Bloor (Deans Rough Farm) and Mrs Samuel Bloor.

Included on the back row are: - Thomas Thorley, Mrs Thomas Thorley, Mrs Peter Mee, Miss Emme Mee and Addy Kennerley.

BAND OF HOPE – 1883 – LOWER WITHINGTON CHAPEL

PLEDGE SIGNED BY LOCAL RESIDENTS

PLEDGE: - By Divine assistance, I will abstain from all Intoxicating Drinks as Beverages and discountenance all the causes and practices of Intemperance.

1883	No.	Name	Address	Remarks
12.2.83	1	Thomas Bradley	Lower Withington	Broken the pledge
12.2.83	2	Thomas Bickerton	"	Broken the pledge
27.1.83	3	Elija Ward	"	
27.1.83	4	Mary Jane Ward	"	
27.1.83	5	Ann Emily Mottershead	"	
12.2.83	6	Albert E Hughes	"	
15.2.83	8	Isaac Blackhurst	"	Broken the pledge
15.2.83	9	Robert Norbury	"	
15.2.83	10	William H Bickerton	"	
15.2.83	11	John Bickerton	"	
15.2.83	12	John Carter	"	Broken the pledge
15.2.83	13	Samuel H Clarke	"	
10.3.83	14	Hannah Bickerton Junr	"	
10.3.83	15	Alice Bickerton	"	Broken the pledge
10.3.83	16	Elizabeth Ann Bickerton	"	
12.3.83	17	Mary Ann Potts	"	
12.3.83	18	Sarah Lennington	"	
12.3.83	19	Elizabeth Thorley	"	
12.3.83	20	Samuel Mee	"	Broken the pledge
12.3.83	21	Emily Foden	"	
12.3.83	22	Frank Bickerton	"	Broken the pledge
12.3.83	23	William Gradwell	"	Broken the pledge
12.3.83	24	Maria Dutton	"	
12.2.83	25	Nathan Foden	"	Broken the pledge
13.1.83	26	Ellen Blackhurst	"	Broken the pledge
13.1.83	27	Emma Jane Robinson	"	
13.3.83	28	Mary Bickerton	Siddington	Broken the pledge
13.3.83	29	Elizabeth Bickerton	"	
13.3.83	30	Herbert Blackhurst	"	Broken the pledge
13.3.83	31	Arthur Hough	"	Broken the pledge
18.3.83	32	William Wood	"	Broken the pledge
18.3.83	33	Charles Wood	"	Broken the pledge
23.3.83	34	Aaron Cooper	Lower Withington	Broken the pledge

Date	No.	Name	Place	Note
23.3.83	35	Henry Hulme	"	
23.3.83	36	Martha Hulme	"	
23.3.83	37	William Cooper	"	Broken the pledge
23.3.83	38	Elizabeth Cooper	"	Broken the pledge
25.3.83	39	John Story	"	Broken the pledge
1.4.83	40	Lucy Bickerton	Siddington	
2.4.83	41	John William Blackhurst	Lower Withington	
12.3.83	42	John Kennerley	"	
12.3.83	43	John Calaghan	"	Broken the pledge
12.3.83	44	Matthew Potts	"	Broken the pledge
12.3.83	45	Emily Cooper	"	
12.3.83	46	Martha Taylor	"	
12.3.83	47	John Bell	Old Withington	
12.3.83	48	Frank Coppack	Lower Withington	Broken the pledge
12.3.83	49	John Mee	"	Broken the pledge
12.3.83	50	Martha Parrot	"	
12.3.83	51	Eleanor Carter	"	
12.5.83	52	John B Kennerley	"	
13.3.83	53	Robert Kennerley	"	
13.3.83	54	Thomas Kennerley	"	
18.3.83	55	Samuel Clarke	Over Peover	
19.3.83	56	Peter Mee	Barnshaw	
19.3.83	57	Mary Helena Hocknell	Barnshaw	
19.3.83	58	Cyrus Hocknell	Barnshaw	
19.3.83	59	Edward Hocknell	Barnshaw	Broken the pledge
19.3.83	60	Henry Hocknell	Barnshaw	Broken the pledge
19.3.83	61	Sarah Hocknell	Barnshaw	Broken the pledge
19.3.83	62	Thomas Foden	Blackden	
19.3.83	63	Mathew Eaton Faulkner	Goostrey	Broken the pledge
21.3.83	64	Martha Moss	Lower Withington	Broken the pledge
21.3.83	65	Elizabeth Venables	"	
21.3.83	66	Sarah Venables	"	
21.3.83	67	Mary Venables	"	
21.3.83	68	Annie Venables	"	
24.3.83	69	William Stanier	"	
24.3.83	70	Emily Ann Mee	"	
24.3.83	71	Alfred Mee	"	Broken the pledge
24.3.83	72	John Venables	Over Peover	
26.3.83	73	Samuel Bloor Junr.	Alderley	Broken the pledge
25.3.83	74	Ellen Thorley	Lower Withington	
10.3.83	75	James Goodier	"	

Band of Hope - 1883

Date	No.	Name	Place	Status
10.3.83	76	Elizabeth Goodier	"	
10.3.83	77	Louis Goodier	"	
10.3.83	78	Joseph Norbury	"	
12.3.83	79	Thomas Slater	"	
12.3.83	80	Samuel Bloor	Old Withington	Broken the pledge
12.3.83	81	Helen Bloor	"	
12.3.83	82	Herbert Walker	"	
12.3.83	83	Charles Goodier	Buglawton	
12.3.83	84	Emily Ward	Lower Withington	
12.3.83	85	Josiah Stonier	Siddington	Broken the pledge
12.3.83	86	Stephen Bloor	Lower Withington	Broken the pledge
12.3.83	87	Arthur Bradley	Lower Withington	Broken the pledge
12.3.83	88	William Norbury	"	Broken the pledge
12.3.83	89	George Norbury	"	Broken the pledge
12.3.83	90	Ellen Norbury	"	
7..4.83	91	Jane Foden	"	
7.4.83	92	Annie Foden	"	
7.4.83	93	Pheobe Foden	"	
7.4.83	94	James Foden	"	Broken the pledge
7.4.83	95	Annie Venables	"	
7.4.83	96	Hannah Venables	"	
9.4.83	97	Thomas Venables	"	Broken the pledge
9.4.83	98	Charles Venables	"	Broken the pledge
9.4.83	99	Peter Bloor	"	Broken the pledge
9.4.83	100	Richard Davies	"	Broken the pledge
9.4.83	101	Elizabeth Dean	"	
9.4.83	102	Fred Snelson	Old Withington	Broken the pledge
9.4.83	103	James Snelson	"	Broken the pledge
9.4.83	104	Elijah Bloor	"	Broken the pledge
9.4.83	105	Mary Kennerly	Marton	
10.4.83	106	Hannah Baskervyle	Old Withington	Broken the pledge
11.4.83	107	Henry Pimlott	"	Broken the pledge
19.4.83	108	Sarah Baskervyle	"	Broken the pledge
19.4.83	109	Mary Baskervyle	"	
19.4.83	110	Thomas Baskervyle	"	
23.4.83	111	Annie Dean	"	
7.4.83	112	Richard Bloor	Lower Withington	
7.4.83	113	Mary Bloor	"	
9.4.83	114	Olive Adshead	"	
9.4.83	115	Noah Adshead	"	Broken the pledge
9.4.83	116	William Sumner	"	
9.4.83	117	Charles Bailey	"	Broken the pledge

Band of Hope - 1883

9.4.83	118	Elizabeth Norbury	"	
14.5.83	119	Sarah Ann Baskervyle	"	
14.5.83	120	Margaret Baskervyle	"	
11.6.83	122	Arthur Holden	"	Broken the pledge
11.6.83	123	Thomas Henry Slack	"	
11.6.83	124	Charles Hall	"	
11.6.83	125	William Challinor	"	Broken the pledge
26.9.83	126	Annie Bell	Row of Trees Lindow	
11.6.83	127	Thomas Foden	Lower Withington	Broken the pledge
12.2.83	128	Samuel Kennerley	"	Broken the pledge
12.3.83	129	John Robinson	"	Broken the pledge
12.3.83	130	Jane Snelson	"	
14.5.83	131	Ellen Hastel	"	
14.5.83	132	Hannah Baskervyle	"	
15.5.83	133	Emily Walker	Old Withington	
15.5.83	134	Mary Ellen Holden	Lower Withington	
23.5.83	135	Samuel Ward	Capesthorne	
23.5.83	136	James Baskervyle	Old Withington	
23.5.83	137	James Pimlott	Lower Withington	
4.6.83	138	Fanny Slater	"	
6.6.83	139	Jessie Snelson	Old Withington	
11.6.83	140	Edwin Bickerton	Siddington	
9.9.83	141	Lee Parsons	Old Withington	
9.9.83	143	Mary Ann Brooks	Chelford	
9.9.83	144	Sarah Gallie	Marton	
19.10.83	145	John Norbury	Old Withington	Broken the pledge
19.10.83	146	William Venables	Over Peover	
19.10.83	147	John Bickerton	Siddington	
19.10.83	148	William Challinor	Lower Withington	
17.12.83	149	Elizabeth Ann Unwin	"	
31.3.84	150	Joseph Birchall	"	
15.5.83	121	George Moss	Chelford	Broken the pledge
31.3.84	151	Mary Birchall	Lower Withington	

Information obtained from Lower Withington Chapel Wesleyan Records 1857-1972

CRO Ref: EMS84 Book 2.

EARLY METHODISM IN OVER PEOVER AND SNELSON

Thanks are due to Mr Donald Read of Mobberley and Mr Frank Wilding of Chelford for information used in this chapter.

Methodism first made its mark in Over Peover and Snelson very early on in the 19th century when local preachers visited the area, preaching in the open air and in various cottages.

The first Preaching House was a cottage in Green Lane followed by a farm, said to be in the same locality (possibly Green Lane Farm). As the congregation grew it became necessary to move to larger premises and a large loft, situated mid-way between Green Lane and the present Snelson Chapel, was made suitable for the services. This preaching room near the roadside pump continued to be the home of the Methodists until the present Snelson Chapel was built. Snelson Chapel is only a very short distance from the preaching room, but in another township. See map on next page.

At some time before 1760 the Mainwarings of Peover Hall gave £280 for the building of a school on Snelson Common, supported by freeholders in the area who also contributed to the cost.

In 1776 the school paid £1.8s.6d for straw and wood for the 'intack' hedge. The field belonging to Snelson House was anciently known as the 'Intack' and a property known as Sycamore Cottage, at right angles to the road overlooked the field. It has been said that this cottage had a large lofty room, which was a meeting place of the Methodists prior to Snelson Chapel being built.

Not long after the Preaching Room was opened a Sunday school was established. Active in the cause at that time were Mr and Mrs Gibson, Mr and Mrs Shatwell, Mr and Mrs Acton and Mr and Mrs Ashton.

One of the Sunday school teachers was Miss Brentley of Chelford. Born at Siddington in 1789, she moved when she was quite young with her parents to Chelford, becoming a Sunday school teacher when she was 15. Some time after, her parents moved to Gawsworth but despite the distance involved, she continued to attend the Sunday school in Peover. As there was no preaching at Gawsworth until the evening, every Sunday she attended preaching in the then new Chapel at Withington.

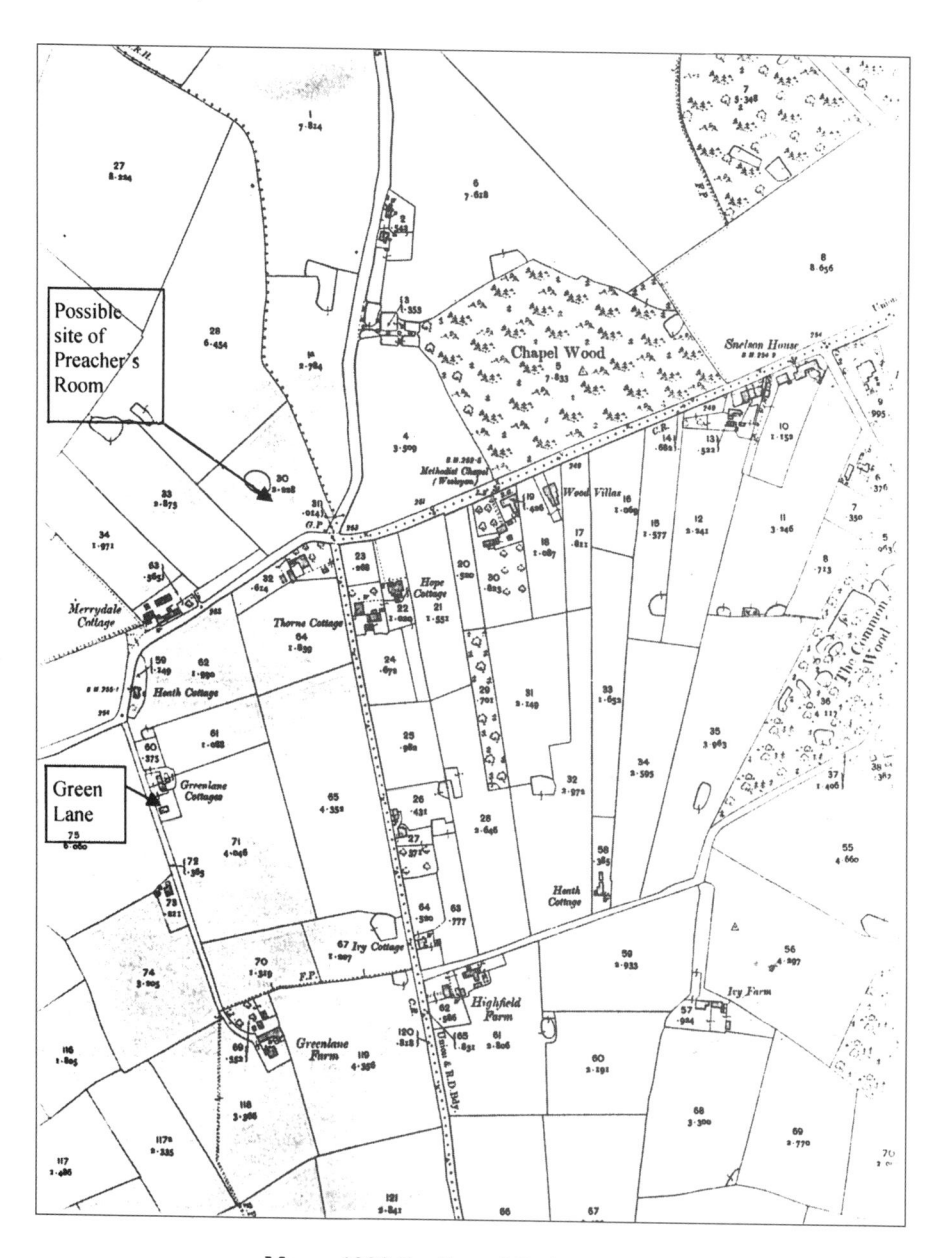

Map – 1909 Section of Ordnance Survey
Showing Snelson Chapel and Green lane

125

In 1813 she became engaged to the Rev. William Ault of Congleton and on 30th November of that year they were married at Prestbury church. Mr Ault offered himself for missionary work and on 31st December 1813 set sail for India to take up an appointment in Ceylon. Prior to the voyage Mrs Ault had not been very well. The voyage did not improve her condition and on the 9th February she passed away and was buried at sea.

One of Miss Brentley's friends when in Chelford was Miss Mary Dale and it was said that they were great company for each other and went everywhere together. However, she didn't last long after her friend's death. Maybe she was affected by it, for she passed away on 9th May 1814, just three months after her friend.

The Sunday school became, in those early days, of great benefit to the children of the area. Not only were they taught to read but also to write.

Over the succeeding years a number of 'well to do' farmers and others had joined the Society and had become dissatisfied with the facilities at that time. The loft was now too small for their requirements and it wasn't a pleasant place to worship in. The room was over a shippon, which was not very conducive to the act of worship. It was therefore decided to create a purpose-built chapel.

A suitable plot of land on the border of three parishes, Snelson, Chelford and Higher Peover, was offered by Mr Ashton and a chapel was built in 1825. The builder was Mr Slater, of Pine Cottage, Higher Peover and the trustees of the chapel were William Gibson, Edward Ashcroft, William Dale, Peter Faulkner, William Brown, Joseph Chantler, Peter Bentley, William Roylance, William Shatwell and William Bailey.

When the chapel was built a gallery for use by the singers was erected behind the pulpit, the singing, for many years, being led by Mr Richard Acton.

Amongst the early preachers was the Rev. John Rattenbury who, more than anybody, was responsible in the mid 1830's for what was called 'the great revival'. During this period the number of villagers converting to Methodism increased considerably and the chapel was, on many occasions, completely full.

Another 'great revival' occurred in 1858 when the Rev. Edward Jones was appointed to Macclesfield as the second minister. He visited Snelson on a number of occasions during that year making many conversions as a result of his powerful preaching.

It would appear that generations of families were involved with the Methodist cause. These included the Gibsons family with William, his son John, and his sons and daughters, and the Shatwells. Thomas Shatwell, (the son of William Shatwell, one of the first trustees), whose house was close to the chapel, paid off a debt of £95 outstanding on the chapel.

Other families involved with the cause were the Acton family and the Higham family of Snelson.

Another pillar of the chapel at that time was Samuel Read, formerly of Higher Peover, and later of Manor Farm, Chelford. It was while listening to a sermon preached at Snelson chapel by the Rev. Edward Jones that he yielded to be saved by grace. Soon after his conversion he was requested to go and call sinners for repentance. The first time he preached at Snelson the chapel was full, he being so well known in the district. It is recorded that his sermon was so effective that many converts came forward and marked the date of his sermon as the date that they were saved. Mr Read was made a class leader and meetings were held in his own home for many years. He died at Alderley Edge in 1893 and was interred at Snelson.

Other members of the Read family, James and his brother, Cragg, were most devoted and loyal workers, both filling the positions of Sunday School Superintendent, Class Leader and Stewards.

Mr Pryce Jones, writing in 1907 on the History of Methodism stated: -

> 'A new chapter in the history of Methodism at Snelson was begun when the circuit was divided. Until the year 1864, Snelson formed a part of the Macclesfield circuit, and the pulpit was supplied by the preachers of that circuit. Snelson was a favourite child, and right well did the ministers and local preachers look after it and nurse it. Many of the preachers walked the eight miles with joy, for they knew that when they entered the chapel they would be well received by the people, for they were the most charitable hearers. No seat was found there for the critic or the scornful. It was generally affirmed by the local preachers that Snelson was the best place in the circuit to launch a new sermon.'

The Jubilee of Snelson Chapel was commemorated in 1875 when the chapel was enlarged and a Sunday school built. The gallery was removed and a minister's vestry added to the chapel. The old tall pulpit was replaced with one of a more modern shape, made of pitch pine, as were the seats. The school was divided from the chapel by sliding doors, facing the pulpit. The chapel was re-opened in November 1875.

The Chapel was first licensed for marriages in the year 1889, the first marriage to be solemnised on 20 March being that of Hannah, daughter of Richard Acton to Mr James Snelson. Baptisms had however been carried out since 14 February 1827 when Thomas, son of Samuel Morris of Over Peover, was baptised.

To understand what life was like during the latter part of the 19th century and the early part of the 20th century, it is well worth referring again to Mr Pryce Jones 1907 article which included the following: -

> "As the chapel was on the border of three parishes, Chelford, Marthall and Higher Peover, the congregation came from each of the parishes, but the majority from Peover. It is only right to acknowledge that as a rule the vicars of these parishes have not been, as in some places, antagonistic to the Methodists. If they did not join hand in hand with them, they did not oppose them. They visited the sick Methodists and they helped them in other ways. The Vicar of Chelford, the Rev. A L Royds, showed a most beautiful Christian spirit when he held a week of special prayer in his parish, and held prayer meetings in the schoolroom. He gave a hearty invitation to the Nonconformists to attend as well as his own Church people. He also requested some of the Methodists to take part in the services. Earnest extempore prayers were offered by the Vicar, also by some of the Methodists, and their united prayers ascended to heaven. It is no wonder that the people said, "It was good to be there," and "Behold, how good and how pleasant it is for brethren to dwell together in unity." It was the custom with the Snelson people to attend the sanctuary twice on the Lord's Day. There were not many half-timers there. It was a beautiful sight to witness the whole family leaving the home, perhaps only in charge of the dog, and wending their way to the chapel from the farm, and from the cottage in the afternoon, then hastening home to tea and to milk the cows, and then returning to the evening service. The Sabbath to them was "a day of delight" and a "day of rest" to body and mind.
>
> From Merrydale Farm they went in numbers; Mr and Mrs Worthington and family, then Mr and Mrs Leigh, and of later years, Mr and Mrs Dale. Mr Dale holds a number of offices in the church and is a liberal supporter. Mrs Dale, in her early days, excelled as a singer and as a player on the harmonium in the house of God. Their son and daughters follow in their footsteps. From Bate Mill Farm they went into the sanctuary in numbers. Mr and Mrs Thomas Venables and their sons and daughters, and they also were liberal to the cause. And when the family removed to Withington, Mr Peter Venables also attended Snelson Chapel. One of their sons, Thomas

Venables, became a local preacher early in life; he was for some time at Mr Thomas Champness's Training Home for Local Preachers, and he laboured most earnestly for the Master, and was well received everywhere. He was very modest, therefore of a peaceful spirit. After labouring in his own circuit for so many years, he emigrated to New Zealand. He had not been there for many months before he met with an accident, and he was suddenly removed to the Church above. The Bate Mill Farm is still occupied by Methodists, Mr and Mrs Peter Mee are both zealous for the cause, and most liberal in their gifts. Mr Mee holds various offices in the circuit and at Snelson.

Not only has Bate Mill Farm been a noted Methodist home, but Bate Mill has also been the home of various Methodist families, and some born there are today most honourable members in the Methodist Church. Mr and Mrs Samuel Clarke, of Foxwood Farm, and their sons and daughters have been good helpers at Snelson Chapel. Also Mr and Mrs Joseph Clarke of Peover; Mr and Mrs Simcock formerly of Ollerton; Mr and Mrs Joseph Street of Peover Heath. Also the various branches of the Street family have been connected with Snelson Chapel from its beginning, and some of the family are still members of the society. The Read family have also attended the Chapel from its early days. Mr James Read is still in harness as a class-leader and Sunday school teacher. Mrs Read was also a good helper before her removal to the Church above. Their sons and daughters are of the same spirit, and are active members in the church and circuit. Mr and Mrs Cragg Read also have been associated with the school and chapel from childhood; Mr Read is a steward and a Sunday school teacher.

Also Mr John Acton, Mr and Mrs Darlington, Mr Blackshaw, Miss Handforth, Mr S Clarke, Mr and Mrs Kinsey, Mr and Mrs Thorley, Mrs Gibson, Mr and Mrs Garner, Mrs Wyatt, Mr Young, Mr Burgess, Mr Mottershead, Mr Baskerville, Mr J Read, Mr S Read, Mr Steele, Mr A Clarke and Mr and Mrs Dean and prominent members of the Chapel.

One of the most prosperous institutions at Snelson has been the Band of Hope. It began some 28 years ago, and it is now by far the foremost in the circuit as far as numbers. About three hundred persons have signed the pledge there, and some of the most active members are those who have been reclaimed.

Their annual festival is held towards the end of May, and the day is spent in visiting various localities, headed by the Snelson Brass Band. In the procession are little children in carts, a number of friends in traps, and the majority walking. They visit the various halls and homes of the gentry, who contribute liberally to the funds of the society. In the afternoon, they have a substantial meal in the schoolroom, and in the evening they hold a public meeting, which is always well attended.

Not only is Snelson Chapel a sacred place to a number of people, but also its surroundings. For it is God's acre, and a great number have been laid to rest there. The graveyard is now nearly full. The schoolroom is also becoming too small for the Sunday scholars, and cannot be enlarged. The trustees were called together to consider the situation some months ago, and they came to the conclusion that it was expedient to build a new chapel and school in the near future, as near as possible to the present chapel, and that sufficient land be procured for the cemetery. Colonel Dixon, of Astle Hall, was approached on the matter – he without any hesitation willingly consented to sell as much land as was required, and at a very reasonable price. The money was soon collected, and the land transferred to the trustees. It is now enclosed by railings. A statute acre was procured not many yards from the present chapel, only further from the road and on higher ground. It is anticipated that before many years are passed away a new chapel and school will be erected on this desirable spot."

It appears that a new chapel was not built[1]. However, money was raised to renovate the Chapel and purchase a new pipe organ in part exchange for the old instrument. The cost of the new organ being £220. The re-opening service took place in April 1914 when Miss Moxon of Alderley Edge unlocked the organ with a gold key presented to her by the Trustees.

During the First World War members of the chapel concentrated on patriotic objectives, raising money for the benefit of serving soldiers.

The Annual Flower Service, which was held for the first time in 1926, became very popular and the gifts of flowers and fruit were given to the Manchester and Macclesfield infirmaries.

In 1931 the chapel was honoured when one of the evening services was preached by Sir Edwin Stockton and the lessons were read by Viscount Hailsham, a former Lord Chancellor, who was the guest of Sir Edwin Stockton of Jodrell Hall.

---

[1] A programme celebrating the Centenary in 1925 states 'The plot of land is still vacant. It has been drained, cleared and made ready for the purpose for which it was bought but, it still waits.

Mothering Sunday – 1975 – Snelson Chapel

Snelson Chapel 1913

Mr Cragg Read    Mr James Dale    Mr James Read

Mr John Gibson    Mr Richard Acton    Mr Robert Higham

Mr Samuel Read    Mr Thomas Garner

Prominent members in the early years of Snelson Chapel.

The Second World War brought many new faces into the chapel. First came the evacuees from Manchester, London and the Channel Isles, joined later by American soldiers serving with General Patten.

Family worship was introduced in 1963.

The Methodist cause was also being promoted at the nearby United Methodist Church situated in Cinder Lane, Over Peover.

The foundation stones for the United Methodist Church were laid on Wednesday 11th June 1913 and the church doors were opened on Wednesday 10th September 1913 by Mr Samuel Clarke of Foxwood. The school doors were opened by Mrs Earlam.

The cost of building was met mainly by subscriptions for stones and bricks which are recorded as follows: -

United Methodist Church, Over Peover,
Foundation Stones were laid on 11th June 1913
In Memory of

Mrs Betsy Baskerville, Mr Joseph Baskerville, Mrs Stephen Bloor, Mr James Clarke, Mr James Dale, Mrs James Dale, Mr Thomas Earlam, Mr Joseph Steele, and by Mr and Mrs John Bloor, Miss Lilian Baskerville, Mr and Mrs Allan Callwood, Mr Samuel Clarke, Mr and Mrs Edwin Clarkson, Mr and Mrs John Clarkson, Mr and Mrs Dale, Mrs E Mackintosh, Mr Peter Mee, Mrs Peter Mee, Mrs George Moss and Mrs Snelson.

Bricks were laid by, or on behalf of, the following: -

Elsie Bailey	Samuel Bloor	Amelia Broome
James Bailey	Mrs Bloor	Charles Burgess
Mrs William Bailey	Anna Bracegirdle	Mrs Charles Burgess
Jack Baxter	Joyce Bracegirdle	John Burgess
Richard Baxter	Willie Bracegirdle	G N Callwood
Vera Baxter	John E Braggins	Henry James Callwood
J E Barstow	Wilfred Braggins	Alfred Clarke
Florrie Blackshaw	Mrs Joseph Brandreth	John Clarke
James Stanley Bloor	S Brandreth	Janet Clarke
Jesse Evyline Bloor	William Brocklehurst	Mrs J O Clarke
Richard Ashton Bloor	Mrs William Brocklehurst	Leslie Clarke

Mary Clarke	Samuel Groves	John Rhodes
Marion Alice Clarke	Sarah Ellen Groves	William Riley
Samuel Clarke	William Groves	Anna Robinson
Mrs Samuel Clarke	Mrs William Groves	Eveline Robinson
Miss Clarke	Rev. F W H Guttridge	Henry Robinson
Gertrude Clarkson	Mrs F W H Guttridge	William Robinson
John Thomas Clarkson	John Hale	Regd. Roland Seddon
Winifred Edna Clarkson	Sarah Hale	Ida Slater
Joe Cragge	Mrs William Harrop	Jesse Slater
John Cragge	Mrs Hudson	Mary Anna Slater
Charles Crimes	Harriett Jackson	Miriam Slater
Joseph Crimes	Madge Jackson	William Slater
Mrs Joseph Crimes	Nellie Jackson	Mrs William Slater
Mrs Sylvia Crimes	Nellie Jackson	Catherine Steele
Thomas Crimes	Polly Jackson	Hector Steele
Thos Arthur Crimes	James Jervis	Angelina Street
Thomas Crimes	Martha Jervis	Blanche Street
J B Cooke	J B Kennerley	Gilbert Street
Algernon Dale	Emma Lomas	Mrs Sutton
Mrs Algernon Dale	Eunice Lomas	Fanny Thorley
Allen Dale	Margaret Lomas	Thomas Thorley
Ernest Dale	Rev J E Mackintosh	Maggie Twiss
Norman Dale	Clifford Massey	Ruth Twiss
Peter Davenport	Thomas Massey	Arthur Venables
Arthur Dawson	Albert Edward Mee	Henry Venables
John Foden	Alfred Mee	Mary Venables
Williamson Foster	Mrs Alfred Mee	Samuel Venables
Thomas Garner	Edward Mee	Thomas Venables
Arthur Groves	Elsie Mee	Arthur Wainwright
Charles Groves	Ivy Mee	Milly Ward
Charles Groves	Abraham Moores	Charles Ward
Mrs Charles Groves	Eaton Moores	Ernest Ward
Edith Groves	Joseph Moores	Florence Ward
Ethel Groves	John Myers	Samuel Ward
Gertie Groves	Donald Pilkington	Thomas Ward
George Groves	George Ravensdale	Walter Ward
Jesse Groves	Helen Read	Dorothy Webb
Sam Groves	Thomas M Read	

Bricks were laid in Memory of the following: -

Charles Allen	Joseph Baskerville	Peter Brandreth

Mrs Peter Brandreth	Mrs Joseph Mottershead	Mr Thomas Walton
Marjorie Burgess	Henry Robinson	Mr James Ward
William Emsley	Mrs Henry Robinson	Mrs James Ward
Mrs John Foden	Mrs Sant	Henry Ward
Robert Higham	Mrs Thomas Thorley	Mrs Samuel Ward
Mrs Caroline Holt	Joseph Tomlinson	Mrs Wyatt
William Kinsey	Mrs Joseph Tomlinson	Richard Young
Mrs Thomas Massey	Mrs Samuel Tomlinson	Mrs Richard Young
Joseph Mottershead	Mrs Walton	

The Trustees offered the Chapel to the Alderley Edge and Knutsford Circuit who declined the offer, the chapel then being offered to the Macclesfield UMC who accepted. On the introduction of the Methodist Union the Macclesfield Park Street Circuit ceased to exist and Over Peover was allocated to the Alderley Edge and Knutsford Circuit.

Following the opening of the doors of the Chapel, two tablets, erected by the congregation and friends to the memory of Mr James Clarke and Mr and Mrs James Dale, were unveiled by Messrs Algernon Dale and A Moores.

The Rev. James Hooley of Durham preached and afterwards tea was served for approximately 350 people.

A large meeting was held in the tent during the evening. Mr J Young of Arclid, presided and addresses were delivered by the Rev. James Hooley, Rev. J E Mackintosh, Messrs Alernon Dale, Alfred Barber, James Hill, Peter Slater, Joseph Steele and Alfred Clarke.

The total proceeds taken for the day amounted to £45.

The opening services were continued on 14th September. The inauguration of the Sunday School took place at 10.30 when the Rev. J E Mackintosh delivered an address. Large congregations attended the chapel in the afternoon and evening and the collections for the day amounted to £57.0s.4½d.

Prior to the opening, the amount standing to the credit of the building fund was £698.18s.6d. With Wednesdays total this was increased to £743.18s.6d thus leaving a debt on the Chapel of £48.17s.6d. Sunday's collections, however, cleared the debt and left a balance of £9 in hand.

United Methodist Church,
OVER PEOVER.

— THE —

FOUNDATION STONES
:: Of the New Chapel ::

Will (D.V.) be Laid

On Wednesday, June 11th, 1913.

Stone & Brick-laying Ceremony at 3 p.m.

ADDRESS by the **Rev. E. D. Cornish,**
(CONNEXIONAL CHAPEL SECRETARY.)

TEA AT 4-30 P.M.

Public Meeting in Tent, at 7 p.m.

Chairman: F. H. JOHNSON, Esq., (of Holmes Chapel).

Tickets for Tea, One Shilling; Children Half-price.

COLLECTION AT EVENING MEETING.

UNITED METHODIST CHAPEL,
OVER PEOVER.

... THE ..
Chapel Opening Ceremony
WILL TAKE PLACE

ON WEDNESDAY, SEPTEMBER 10th, 1913.

The Chapel and School Doors will be opened at 3 p.m.,

AFTER WHICH

TWO MEMORIAL TABLETS WILL BE UNVEILED.

DIVINE SERVICE at 3-15 P.M.,   SERMON by the Rev. JAMES HOOLEY
(of Durham)

TEA AT 4-30 P.M.

Public Meeting in Tent, at 7 p.m.
Chairman - J. YOUNG, Esq. (of Arclid.)

Tickets for Tea One Shilling;   Children half-price.

Collection at Service and Public Meeting in aid of the Building Fund.

THE SINGING WILL BE LED BY THE SIDDINGTON AND WITHINGTON BRASS BAND.

THE OPENING SERVICES

will be continued on Sunday, September 14th, when Sermons will be preached by the
REV. J. E. MACKINTOSH, OF MACCLESFIELD.

SERVICES AT 2-15 AND 6-30 P.M.

THE SUNDAY SCHOOL WILL BE OPENED ON SUNDAY, SEPTEMBER 14th, 1913.

1909 OS MAP

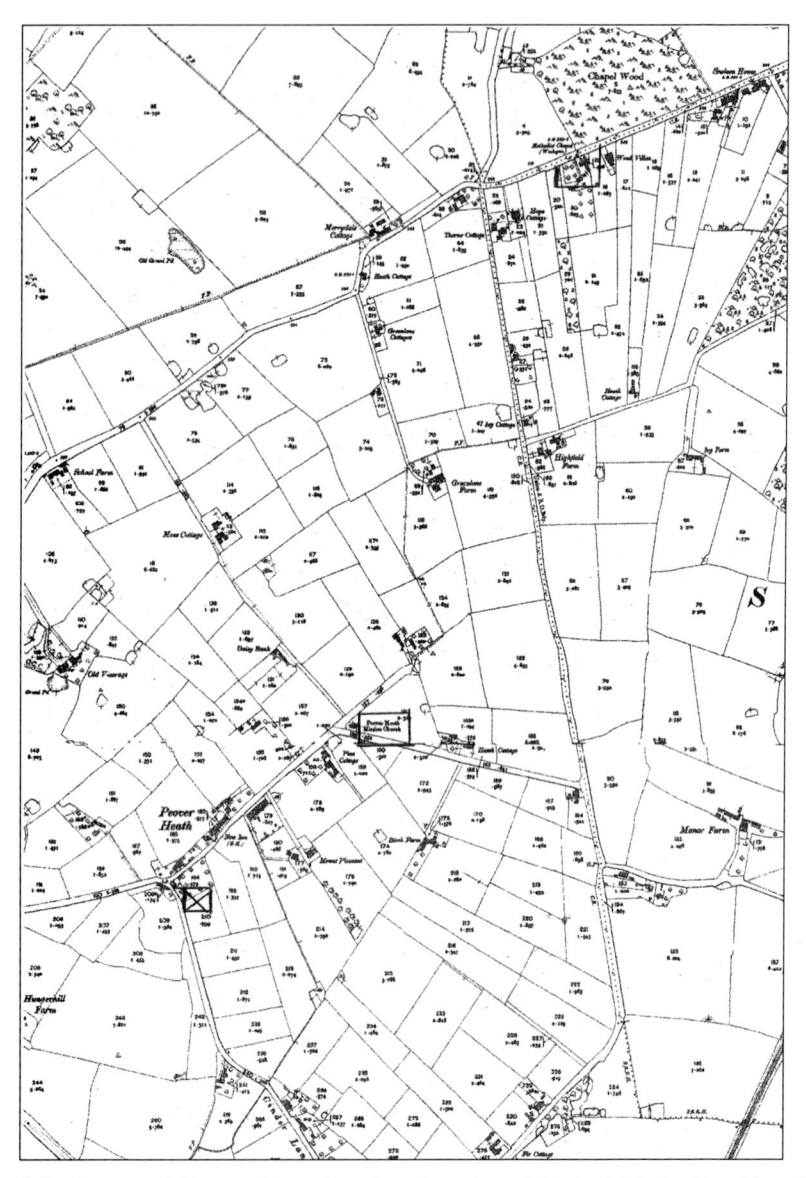

Map of Snelson and Peover Superior showing site of United Methodist Church, Peover Heath Mission Church and Weslyan Chapel. Note – United Methodist Church built in this area 1913.

LOWER WITHINGTON WALKERS
6th June 1969

TWENTY-THREE PROUD WALKERS

Pictured Left to right: -Anne Yarwood, Pauline Kennerley, Irene Kennerley, Anne Bradley, Stan Kennerley, Hilda Bloor, Front: Charles Yarwood

Twenty-three members of Lower Withington Methodist Guild last Thursday evening tackled a ten mile sponsored walk in aid of their Guild and Sunday School funds. Stephen Kennerley and John Nicholas decided to run the course, which they completed in one hour ten minutes. Taking part were Mr and Mrs S B Kennerley, Mr and Mrs John Carter, Mr and Mrs John Sproston, Mrs Margaret Yoxall, the Misses Rita Snelson, Anne Yarwood, Ann Bradley, Catherine Carey, Helen Bell, Ruth Bell, Jean Bell and Pauline Kennerley, Mrs Phyllis Kennerley, Messrs J S Bloor, David Kennerley, Stephen Kennerley, John Nicholas, Brian Jones, George Yarwood and John Venables.

Starting from Lower Withington Methodist Chapel the route was via Withington, Siddington and back via Chelford. Cold drinks were served at the two-mile checkpoints and, back at the chapel, refreshments were served by Mrs J S Bloor. The check-point officials were Messrs. Charles Yarwood, Charles Sproston, Percy Kennerley and Robert Kennerley. The event was organised by Mr John Sproston.

At the close, the sponsors and Mrs Bloor were thanked by Miss Ruth Bell on behalf of the competitors.

LOWER WITHINGTON CHILDREN
Pictured outside original village hall.

LW-WOMEN'S INSTITUTE

18th April 1970
County Express

THEY'RE THE TOPS

Withington Women's Institute members, Mrs Mona Turnock, Mrs Doris Dakin, Mrs Hilda Bloor and Mrs Dorothy Monks with their winning entry in the produce section at last week's area final of the Golden Jubilee "Top of the County" competition.

The area competition, in which 12 other institutes competed, was held at Chelford and the produce contest was for an arrangement of flowers, an iced cake and a salad all prepared and staged in 30 minutes. Dean Row W.I. was awarded reserve and Row-of-Trees won the handicraft section. The winners now go forward to the regional contest to be held at Winsford later in the year.

Judges were Mrs D Furber, Mrs M Goodwin and Miss Clare.

ARTHUR BURGESS

Arthur Burgess was born in a house, since demolished, where Chelford roundabout stands today, his father being the village blacksmith. When he was 13 Arthur started the first newspaper delivery service, copies being collected from Chelford Station and delivered throughout the village. During the Great War Arthur drove a Fordson tractor on the farm. His tractor was supplied by Knutsford Motors.

Later in life Arthur made his home at Highway Garage, the garage now being run by his grandson, Graham Dale.

LOWER WITHINGTON ROSE QUEEN FESTIVAL

The first Rose Queen Festival was held on Saturday June 11th 1949. The procession started at 2.15pm near Dicklow Cob and paraded around the village green to the Red Lion Inn, back on to the main road, past the Parish Hall to the field kindly lent by Mr Ted Moston. Escorting the Rose Queen, Miss Alice Shufflebottom, were a number of characters in spectacular costume.

The coronation of Queen Alice took place at 3.15pm by Mrs Baskerville Glegg. Entertainment by the Kathleen Davies School of Dancing from Withington, Manchester and Lower Withington Women's Institute Country Dancing team followed the coronation.

There was Uncle Fred from Manchester with his Punch and Judy Show and sideshows and a fancy dress parade. Refreshments were served in the Parish Hall. Admission to the festival ground was 1s 6d for adults and 6d for children.

A dance was held in the evening at the Parish Hall, where the admission was 2s 0d.

The first Lower Withington Rose Queen Festival committee were: -

President	Mr J Wilson	
Chairman	Mr W Buckley	
Committee	Mr E Moston	Mr K Snelson
	Mr R Massey	Mr H Rigby
	Mr A Newton	Mrs J Wilson
	Mr H Bell	Mrs J Bailey
	Mr P Kennerley	Mrs F Fisher
	Mr T Dyer	Mrs G Hamner
Hon Treasurer	Mr A Turnock	
Hon Secretary	Mr J Bailey (Hodge Hill Cottages, Lower Withington	

To celebrate the 16th Rose Queen Festival in 1964, none other than Coronation Street's own Miss Nugent (later to become Mrs Bishop!) – namely Miss Eileen Derbyshire opened the event.

One quite unique aspect of the fancy dress was the best decorated bicycles. Annually children, and their parents and grand parents, made dozens of crepe paper roses to proudly show off their treasured bicycles.

ROSE QUEEN FESTIVAL

LOWER WITHINGTON

proudly presents to you its first

Rose Queen

SATURDAY, JUNE 11TH

THE PROCESSION STARTS AT 2-15 p.m., NEAR DICKLOW COB, and will Parade round the Triangle to the RED LION, back on to the MAIN ROAD, past the Parish Hall to the FIELD kindly lent by Mr. Ted Moston). Escorting the ROSE QUEEN will be numerous characters in spectacular costumes

CORONATION OF THE QUEEN at 3-15 p.m., by MRS. BASKERVILLE GLEGG.

Charming performances will afterwards be given by the Kathleen Davies School of Dancing from Withington, Manchester. The Lower Withington Womens' Institute members will give a Display of Country Dancing.
UNCLE FRED from Manchester will entertain with his PUNCH & JUDY SHOW.
SIDE SHOWS.   FANCY DRESS PARADES.
PROFESSOR REGAN, from Stockport ::: VENTRILOQUIST & CONJUROR.
REFRESHMENTS will be served in the Parish Hall.

Admission to Ground, 1/6;   Children, 6d.

DANCE IN THE PARISH HALL IN THE EVENING   :::   ADMISSION, 2/-

PRIZES for the BEST CHILD'S and ADULT'S FANCYDRESS COSTUME. There will be separate Parades on the Field so make it a day to remember, b being just what you want to be for a day

Poster for Rose Queen Festival 11th June 1949 or 50.

The tableaux were exceptional every year. Weeks of preparation preceded the festival, with all the village organisations having secret meetings to decide on the theme for their tableaux. The standard was exceptionally high, and the atmosphere in the village was electric. The anticipation of what the competition was from each organisation and who would win the prestigious trophies.

Carole Jenkinson – Rose Queen 2000

Youth Club Float 5 July 1969

Standing back row: - *Bill* – Steven Masser, *Weed Head* – Jennifer ?, *Ben* – Martyn Corbishley, *Alice* – Fiona Baker, *Doormouse* – Carole Barber, *Looby Loo* - Ann Hastings, *Andy Pandy* – Andrew Barber, *Popey* – Paul Jenkinson,

Front row: - *March Hare* – Julia Barber, *Mad hatter* – Juliette Cummings, *Jack-in-the-Box* – Geoffrey Blomfield.

Anne Perry – Rose Queen 1950

Rose Queens Past and Present

1949	Alice Shufflebotham	1975	Jacqueline Lewis
1950	Anne Perry	1976	Wendy Fairhurst
1951	Barbara Fisher	1977	Nichola Bacchus
1952	Brenda Booth	1978	Elaine Lewis
1953	Mary Bayley	1979	Susan Moore
1954	Celia Bayley	1980	Julie Barber
1955	Joy Kennerley	1981	Paula Fairhurst
1956	May Fairhurst	1982	Claire Baskerville
1957	Christine Snelson	1983	Lisa Kennerley
1958	Elizabeth Dyer	1984	Alison Swan
1959	Isobel Mitchell	1985	Melissa Buxton
1960	Gwendoline Newton	1986	Charlotte Slater
1961	Jean Bell	1987	Hannah Benoy
1962	Joan Massey	1988	Lorraine Brown
1963	Phyllis Thornley	1989	Donna Massey
1964	Phyllis Heath	1990	Elizabeth Slater
1965	Christine Jackson	1991	Kelly Massey
1966	Pamela Johnstone	1992	Gemma Jefferies
1967	J Anne Hastings	1993	Briony Benoy
1968	Anne Murtagh	1994	Claire Howard
1969	Michelle Barratt	1995	Tracy Howard
1970	Shelia Lawrence	1996	Dawn Kennerley
1971	Mary Kitching	1997	Rebecca Stevens
1972	Alison Jackson	1998	Rebekka Mitton
1973	Adrienne Tallentire	1999	Natalie Robinson
1974	Karen Butters	2000	Carole Jenkinson

Rosedays Remembered

A Set of two videos produced by Chris and Julia Slater with Mike Cliffe, using videos of past Rosedays kindly lent by Bill Moston and Julia Slater. These videos span from 1964 to 1992 and are a unique record of the village Rosedays. They also include footage of the old Parish Hall, which was built in 1925, being demolished in 1965 to make way for the current Parish Hall. These videos are still available today, from the authors of the book. The video commences with the following verses, which reflect the sincerity and affection for this unique village and its Rosedays.

Here in 1995 Lower Withington is still alive
With happy hearts and friendly folks
Sharing laughter, sadness, tears and jokes.
A village of families caring and giving
Protecting its future, at least whilst they're living.

We remember the times at the old Village Hall
The dances and socials were fun for all
But sadly the hall was getting old and decayed
'A new Village Hall' was what everyone said.

No challenge too great for Withington folk
We'll soon raise the money – and that's no joke.
So Traction Engine rallies were an annual event
And delighted spectators their money spent.

Money rolled in from other village do's
'Til the opening of the new Village Hall made the news.
Its modern exterior caused folks to stare
But the villagers were delighted, what did they care.

The village school closed causing sadness to all
Our village life will go was the villagers call.
But alas our village will never die
'Cause the village is made up of folks like you and I.

This wonderful village is captured for all
By a remarkable young man with a camera so small
The invention of 'cine' fascinated young Bill
And our thanks go to him and always will.

He developed a history unique and so clear
Of the way we were, year after year
As you sit and watch our history unfold
Of friends past and present, young and old
Look, there's Frank Foden you're bound to recall
He was a treasure no longer with us all.

But alive they all our in our memories today
As we watch them enjoy each different Roseday
This village is made not by houses and farms
But by caring people with outstretched arms

We are lucky to be part of this picture today
And hope that it always remains this way.

So sit back and relax and enjoy our show
And remember the friends that you used to know
So on with the films, no more to be said
Let all the fond memories re-enter your head.

Julia Slater 1995

All past Rose Queens

Picture taken at Rose Queen Festival 1989

Cinderella performed in Village Hall 1950. Principles – Ann Perry and Barbara Fisher.
Second pantomime organised by Mrs Wilson to raise money to finance the launch of the Lower Withington Rose Days.

SLATER FAMILY

Charlotte Slater in Bassinet with William Slater on her knee
C 1916 – pictured outside Bate Mill Cottage

**The Landlord – Mr Freddy Fisher outside the
Black Swan at Lower Withington March 1980**

Norfolk Farm

Originally in Lapwing Lane, demolished as part of the Sand Quarry development.

Lapwing Cottage in Lapwing Lane

Trap Street, Lower Withington 1918

Holmes Chapel and Lower Withington Worthies
The picture above was taken in July 1902 and shows a group of Holmes Chapel and Lower Withington 'worthies' who were visiting Northwich. Included in the picture are: - Mr Yarwood, Mr Hulme and Mr Massey of Lower Withington.

HOLLY TREE FARM LOWER WITHINGTON
Picture taken following a heavy fall of snow in 1953

DAISY BANK FARM – LOWER WITHINGTON 19th CENTURY

Part converted into a Chemist shop c1870.

Daisy Bank Farm was occupied in 1841 by: -

    Ann Gilbert   age 40   Independent means
    John Gilbert   age 18
    James Gilbert   age 14
    Joseph Gilbert   age 8
    Elizabeth Gilbert age 11
    Ann Gilbert   age 5
    Esther Gilbert   age 3
    Ann Barber   age 18   Female Servant

By 1851 the farm had been taken over by John Gilbert age 28, living there with his wife Alice and three children, Edwin 6, Ann 4 and Alice 2. Also present on the night of the census were Mary Dumville, aunt, a widow aged 63 and two servants, Joseph Buckley and Margaret Wood.

Between 1851 and 1861 John Gilbert must have died and Alice re-married Samuel Appleton. The 1861 Census shows the following information.

1861 (No name)	Samuel Appleton	Head	M	30	Farmer of 25 acres	Born Barnshaw
	Alice Appleton	Wife	M	36		Born Goostrey
	Caroline Appleton	Dau		3		Born Lower Withington
	Ann Gilbert	Step Dau.	U	14		Born Lower Withington
	Alice Gilbert	Step Dau		12	Scholar	Born Lower Withington
	Hester Gilbert	Step Dau		10	Scholar	Born Lower Withington
	Ann Bell	Serv.	U	36	House Servant	Born Goostrey
	George Dale	Serv.	W	67	Farm Servant	Not known

Ten years later in 1871 Edwin Gilbert age 26, (son of John Gilbert deceased) was running the farm living there with his sister, Alice aged 22, his step father, Samuel Appleton and his mother, Alice Appleton. Edwin's occupation is listed as a Farmer and Druggist and it was probably about this time that the farm was also a Chemist Shop as shown in the picture.

Edwin subsequently married and lived with his wife, Hannah, at Daisy Bank Farm at least until the end of the 19th century.

FRANCES ELIZA CROMPTON 1866-1952

Frances Eliza Crompton was born in 1866 at Butley near Prestbury, the middle child of a family of five children born to Richard Ellis and Alice Morris Crompton. The family moved to Lindow House, Wilmslow and Frances grew up in a 'well to do' Victorian family complete with governesses, maids, cooks and gardeners.

The 1881 Census gives the following information relative to the complete family.

Name	Relationship	Status	Age	Occupation	Birthplace
Richard Ellis Crompton[1]	Head	M	51	Dividends interest of money (no occupation)	Salford, Lancs
Alice Morris Crompton	Wife	M	51	Dividends interest of money	Whittington, Staffs.
Alice Josephine Crompton	Dau	U	21		Prestbury
Elliott Atkins Crompton	Son	U	19	Articled Pupil to Surveyor	Prestbury
Francis Eliza Crompton	Dau	U	15	Scholar	Prestbury
Agnes Crompton	Dau	U	13	Scholar	Prestbury
Richard Crompton	Son	U	9	Scholar	Prestbury
Catherine E Heaton	Serv.	U	21	Cook Domestic Servant	Ardwick, Lancs
Elizabeth Bradley	Serv	U	18	Housemaid Domestic Servant	Wilmslow

It can be seen from the above that Frances' parents both had money and were living off the interest generated by this capital. In the census, Richard Ellis Crompton is shown as having no occupation.

It was within this sort of society that Frances grew up and it is not surprising that she developed an interest in the countryside as an observer of birds, a student of wild flowers and gardening.

This interest stood her in good stead when she later wrote a series of children's stories that made her a well-known and respected figure in the literary circles of the day. Between 1888 and 1903 a total of 29 stories were written and published, the

---

[1] Richard Ellis Crompton was a descendant of Samuel Crompton, the inventor in 1799 of the Spinning Mule.

first entitled 'Friday's Child', receiving critical acclaim when it was reviewed in the Manchester Guardian.

The family made a number of visits to Europe, all meticulously recorded in Frances's diaries.

In 1915 Frances commenced her Gardening Diaries in which she records the day to day events of this difficult period including her feelings for her children, two of whom were on active service in France. In December 1916 she wrote of her son, Geoffrey:

> "He looks very well indeed and though still a cadet is dressed as an officer and presents a most spick and span appearance after Arthur's (her eldest son) war-worn clothes who came straight from his dugout on the Somme."

In fact Arthur had been on the Somme on three separate occasions. However, Arthur survived the war and it was Geoffrey who did not, being posted missing in June 1917.

Geoffrey's death must have had a profound effect on Frances. She did not write her diaries again until New Years Day 1919, obviously making an effort to start life anew when peace was regained. The diaries continue through to 1922 at which stage she must have decided not to continue with them or perhaps destroyed them at a later date.

All through her life Frances retained an interest in painting, producing a collection of water-colours and black and white sketches, many of the area around Chelford. The cover illustration on the front cover of this book and the earlier book, 'Chelford - A Cheshire Village' are from her brush.

Her life of 86 years encompassed the Victorian and Edwardian eras and the First and Second World Wars. The war time diaries were written when the family lived at Larchwood, in Pepper Street, Snelson, having moved there at the turn of the Century after living in Holmes Chapel for a period.

In all her writings and her work as an artist, Frances retained her maiden name of Crompton, though she had married John Leopold Walsh in the late 1880's or early 1890's. She had four sons, Arthur, Roger, John and Geoffrey and three daughters, Eleanor, Audrey and Gwenifer.

Frances died in 1952, just two years after the death of her husband, John Leopold Walsh.

All the surviving diaries, paintings and other artifacts are now retained in the archives of the Cheshire Record Office, Duke Street Chester under the Frances Crompton collection, ref., D5453.

Extracts from Diary (First World War Period)

13 Jan 1915

It was calm, mild and very pleasant in the garden today and I had quite a nice gardening time. I picked up a hamper of dead wood and Roger sawed out for me the dead branches amongst the laurels, and some living boughs which I had planned beforehand to be removed as they were not ornamental and were in the way of other things. The wind had swept up dead leaves into heaps which lay still in quiet corners, so I picked up a hamper full or two of these while they lay to hand. In the afternoon Read came to help Evans to pull the trees back into place in the orchard and secured them with props and stays. This was done and Read determined to move the Victoria Plum tree in the orchard also , which I proposed in the autumn should be put a little on one side of its present position. It is very much in the way at present, being right in the middle of the path down the grass when one wheels a barrow to the rubbish yard, and just two yards or so would make such a difference.
So the tree was dug up and the hole dug, the tree planted and staged, the hole filled in, covered with sods and then rolled, and we all three agreed that it was a very great improvement I am sure that any able bodied man would smile if he saw the three of us working together. Read is nearer eighty than seventy , Evans has only one good arm and one good leg, and I like the psalmist was small and of no reputation for strength. Still I am very thankful to have some such help, and consider that we are very fortunately situated, when many people are left in such plights for the lack of labour. They now have no man at all, at the Bowyers, for instance, where formerly they had two, and very little prospect of getting anyone either as a long as the war lasts.

In the intervals, when I was not needed to hold the tree steady, I was making the most of my time by mending the rose trellis between my flower border and the grass of the orchard. The storm had blown it about, and loosened the roses in places, so I made all secure. It was very pleasant out today; I stayed in the orchard till nearly four o'clock, and Read remarked that "Now the year had turned the afternoons were lengthening by a cock's stride", a queer old country expression that I have not heard for years.

Thursday 24th June 1915

Midsummer Day

"Summer is not fully established until the elder is in flower, and it ends when the berries are ripe." So I find I have at some time written on the margin of my Brand's "Antiquities", but cannot give any reference for it. The elder is in flower now, has been for a few days, and as summer only truly commences on June 22, this is quite accurate. I like an old fashioned "Elder" bush, as the country people in Cheshire call them. We have five good sized bushes in the garden, always full of bloom at this time; the flowering, by the way, is said to keep flies at a distance, but I have never quite found this to my satisfaction - nor yet disproved it. As for the berries, they are not allowed to adorn the trees long, being devoured by flocks of starlings and other birds, the starlings in particular seeming to be ravenously fond of them. The old gardener who planted much of this garden in 1898 and 9 brought these elders out of the coppices round about, to make quick shelter, and they do grow very fast in their early years, but I think ours have grown almost as large as they ever will; at least, I cannot remember that I have ever seen any much larger.

Monday 11 October 1916

It being wartime, only the painting outside absolutely necessary to preserve the premises and keep them weather-tight - which they had ceased to be - had been done, but I asked the painters to mix and leave for us a can of dark green and one of white. Roger and Audrey undertaking to paint the garden seats and my frames. So today they began, the seats, garden table, etc., ranged round on the tennis lawn as if for a garden meeting; they achieved a fair amount of success at the painting, but made a fearful mess of themselves.

Friday 3 March 1916

Yesterday was wet, pouring wet, almost all day. My bundle of roses etc., came from Caldwell's but I could not even unpack it in the rain, so they were put in the outhouse till morning. On Wednesday night, or in the small hours of Thursday morning, we had a very unwelcome visitor. I was wakened between twelve and one o'clock by violent shouting in the garden under the window, "Hey! Hey! Hey!" repeated loudly. I thought at the first moment that it was the policeman who perhaps saw a light in the maid's room - I know that the rest of the house was in darkness - and that he was warning us to extinguish it, under the new regulations against displaying lights which may be a source of danger from hostile aircraft - regulations which have caused me some trouble lately in me providing curtains to darken the windows to a greater extent than blinds alone will do. However, Leo remarked with perfect calm, "It is that wretched Man", and then I distinguished that he was calling to his dog (whether it was really there or only in his drunken imagination, I cannot say), threatening it with "a bomb after it". Whether I wished for a bomb after him is better left unwritten, but my feelings may be guessed when I heard him tramping about and still shouting for some time longer, and thought of my poor flower borders under his great boots, on a pitch dark night, at one o'clock in the morning! Sure enough, daylight revealed his tracks. He had stumbled down the garden leaving clods of damp soil about the gravel walks, as far as the roses, but had pulled up on the first border - because he had got his face scratched by Thalia, I hope, but there were no return tracks, so what became of him after that point is wrapped in mystery. It seems that Leo heard him stumbling about the garden about midnight, before he came to bed, but thought he had melted away safely into the road; whereas, it seems more probable that he had been taking a nap under a bush, or something of the sort. At any rate, he reappeared on the scene about one o'clock, trampling on the borders I have made up afresh under the window; here and there he has planted a foot on the poor dear springing daffodils, and he has missed the peonies by inches, but by far the worst mess is on the azalea and iris beds, where he has broken off whole growths of the latter, and appears to have walked round and round in a circle on the former, treading on the lilies amongst the bushes (though fortunately the growth was not far advanced). Here lay his stick trodden into the soil, a nice green hazel sapling which I shall keep as a trophy, so I suppose he walked about to look for it. He had also burst through the light fence of oak branches on which my cyclonias are trained, and had planted a cruel foot in the middle of St Dabesc's heath, but what prevented him falling head first into the little "valley" between the heath and the saxifrage banks, I cannot imagine. Nor how he finally got out of the garden at all in the end, the gate of which he thoughtfully left open to be ready for the postman in the morning. It has since transpired that he was at the Hardwick's sale, then at the little inn at Peover Heath (which calls itself the New Inn, but is always alluded to by the country people as The Dog and Rat), and after that there is a gap in the chain of events until he turns up in our garden about midnight. Well, that is enough about disreputable old Thomas, who will certainly be picked out of a pond some morning but Evans has had to clear the clods of sticky soil from the gravel with a shovel, and it will take me I do not know how long to efface his traces from the borders.

On Monday evening also a very curious thing happened to Leo. He was late at the Bank, and reaching our own station from the train after nine o'clock, stood for a moment on the platform to pull his coat up against this cold wind. While drawing it upward and backward at the collar to pull it more comfortably about his throat something appeared to strike him between the shoulders, but supposing it to be only his scarf, he paid no attention to it and moved on. Instead of cycling home as usual, he walked with a neighbour, and on the way felt something like a pad on his back under his coat, but again thought that his scarf was disarranged, or that some friend had pinned something to his back for a joke. But on reaching home, he took off his coat in the hall, and out flew a thrush! The poor little thing had probably been

Larchwood Garden September 1941

disturbed by the storm, and dazzled by the porter's lantern, had made for what it thought would be cover, but it was a most extraordinary circumstance that it should be absolutely buttoned up inside a coat and the wearer be unconscious of what had happened! It flew into the coat room off the hall, and was found resting on a hat peg, from which it was transferred to Geoffrey's finger, and so to a tree in the garden, apparently none the worse for its odd experience.

Wednesday, Ash Wednesday 8th March

Wednesday was another dreadful day, snow almost from dawn to dark without stopping, but melting on the ground. Audrey, Roger and I waded to morning service, but the road was in such a state with slippery snow under the half melted slush that I fell down twice, the first time so hard that one of my snow boots flew off my foot, and in company with my open umbrella, whirled up the road. Geoffrey has now joined the Manchester University Officers' Training Corps, so had to attend a drill in the wind and sleet.

CHELFORD MINISTERS/LOCAL PREACHERS
1648 TO 1678

In 1648 when the Cheshire ministers subscribed their 'Attestation' (*taking of an oath*), one of those who appended his signature to the document was Nehemiah Worthington, minister of Chelford. However, in some documents the minister of Chelford at that time was stated to be a Robert Worthington. Whether this is the same person is not clear – possibly over the years the records have become distorted. What we do know for certain is that on 9 December 1651 Mr Joseph Ottiwell was presented to the Manchester Classe of Presbyterian Ministers for ordination to serve the congregation at Chelford. He was accordingly examined in logic, physics, ethics and metaphysics and was approved. He was directed to preach before the Association at their next meeting on 13 January 1651/2, having received a thesis to defend and also an 'Instrument' (*A contract in writing*) to be fixed to the church door at Chelford. The Instrument, signed by the elders of the congregation, was returned on 10 February. Ottiwell expounded his thesis to the satisfaction of the Classe and received notice that he would be ordained at Manchester on the 25th inst. Accordingly Joseph Ottiwell was appointed to the ministry. Mr Hollinworth opened the service with prayer, Mr Walker preached, Mr Walton prayed, Mr Heyricke proposed the questions, prayed at the laying-on of hands and gave the exhortation. The newly ordained pastor then received a certificate, signed by ten ministers, testifying to his ordination to serve the church at Chelford.

However, Joseph Ottiwell only remained at Chelford for a period of two years subsequently resigning his position, and the village of Chelford was again without a minister.

On 28 April 1653 however, Mr Ralph Worsley, BA of Cambridge, sought ordination from the Classe to serve the church Mr Ottiwell had left. As in the case of Joseph Ottiwell, Ralph Worsley was given an 'Instrument' to be fixed to the Church door and a question to argue at the next meeting of the Association. He was examined in classics, history, metaphysics, logic and divinity, and approved. On 14 June 1653 he brought to the Association his 'Instrument' duly signed by the elders of the church and was ordained with two other candidates on the following day at the parish church of Manchester (*probably now Manchester Cathedral*). In the certificate subsequently given to him he is said to have been about twenty-two years old.

From the records it appears that Ralph Worsley had some problems and against the date 17 January 1653/4 we read 'Mr Ra Worsley was then at Chelford and was of very light carriage, and to keep him from imposing hands at the ordination, they proposed to have some three or four of such as were nominated to impose hands. I was left out, and the baseness of my heart was such that I had great tugging with myself.'

Mr Worsley did not remain long at Chelford. He was succeeded in 1657 by Mr Hugh Henshaw.

Again there appears to have been some problems, certainly at the beginning of his ministry. At this time the living at Gawsworth was vacant and Hugh Henshaw was amongst the candidates for the appointment. It appears that the people of Gawsworth would have chosen him, had he not been allocated to Chelford. There was a feeling that he had encouraged the invitation from Gawsworth and that he would have preferred the living of Gawsworth to Chelford.

How long Hugh Henshaw stayed at Chelford is not known but by 1678 Reginald Bancroft was Minister of Chelford as well as Siddington.

The period of Hugh Henshaw's ministry was fraught with difficulty. It has been recorded that the Church was kept together through the labours of Mr Thomas Edge, who resided in the vicinity following his ejection from Gawsworth in 1662. Though prevented from continuing his public ministrations, Mr Edge appears to have been very active in promoting his beliefs. There is a reference dated 28 October 1678 in the diary of a Mr Newcome (a previous minister at Gawsworth but at that time in Manchester) as follows: "My brother, Leadbeater, had been over here a little before and had engaged me to come amongst some good people in Cheshire (whom Mr Edge had kept together) once a quarter, to keep them from scattering, or closing with some unfit man that might mislead them. And I went to them this first time on 1 November and met with some of the people that were of my charge at Goosetree; and was glad to have opportunity to see them and do them service this way".

On the passing of the Act of Uniformity in 1662[1] Thomas Edge, who refused to sign, left Gawsworth and came to live in Chelford. In 1672 he preached at a meeting house, specifically prepared for him, at Withington. He appears to have been a very effective and popular preacher. It was said at the time that 'No meeting in the country was more crowded'.

In addition to general meetings Thomas Edge preached privately in the neighbourhood of Chelford and other parts of Cheshire and Staffordshire, the times

---

[1] As part of the Restoration settlement a bill was passed re-introducing the Book of Common Prayer. Ministers were required publicly to give assent to the Book. All ministers and schoolmasters were also required to make a declaration of the illegality of taking up arms against the King. Some 2000 ministers who refused to conform were ejected from their livings.

and places of his meetings being as far as possible, kept secret. It was his practice to gather his people together before their neighbours were out of their beds and complete his preaching before the public worship began. In the afternoon he usually heard the parish minister at Chelford.

Thomas Edge died on 22 June 1678, continuing to preach to the very last day of his life. He rose on the day of his death as usual but, finding himself ill, he lay down on his bed and called for his will, which was then drawn up. He sealed it and died soon afterwards.

His will was, in form, typical of the period.

TRANSLATION OF WILL OF THOMAS EDGE OF CHELFORD 1678

*Know all men by those present that I Thomas Edge of Chelford in the
County of Chester (being through the mercy of God at present in perfect memory
And good health of body, yet considering my frailty and desiring both to keep my heart
Prepared and to set my house in order that I may be ready for any change when it comes)
Do by this my last will and testament dispose of that temporall estate God hath
Given to me in manner following
First I give unto my dear wife Mary Edge the silver tanker and silver spoons that
Were her mothers. I also give unto her that bed with all belonging to it as it stands in
the chamber, as also that bed of servant lieth in and all the linnen that are hers
at Chelford and all the linnen at Blackden and the trunk they are in. And of my books
I give unto her those English practical books she shall make choice of. I also give
unto her of the rest of my goods which she shall make choice of to the value of five
pounds. It is next by my will that the rest of my goods be sold by my exec -
tors herein after mentioned, and the money they are sold for as also what money I
have by me, or owing to me (my funeral expenses being first paid) I committeth
management of solely to my dear brother Oliver Edge to be disposed of by him
in the manner following.   First it is my will that my brother pay to my
wife yearly during her natural life out of the profits of the money committed
to his management the sum of twelve pounds the payment whereof I have
obliged myself by my bonds given to Mr Thomas Bagnall of Newcastle in the
County of Stafford, and it is my will that this said twelve pounds be paid at the times
mentioned in the aforesaid bond.   After the decease of my wife I do by this my
last will dispose of the money, the management whereof during my wife's natural life
I have committed to my brother Oliver Edge, in manner hereinafter expressed viz
First to my cousin Ebenezer Edge, Mary Gaytherne and Hannah Edge children of my
aforesaid brother Oliver Edge I give each of them twenty pounds. Item, to my cousin
Hannah Ashton the only child now living of my sister Katherine deceased I give the sum of
twenty pounds. Item, to my cousins Samuel Grantherne and Hannah Grantherne
children of my sister Mary deceased I give either of them twenty pounds. The legacies
mentioned to be paid within six months after the death of my wife. Item, if my sister
Elizabeth Knot survives my wife it is my will that my brother lay out in necessary*

towards her maintenance three pounds a year during her natural life. Item, to my cousins John Knot, Mary Knot and Elizabeth Knot children of my sister Elizabeth Knot I give each of them twenty pounds to be paid to them within six months after the decease of my wife Mary Edge and sister Elizabeth Knot. It is further my will that if any of my cousins before named die before the time appointed for payment of the forementioned legacies given to them, if they have any child or children, the legacy given to them shall be disposed of by my brother Oliver Edge for the use of such child or children: But if they die without any issue surviving, that then the legacies given to them shall be given to their surviving brothers or sisters. Item, I give to Philip Wright of Over Peover in the county of Chester yeoman one twenty shilling piece of Gold to be given to him immediately after my decease. The remainder of my estate I give to my brother Oliver Edge. And I nominate and appoint my brother Oliver Edge and the aforementioned Philip Wright executors of this my last will and testament. Witness my hands and seal.

Thomas Edge

Signed sealed and published Of the 21st day Of June 1678

It would appear that the period of the Commonwealth followed by the Restoration was a difficult time for Chelford Ministers. In 1678 a Reginald Bancroft was Minister of Chelford as well as Siddington and it wasn't until 1719 when John Dean was nominated by the inhabitants – 'who say they have a right to do so' – that matters appear to settle down. John Dean was Minister of Chelford until 1772 when John Parker was appointed.

Prior to the appointment of John Dean as Curate of Chelford the following villagers signed the letter[2] to the Lord Bishop of Chester recommending John Dean as Curate of Chelford.

William Baskerville }	Church Wardens
John Foden }	
Mary Lowe	John Branford
Thomas Wilson	Nathaniel Booth
Samuel Tomson	Edw. Snelson (by mark)
William Wilson (by mark)	John Dale
Mary Baskervyle	Peter Summerfield
Wm Stanley	Edward Leigh
Tho Brooke	Geo Heald

Signed on 18 Feb. 1719/20

Certain information included above has been extracted from Historical Sketches of Noncomformity in Cheshire by William Unwick published March 1864 Copy held in the Alderley Edge Research Library of the Family History Society of Cheshire.

---

2   Cheshire Record Office - Chelford Parish Bundle ref: EDP 68/1/1.

Will of Thomas Edge of Chelford 1678

OATH OF ALLEGIANCE 1723

The Act of 1722 made it necessary for all persons in England over 18 to swear an oath of allegiance to the crown at Quarter Sessions if they had not already taken it; and those refusing to comply were required to register their names and real estates as Papists.

The names of persons who took the oath and were resident in Chelford, Lower Withington, Old Withington and Snelson are as follows: -

(Note 'c' against a name indicates that a certificate was produced).

Joseph Acton	de	Lower Withington		Philip Antrobus	de	Snelson	
Thomas Bailey	de	*Lower Withington*	c	Samuel Barber	de	*Lower Withington*	c
Robert Barns	de	Lower Withington	c	Daniel Bartington	de	Lower Withington	
Mary Baskerville	de	Old Withington		Thomas Berrisford	de	Chelford	c
Richard Booth	de	Chelford	c	Mary Bostock-widow	de	Chelford	c
John Bradford	de	Old Withington	c	Thomas Brookes-gent	de	Chelford	
Charles Bunn	de	Lower Withington		Jane Dale	de	Lower Withington	
John Dale	de	Over Withington		Mary Davenport	de	Lower Withington	
Thomas Davenport	de	Lower Withington		Anne Davenport	de	Lower Withington	
Richard Davenport	de	Lower Withington		John Davies	de	Lower Withington	
Thomas Davies	de	Lower Withington		William Davies	de	Lower Withington	c
John Dean	de	Lower Withington	c	Edward Ellis	de	Lower Withington	
Edward Foden	de	Lower Withington		John Foden	de	Chelford	
Randle Foden	de	Lower Withington	c	Sarah Foden – widow	de	Lower Withington	
Isaac Gallymore	de	Lower Withington		John Gallymore	de	Lower Withington	
John Henshaw	de	Lower Withington		Margaret Henshaw	de	Lower Withington	
Richard Hope	de	Chelford		Ellen Kettle	de	Lower Withington	c
John Kinsey	de	Lower Withington	c	Edward Lee	de	Over Withington	
Zebulon Lea	de	Lower Withington		Edward Leigh	de	Lower Withington	
Thomas Lockett	de	Lower Withington	c	Mary Lowe	de	Chelford	c
Richard Lowe	de	Lower Withington	c	Peter Lowndes	de	Lower Withington	c
Thomas Lowndes	de	Lower Withington	c	John Oakes	de	Lower Withington	
Randle Oakes	de	Lower Withington		Thomas Oakes	de	Lower Withington	
Thomas Pimlott	de	Chelford		John Sandbach	de	Snelson	
Mary Sandbach Spinster	de	Chelford		Nathaniel Sandbach	de	Snelson	
William Shaw	de	Chelford		Thomas Shawcross	de	Lower Withington	
Hannah Smallwood	de	Lower Withington	c	Hannah Smallwood-widow	de	Lower Withington	
John Smallwood-gent	de	Chelford		Joshua Smallwood	de	Lower Withington	
Randle Smallwood	de	Lower Withington		John Stubbs	de	Lower Withington	
Eliz Summerfield	de	Over Withington		Peter Summerfield	de	Lower Withington	
Sarah Tompson	de	Lower Withington		Jonathan Walker	de	Chelford	
John Ward	de	Chelford		Edward Whitaker	de	Withington	
Anne Whitehall	de	Chelford	c	Thomas Wilson	de	Chelford	
William Wilson	de	Over Withington	c	Thomas Wood	de	Snelson	

There do not appear to have been any Papists in the Chelford area at that time. Certainly in 1767 nobody was prepared to admit to being a papist as can be seen from the Returns of Papists 1767 Chester Diocese[3].

Early in 1767, following criticism that the Anglican bishops were becoming lax in restraining the spread of Catholicism, the House of Lords instituted an enquiry into the number of Papists in each parish in England and Wales. The bishops were directed to collect from the parish clergy and forward to the Clerk of the House "as correct and complete lists as can be obtained of the Papists, or reputed Papists, distinguishing their parishes, sexes, ages and occupations and how long they have been there resident".

The following is the entry for Capesthorne and Chelford: -

Entry — Capesthorne and Chelford

I have the pleasure and satisfaction of acquainting your Lordship that I have not any papists or reputed papists in my Chapelry.

Mr Dean of Chelford[4] desires his duty to your Lordship – his eyesight failing him, desires me to inform your Lordship that he hath not any papist in his Chapelry.

(signed)   G Everard, Capesthorne 17 August 1767.

---

[3]   Catholic Record Society Family History Society of Cheshire Alderley Edge Research Centre Ref: G899.
[4]   Vicar of Chelford Church 1719 to 1772.

ASTLE ESTATE 1784

The Astle Estate documents retained in the archives of the University of Manchester John Rylands Library include a map of Astle Estate[5] - The seat of the Rev. J Parker, drawn 12 July 1784 by J Pennington. A copy of the map with original spelling is shown in Fig 1.

The apportionment, shown on the map is as follows: -

No.	Field Names	A	R	P
1	Chelford Ground	8	0	15
2	Mill - Pool	6	1	11
3	Chapel Meadow	1	1	10
4	Front	21	3	30
5	Rough below the Mill	1	0	19
6	Nursery between house and Mill	0	3	21
7	Garden yards buildings etc	2	1	12
8	Fish pond meadow	0	2	03
9	Timber yard	0	2	38
10	Big field	14	2	37
11	Warren field	4	2	36
12	Barber's yard Garden woods etc	1	3	14
13	Beswick's fields	3	1	07
14	Marl field	2	1	10
15	Lime field	3	2	15
16	Wood field	1	3	06
17	Orchard	0	1	34
18	Gorsty Croft	2	0	10
19	Great wood meadow	1	3	38
20	Little woods meadow	0	2	23
21	Brick fields	3	1	14
22	Walk Mill field	1	1	37
23	Rough Hays	3	1	05
24	Farthest meadow	1	1	30
25	Middle meadow	1	0	33
26	Little meadow	0	3	09

---

5   John Rylands University Library of Manchester, Astle Estate documents Ref: box No. 6 Bundle No. 2.

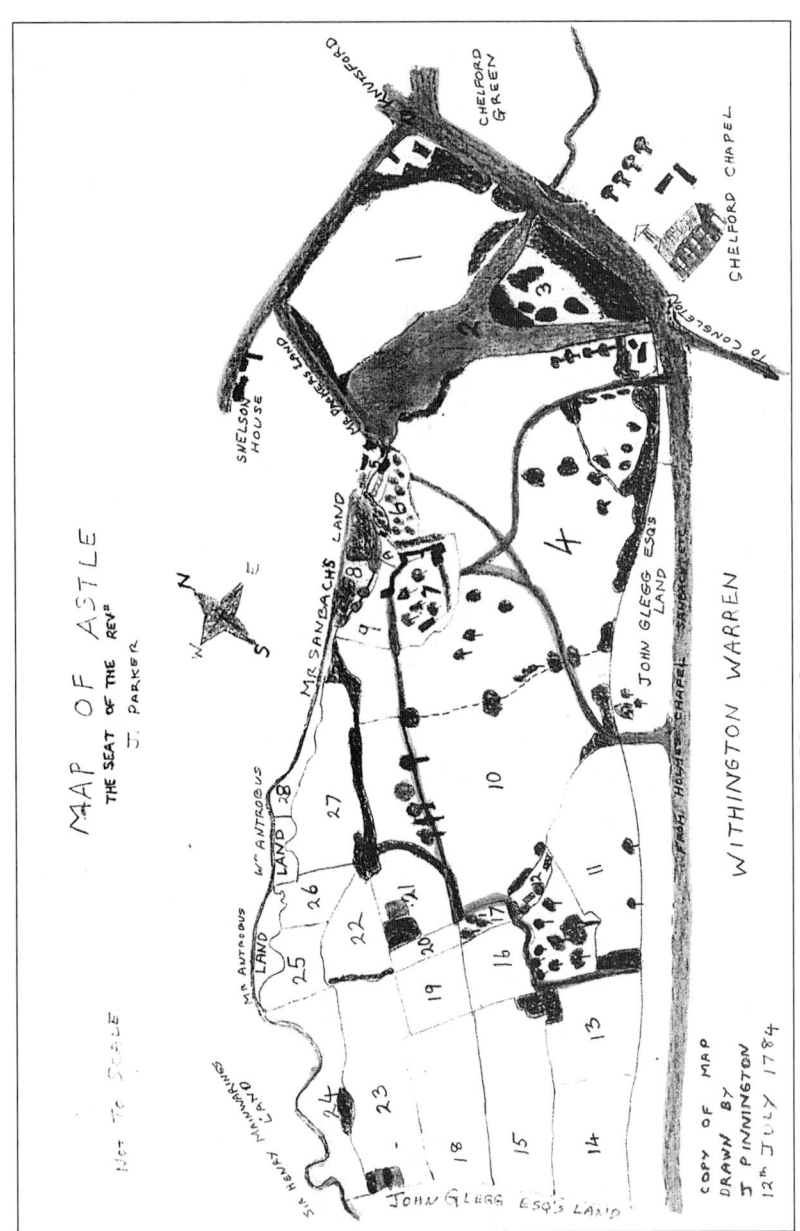

Fig 1. Map of Astle

		A	R	P
27	Great meadow	2	2	36
28	Long meadow	0	3	28
A	Middingsteads pigsties etc	0	0	27
TOTAL		96	0	08

The apportionment also shows the following deductions

	A	R	P
School house + gardens	0	0	28½
Shop house + gardens	0	0	20¼

The fact that the deductions are shown on this map indicates that the school and the village shop were shown on the map but were not included in the estate. Assuming this to be correct, it appears that the school was positioned on the eastern side of the bridle way leading to the hall between the bridle way and Snape Brook, virtually opposite the road to Congleton, according to the map,. If this area did in fact house the School it would then suggest that the original school must have relocated to Alderley Road after 1784.

The map shows Snelson House on the south side of what is now Peover Road and to the west of the road leading to the mill and hall.

It would appear that the mill was originally sited at the west end of the Mill Pool (area 2 on the map), the headrace for the mill being taken off the outlet stream. Area 5 on the map is described as 'Rough below the Mill' and area 6 on the plan, 'Nursery between house and Mill'. Furthermore a building is shown on the map in this area, probably the original siting of the mill. An earlier map of the Estate at Milne House, taken 14th February 1731[6] also shows what could have been a mill in the same position. The area to one end of the mill is referred to as 'The Outlette' and the field beyond the Outlette is referred to as Mill Meadow.

Other interesting observations from the map include: -

---

6. John Rylands University Library of Manchester, Astle Estate documents, Ref: Box No. 3 Bundle No. 2.

a) Confirmation that the Chelford Green was on the left-hand side of the Holmes Chapel road, leaving the village crossroads (now the roundabout).

b) The bridge over Bag Brook was a narrow hump type.

c) There were a number of ponds on the estate.

d) The estate included a Lime Field and a Brickfield.

e) Church Cottages (at least some of them) were in existence.

f) If the plan was accurate in detail, the old chapel had eight windows in one side, four above and four below.

g) The entrance to the chapel was in the end west wall.

h) Area 12 on the plan is designated as Barber's yard. The Barber family was resident in Lower Withington as yeomen at this time, Edward Barber marrying Margaret Goodwin in 1769. Furthermore a John Barber of Astle, a husbandman, married Hannah Stonehewer in 1771 and others of the same name were recorded in the Registers in the latter half of the 18th century.

i) The map was drawn by J Pinnington. A John Pinnington of Lower Withington (Yeoman) married Mary Lowndes of Astbury (widow) in 1771. Perhaps one and the same

CHELFORD & DISTRICT
EARLY 18TH CENTURY

The present day image of the 18th century country cottage with deep overhanging thatch, roses round the door and a garden full of beautiful flowers is a 20th century piece of nostalgia with no basis in truth.

To get an idea of what a cottage was really like in the 18th century we should consider the description given by the travel writer, William Hutchinson: -

> "The cottages of the lower class of people are deplorable, composed of upright timbers fixed in the ground, the intersections wattle and plastered (*wattle & daub*) with mud: the roofs, some thatched and others covered with turf; one little piece of glass to admit the beams of the day; and a hearthstone on the ground for the peat and turf fire."

It was quite common for a rural labourer to share his cottage with his livestock. The cottages were generally small, cramped, ill equipped and badly built. They would be constantly in need of repair and subject to the effects of inclement weather not uncommon in the Chelford area at this time.

One of the difficulties, which arise when exploring 'ordinary' life in these early days, is a lack of information about individuals and their possessions. Until well into the nineteenth century and, in many cases, much later than that, the rural labourer or artisan just did not keep records, letters, accounts etc.

By looking at selected wills and inventories of the period it is possible to build up a picture of rural life during this period.

Inventories were drawn up for the purpose of proving a will and as a basis on which to calculate court fees. They usually listed the furniture and utensils, as well as the livestock, crops, equipment, tools and furnished goods. Crops harvested above ground were included as long as manual labour had been involved in their cultivation.

The contents of inventories also provide information relating to trade and usually list items that were used in the work carried out by the testator. Certain items give an indication of wealth. For example, in the early part of the 18th century, the more affluent people sat at jointed tables and chairs, whereas poorer people managed with stools, benches and trestles. According to Beverley Adams, author of "Lifestyle and Culture in Hereford ... Wills and Inventories 1660 to 1729", a feather mattress was a sign of wealth and sheets were regarded as a luxury. Other indications of wealth in this period include books, window glass, mirrors and clocks.

Chelford was virtually self sufficient in the 18th century. The Parish Registers of the period include, in addition to farmers, labourers and servants, the following: -

Smith	A worker in metal identified by colour of metal used. Blacksmiths worked in iron; Whitesmiths in tin; Brownsmiths in copper; Greensmiths in copper or latten; Redsmiths in gold; though none of the latter were recorded in Chelford.
Ale Seller	Maker and seller of ale.
Shoemaker	A cobbler, or maker of new shoes. Originally a cobbler was prohibited from using new leather. Even though the Chelford records refer to a shoemaker it is more likely that he was a cobbler.
Ropemaker	Rope or net maker.
Wheelwright	Maker of wheels for wheeled carriages.
Grocer	Seller of produce.
Chandler	Originally Candler – Maker or seller of candles.
Dryster	Dealer in salted or dry meats and possibly pickles and sauces.
Joyner	Craftsmen who worked with wood.
Carpenter	A worker in timber.
Brickmaker	A maker of bricks.
Tanner	One who tanned hides and converted them into leather by soaking in liquid.
Pumpmaker	Maker of pumps and pipes for the raising and lowering of water.
Yeoman	Small freeholder, a commoner; one of a class just below the gentry.

Cooper	A maker and repairer of wooden vessels.
Husbandman	A tenant farmer.
Taylor	A worker of cloth.
Schoolmaster	Teacher (note the early 18th century Chelford records refer to a Schoolmaster though the village school was not founded until 1754).[7]
Weaver	A maker of cloth by crossing threads.
Butcher	A dealer in meats.
Miller	Corn miller, cloth miller, saw miller.
Webster	Originally a female weaver only but by 17th century the term applied to any weaver.

In an effort to build a picture of Chelford and district in the early 18th century the surviving wills and inventories of the following villagers have been used.

Hugh Hopwood	Chelford	Cooper	1694
John Smith	Lower Withington	Webster	1703
Thomas Topp	Snelson	Chandler	1701/2
John Lowe	Chelford	Gentleman	1712
John Lawton	Chelford	Blacksmith	1713
Benjamin Hall	Old Withington	Yeoman	1713

The terms used in inventories of this period contain many local expressions. Also the writing and spelling in the inventories varies considerably[8]. The inventories should therefore be read with some caution.

The majority of the furniture mentioned in the inventories of this period would have been made locally from whatever wood was available. This would usually have been oak but also elm, yew, beech if readily available. Chests were common with the majority of cottages having one or more. Large chests were constructed as a complete unit from a solid tree trunk. Smaller chests were made of planks or boards of oak fastened together at the corners. By the sixteenth century, carpenters were

---

[7] The will of John Parker 1711 refers to a schoolmaster at the school in Nether Alderley.

[8] It was not until later in the 18th century that English spelling became standardardised.

constructing chests based on a frame joined by mortises and tenons. It is probable that the chests used in the Chelford area at the turn of the 18th century would have been of the less sophisticated type.

The gradual progression to more sophisticated furniture was a continual process throughout the 17th and 18th century until the arrival of mass production in factories. Chairs and stools for example developed from the dugout method moving through box-like structures to more complex joinery techniques by the 16th and 17th centuries.[9]. Jointed tables superseded board tables (heavy planks of wood on trestles) at a similar period.

Dressers and cupboards were important pieces of furniture in village homes, dressers originally being in the form of side tables where food was 'dressed' before serving. Cupboards were generally used for storage and display of tableware. However, by the 18th century dressers were used both for storage and display having open shelves above the dresser top with drawers and cupboards below.

A typical artisan's cottage in the Chelford area in the early part of the 18th century would have consisted of four main rooms – a living hall with a fireplace and a parlour with a bed, both on the ground floor and two bedchambers above.

If the occupier needed a shop to sell his wares this tended to be a separate structure, though this was not always the case.

Hugh Hopwood lived in Chelford as a Cooper, the inventory taken on his death in 1694 showing that his cottage consisted of a new parlour, a little bedchamber, a shop, a house chamber, a new chamber and a buttery. There was also a barn and a small number of cattle. All in all a not insignificant property. The total value of the inventory was £72.8s.3d of which £17.16s.7d (a significant amount in those days) was in his purse, probably for use in the shop. Whether the shop was part of the house or a separate building is not clear from the inventory.

Extract from the Inventory of Hugh Hopwood of Chelford – Cooper, 1694

The House

The table, the cupboard, the chairs, the stools, the cushions, the pewter, the brass, the linen, the glasscase, the ironworks, the dish cloth, the bassin, the iron chair, the noggin[10], wooden spoons, the chese cloth, the postell and mortar.

---

9   A number of joiners and carpenters lived in the Chelford district at this time and must have been busy preparing furniture for the home and equipment for use on the farm.

10   Small drinking vessel

The will itself, made 1 October 1692 with a codicil of 4 April 1694, contains the names of residents in surrounding areas. Money, usually only a few shillings, is left to the people listed below. One person on the list (Harriet Davenport) was his kinswoman. Whether the rest were customers or friends is not clear.

William Pimlow, James Pimlow and Mary Pimlow sons and daughters of William Pimlow of Great Budworth.
The daughters of John Davenport of Chelford that he had by his first wife.
Harriet Davenport my kinswoman.
Henry Davenport son of John Davenport (when he pays the money he owes to me).
John Davenport of Chelford.
Thomas Topp of Snelson and his children.
Martha Bolchaw of Snelson – William Legh of Snelson
Richard Sandbach of Snelson and Elizabeth, his wife.
Robert Strattell of Snelson – Anne Strattell.
Sarah Wilson of Marthall – Elizabeth Booth of Marthall, widow.
Anne Royle wife of Joseph Royle of Fulshaw.
Ann Crag of Marthall – Margaret Radford wife of Charles Radford of Chelford.
Anne Hoyle wife of George Hoile? of Marthall.
Mary Lowe and Rebecca Lowther.
Elizabeth Birtles of Nether Alderley – Susanna Smallwood of Chelford.
Mary Symcock of Chelford – Mary Booth of Withington, widow.
The three children of Randle Norbury of Chelford which he had by Frances Norbury viz., George, John and Mary.
Richard Fallows of Nether Alderley and his mother.
John Herbert? of Alderley – John Hinlow? of Little Warford.
John Hunt of Mobberley – Christopher Sutton of Lower Withington.
William White of Old Withington – John Burgess and his wife.
Thomas Hoskinson of Pickmere – George Wilson of Marthall and his sister, Mary.
Phillip Beighton of Old Withington
George Lowe of Chelford for his children.
Margaret Groom my servant.
The minister that shall preach my funeral.
Margaret Millington of Moortown – Thomas High ? of Allostock.
John Ward of Capesthorne – Anthony Furnivale of Woodford.
Moses Statham of Astle for carrying my books to my house.
John Hull of Withington and his wife – John Baguly of Knutsford Smith.
Mary Curbishly of Old Withington – Mary Wick ? of Nether Alderley.
Anne Hall of Henbury, widow – The children of Edward Hallows of Toft.
John Bray of Mobblerley – John Birtles of Astle.
Edward ? son of Over Alderley – Dorothy Miller of Hulme Wolford, widow.
The son of Mary Baily of Kermincham – Elizabeth Henshaw of Warford, widow.

John Ward of Old Withington and his wife.
John Drake of Marthall and his wife – John Symson of Adlington and his wife.
Ellen Joyson of Upton – The wife of Jeremiah Lowe of Knutsford.
Thomas Brooke nephew of John Brooke of Chelford.
William Antrobus brother of John Antrobus of Snelson.
Ralph Pick? of Warford – Mary Pick? of Grapenhall.
John Koll son of Robert Koll of Marthall – John Partington of Ollerton.
Edward Jackson of Siddington and his wife.
William Jackson of Toft provided he discharges his debt to me.
George Hallows of Snelson and his wife.
Margaret Williams wife of Charles Williams of Budworth.
The poor of Chelford, Old Withington and Snelson.
The poor of Marthall and Little Warford.

In a codicil to his will the following additional names appear.

Peter Coulthurst of Sandlebridge and Elizabeth his wife.
Peter Barrow of Little Warford and his wife.
John Sandbach of Snelson and his wife.
Anne Partington of Siddington.
Elizabeth Lowe wife of George Lowe of Chelford.
Randolf Mirrill and his wife of Chelford.

There are in addition a number of personal legacies to members of his family including forty shillings to his kinsman, Ralph Hopwood of Great Peover provided he pays a debt outstanding to him of six pounds.

When looking at the inventory of **John Smith** of Lower Withington, a Webster by occupation, taken on 4 June 1703 we find that his accommodation consisted of a dwelling house, a little parlour, a further parlour above the house, a chamber, a further chamber, a chamber over the shop and a buttery. Again quite a large cottage. There is no reference to a shop other than to a chamber over the shop. As John Smith was a Webster (a weaver) it is possible that the loom on which he worked was situated downstairs in the dwelling house. It was the practice early in 18th century, before mass production, for weavers, spinners and carders to work at home. The small children carried out the carding operation, the adult female members of the family the spinning operation and the adult males, the weaving operation. As it would take six spinners to keep one weaver going it was common for the weaver to have a day job (in this area, probably farming) and to carry out the weaving in the evening. They were paid by the piece (where the term piece work originated). The total value of the inventory was £115.19s.0d of which £82.10s.10d was stated as

Money upon Bonds. As in the case of Hugh Hopwood, John Smith had a small number of cattle in his care, a mare, two cows and one calf.

Extract from the inventory of John Smith of Lower Withington 1703.

In the Dwelling House
A table, cupboards, brass and pewter and other implements.
In the little parlour above the house.
One bed, a chair and little coffor[11].
In the further parlour above the house.
One bed, one chest and cupboard, a table with forms and other small things.

The inventory of **Thomas Topp,** a Chandler of Snelson taken on 4 February 1701/2 does not place the contents in the rooms in which they were situated. The inventory was valued at £482.7s.5d, a considerable sum at that time and reflects his occupation as a Chandler with the candles and tallow valued at £40.0s.0d, shop goods at £5.0s.0d, and saddle, bridle, purse and apparel at £10.0s.0d. He was quite a wealthy man with £322.7s.2d due by bonds and otherwise. In common with the majority of villagers he had livestock, i.e., two horses (probably for delivery purposes) two cows and one swine. The inventory includes the tools of his trade including one bowsaw, four augers, two spoke shades, two chisels, two pairing knives, one file, one rasp, three gauges, an holdfast, one wimble board[12], two bitts, one plane and mandrel. He also owned two feather beds (a real luxury in those days) and three additional beds. A further indication of his status can be inferred from the number of household luxury items listed, for example £4.5s.10d worth of linen cloth, brass pans, brass pots, two brass candlesticks, a warming pan, two smoothing irons, four dozen and half spoons, fourteen plates, fifteen pewter dishes, three clocks (one at Hugh Gidmans) and two guns. Quite a prosperous household.

Further up the social ladder was **John Lowe** of Chelford, a Gentleman, whose inventory was valued and appraised by John Norbury and John Sandbach on 24 October 1712.

The Lowe family were very well established in Chelford at this time. Joseph Lowe and his father George Lowe living in Milne House (the original site of Astle Hall) until c 1720. George Lowe had at least three sons and it is therefore possible that John Lowe was one of the sons. It can be learned from John Lowe's will that he had a brother, George Lowe, who with

---

11	A small chest or box.
12	Gimlet, auger or brace

John's uncle Jonathan Lowe of Bonmingham in the County of York, was overseer of John's will.

Inventory of John Lowe of Chelford 1712

A true and perfect inventory of all the goods and chattels and personal estate of John Lowe late of Chelford, Gent: Valued and approved by John Norbury and John Sandbach.

	£	s	d
Fourteen milk cows	42	00	00
Three horses with grass	10	00	00
Four sheep	1	04	00
Barley	14	00	00
Oats & fresh wheat	*12*	*00*	*00*
Hay	*07*	*10*	*00*
Seventeen hundred of chaff	17	00	00
One corn cart, two dung carts, Two plows and three harrows	05	00	00
The old miln and ark[13] and an old Hogshead[14]	01	00	00
Four swine or hoggs	04	00	00
One table and one looking glass	01	15	00
The horse brought from [15]Haywood Hall and now lyeing in the Hay bay	01	10	00
Chest of drawers	01	10	00
One bed	03	00	00
Linnen	05	00	00
Boards, earthen vessels Old lumber[16]	01	10	00
Pewter plates and apparel	10	00	00
Debts owing to the above named Deceased John Lowe	-	-	-

It is apparent from this inventory that John Lowe was a farmer, although he describes himself as a Gentleman in his will.

---

13 A chest or coffer with domed lid.
14 Large cask.
15 Haywood Hall in Nether Alderley.
16 Furniture stored away out of use.

The value of the inventory probably only covers the farming element of his estate[17]. Certainly he had property elsewhere, his will containing a clause to cover the possibility that his estate could not meet the funeral expenses and that his eldest son would not pay the difference.

'I do hereby give and bequeath unto my younger children the revision of a tenement in Higher Peover which I lately purchased from Sir Thomas Mainwaring of Peover aforesaid and do hereby order and appoint that my said younger children shall pay and discharge the remainder of such debt out of the remainder or revision of my tenement aforesaid.'

His three younger children were Elizabeth, John and Mary

John Lawton was a blacksmith who died intestate in 1713. He lived in Chelford. Mentioned in the administration of his estate is his wife, Katherine, and a Thomas Lawton of Marton, a joiner.

According to the inventory, the property consisted of the Smithy and a dwelling house. There is no mention of any bed, bedding or items normally associated with a parlour. It is possible that he lived with one of his children in a cottage and that the child owned the bed and bedding etc. However, only one child is mentioned in his administration and he lived in Marton.

If the appraisers who drew up the inventory are to be relied on, John Lawton was by no means prosperous. The list of items from the Smithy includes working equipment such as grinding stones and frames, a smoothing steady, iron plates, two old sword blades, weights, old iron and some new iron. Apart from one long table and form, four turned chairs, one bulrush chair and four stoves, the dwelling house had very little else – an iron pot, a brass kettle, a little cupboard and a frying pan.

Perhaps the Smithy and its dwelling house were used as working premises (the large amount of seating area may have been for his customers), and the family lodged elsewhere. However, in common with the majority of villagers at that time, the inventory showed that he owned some cattle, i.e., one cow and one calf.

The total inventory amounted to £16.14s.02d of which £4.6s.0d was owed to him. His wearing apparel and money in his pocket amounted to £0.10s.0d

---

17 Certain things including real estate and items, which would automatically pass to the heir, were excluded by law.

At the other end of the social scale was **Benjamin Hall,** a yeoman of Old Withington, who also died in 1713. He was a witness to John Lowe's (Gentleman) will, and being a yeoman, probably moved in a higher level of society.

His inventory taken on 30 April 1713 was as follows: -

In house
One long table and forms and benches

In dining room
Table, benches and forms

In chamber over parlour
2 bedsteads and 2 shelves

In chamber over house
2 bedsteads
Shelves.

In little parlour
3 little shelves and 3 benches

In buttery,
? shelves at 6 pence a piece

In bake house,
One moult ash.
A moulding board[18] tub and one shelf

In house behind door
2 long shelves and a bench

In little house
one long table, shelves and settles
One fall table and one ladder

In buttery and parlour
7 shelves

In house
An iron shoetree
One grinding stone
[19]Broad drop
Two ladders and & 8 and half ??

In the barn

Board spokes and tallows plow bed.
Two plows and one pair of irons
Weighs and weigh prams and 3 sickles and a hook
A spoke?? And old shoe, a chattle
A marl pick, 2 pairs fotters
Two hand ?? a clove and hay hook
4 sowes and pair of chains and 2 wheelbarrows
Ropes – 3 pairs pott hooks, rakes & scythe
One hatchet, 1 bill, 1 hammer
5 pikils
One javelin, 1 habbard and pikestaff and 2 chairs
[20]A ripple comb, 4 weeding hooks and 2 turf spades
Two horse pack? A worthing[21] hook corake & thrushing

18	Board on which dough was kneaded.
19	Fine, wide plain black cloth used for men's garments.
20	Instrument toothed like a comb used for cleaning flax and hemps from the seeds.
21	Stout hook.

One silts ?? wheel & trunk – Tow
Rest of the lumber in the barn top

At the mill house
In the house place

One table and form, one little table
Four ash chairs and one cupboard
One brass pan, one grate tongs
And fire shovel
One dripping pan, an iron plate
bellows, a trivet
A chafing dish and goose broach,
Hand hooks, smoothing iron & ?
Two [22]skillets, 2 ladles, a flesh fork, a salt coffer
A hacking knife, skimmer, slice, a
A brass chafing dish[23] a gun
2 cushions, an iron crow[24]
Another brass ladle, a fork and shovel,
a testing iron

In buttery

In pewter 14 dishes and one flagon
Fifteen plates, one little brass pan,
One brass kettle an iron pot a brass pott,
A little brass pot, 2 frying pans
Two pewter chamber pots and 2 cans

In parlour

One bedstead, 2 blankets, 2 bolsters
and two feather pillows

One oval table, 2 sickled chairs
One press, clock and case, one cupboard
One warming pan, 8 pictures, one desk
Two bulrush chairs, a glass case, 7 Cushions
Two looking glasses, 4 yards black woollen cloth, 4 yards and half
In sow?

Chamber over house

A window sheet chair
A turets, tow??, crook
Two little coffers and one box
A long sheet, flax ribbons
A chen, a saddle and housing and 2 bridles
hang broach, a proker?
Bed stock, feather bed, 2 bolsters, 6 blankets and coverlet
One pick halph? Pick and quarter, a pilch and roundty[25]
A childs chair, a wheat riddle and Greeting sieve

In parlour chamber

Four swords and a belt, close stool box
Three coffers, a trunk, a box
A hand whip, little gun
Hangings about a bed, 2 coverlets and 4 blankets
Four pillows and 2 bolsters, a feather
Bed and 2 chaff beds

---

22 A cooking vessel with three feet to stand over the fire.
23 Small enclosed brasier.
24 Strong bar of iron used as a lever.
25 Cask of varying capacity usually used for liquor.

A rug, blankets and new coverlet, A chaff bed stock and mattress
Chaff bed and mat Linen?, wearing apparel
Two bolsters, 3 blankets, 3 pillows, Hay and fuill[26] cow
Featherbed?

In cash £1 8s.

The total value of the inventory amounted to £360.3s.5d revealing Benjamin Hall as quite a wealthy man.

Authors note: - More research is necessary to complete a 'picture' of the village. From the limited information above it would appear that the living conditions in Chelford district may have been above average, although without information concerning the villagers who did not leave a will or where an inventory was not carried out, this cannot be certain.

---

26 Could be young mare or female foal.

STATION ROAD c 1920

Station Road showing bank on left hand side of road with car outside newsagents.

Larchwood in 1921.

Larchwood, Pepper Street, Snelson in 1921 from painting by Frances Crompton

CHELFORD CORNER SHOP AND POST OFFICE

The picture above shows the shop in 2000 following re-painting.

The shop is now run by Eileen and John Burtonwood.

The building dates back to 1675 and has been used as a shop since 1705. The earliest records in the Parish Registers relative to a shop in Chelford are as follows: -

    Burial 1 Oct. 1730 Mary wife of Josiah Furnival of Chelford – Grocer
    Burial 20 June 1736 Josiah Furnival of Chelford -   Grocer
    Baptism 1739 Mary daughter of Samuel & Sarah Tomson   Grocer
    Baptism 21 Jan 1740 William son of Samuel & Sarah Tomson Grocer

For more information relative to the history of the shop see Chelford – A Cheshire Village, published 1999.

Old Vicarage

Chelford

Rear View

c 1975

Old Vicarage

Chelford

Front view

Standing in front

Carol Wilson

c 1975

**JESSIE SLATER'S COTTAGE
MEREHILLS c 1954 – DEMOLISHED 1962**

Viewed from Pepper Street, the cottage was situated where Dixon Drive now joins Knutsford Road.

ASTLE HALL C1900

EXCERPTS FROM THE WILMSLOW AND ALDERLEY ADVERTISER
1874/5 + 1890

Friday 14 August 1874
Tragedy at Chelford

On Saturday afternoon, after the 3.45 train had passed Chelford and within half a mile of Blackton Box, between there and Holmes Chapel station, the driver espied a woman on the upline coming towards the train. He sung out to her as he was able but finding he could not make her hear, let off the steam and endeavoured to stop the engine. She continued to walk in the road the train was going and, though the engine driver continued again and again (*to shout possibly*) she paid no heed. She was consequently killed on the spot. The woman's name was Pollsall and at the time she met with a melancholy and fatal accident, had a husband and nine children. When the news of the sad mishap reached her husband he became like a madman, and it was with difficulty he could be kept from laying violent hands on himself. Mr Dunston, coroner for the district, held an inquest on the body of the woman on Monday at Holmes Chapel and a verdict was given in accordance with the facts.

Friday 18 September 1874
Robbery and Poaching at Chelford

A double case of robbery and poaching was expected to have been heard at the County Petty Sessions on Tuesday, which was alleged to have occurred on the 5th of the present month at Sandle Moss near Nether Alderley, although in the Chelford Police Division. None of the particulars transpired in Court: but on the night of the 4th of the present month, we were told, the keeper of the tollbar at Chelford, Hugh Bailey, lent to Potts, one of Lord Stanley's gamekeepers, a mackintosh, and he had it with him during the night when he was going about his lordship's property with two other gamekeepers. After half past three in the morning, Thomas Hughes, constable at Chelford, who was going on his rounds, came up with them, and after walking a little way along Bollington Lane, parted company with the other two and proceeded with Potts. Presently they heard the cry of a rabbit in distress, when Potts asked Hughes if he would mind accompanying him. He assented: and they went across the little field together, and on looking over the fence that separated the fields, espied two men who appeared to be there for an unlawful purpose, in the next field. The gamekeepers and the policeman got over the fence and pursued them to the far corner where they beheld a gang waiting for them. The poachers then commenced to throw stones at their pursuers. Hughes turned his lamp upon them, when they shouted, "Give it that b.....". As Potts and Hughes were powerless in the presence of so large a number they thought to put a further distance between themselves and their assailants, and they left the ground, Potts forgetting to pick up the mackintosh he had previously cast to the ground. The poachers followed the gamekeeper and the police officer as far as the fence, hurling stones at them the entire distance. When they both got safely over the fence, the two gamekeepers they had previously been in company with came up. The poachers soon discovered the reinforcement, and they beat a retreat. Constable Hughes then went over the fence to look for the mackintosh that Potts had left but no trace of it could be found. While making the search for the coat, Hughes discovered a net one hundred yards long and two rabbits within it and delivered the same to the gamekeeper. On the Wednesday following, Hughes suspecting who had punished them were poachers from Marthall, searched houses for the missing coat but did not find any tidings of it. He then visited Mobberley, as he had received some information that it might have been conveyed in that direction. He went into a house in Moss Lane, kept by a Mrs Sophia Bowers who has a small farmhouse there and deals in rabbits etc., and there discovered she had purchased the mackintosh from Thomas Killer, one of the party of poachers who had been throwing stones the previous Saturday.

The case will be held on Tuesday next.

Friday 16 October 1874
A Little about the Roads

At the meeting of the Highway Board on Tuesday, the roads of Chelford were said to have cost £1.19s during the month of September. On the Chelford and Holmes Chapel Road, £1.7s.7d had been expended. An offer of £62 had been made for the bar house on the Congleton Road and it was agreed that that sum should be accepted.

Friday 16 October 1874
The Last of the Robin Hood

The old established public house situated in the Macclesfield and Chelford Road (*now Ivy House*), a few hundred yards from the Post Office at Chelford, was opened for the last time last week. It appears that Captain Dixon had for some time had a wish that the beer retailing on his property should be confined to one establishment and, accordingly, Mrs Kennerley, who for some 30 years has been the landlady, received notice from him which notice would expire about six months hence. As that lady had determined on giving up an occupation for a long time profitable to her, she did not come to stay until the extreme of the time allotted. The doing away of the house for public purposes must be the means of adding to the connection at the Dixon's Arms and we understand that the proprietor of that establishment will have to make some recompense for the additional trade anticipated.

Friday 30 October 1874
Monksheath – A Remembrance of the year 1807

The Liverpool mail coach which passed through Wilmslow and Congleton used to stop at the inn at Monks Heath to change cattle[*horses*]. On one occasion when Sir Peter Warburton was hunting, the following occurrence took place. The mail had just arrived from Congleton and the horses that had performed the stage were taken off and separated from the carriage when Sir Peter's hounds were heard in full cry. Although none of their harnesses were removed they immediately started after them and followed up the chase until the last. One of them a blood mare, kept the track with the whippers-in and gallantly bore away for a period of two hours, taking hedges and ditches and not missing a leap until Mr Reynard was run to earth in Mr Hibberts plantations. These high spirited horses were afterwards led back to the inn at Monks Heath and, although they had gone through such extraordinary exertion, they managed to perform the stage back to Congleton the same evening.

The inn referred to above would have been Irongate Inn, now a house on the corner at Monks Heath cross road..

Friday 8 January 1875
Foot and Mouth Disease – Withington

We regret to find that the great pest to farms, the Foot and Mouth Disease, is spreading rapidly in Withington. A recent enumeration makes no less than five farms suffering from the disorder.

Friday 8 January 1875
Frightful Mutilation of a woman at Chelford

On Thursday the last day of the old year a frightful accident occurred at Chelford Station to a young woman aged 29, a dressmaker of Over Peover, near Knutsford who, with a female friend had booked from Chelford to Holmes Chapel by the train that should call at the station at 9.35 in the morning. The frost was severe on that day, and the weather rather hazy, and the poor creature, who had been waiting more than half an hour in the waiting room, on hearing the train approaching, hastened to cross the line, by which means she came to her untimely end.

The platforms at Chelford station, as many of our readers are aware, are in a different position to most on that portion of the North Western line between Manchester and Crewe. Instead of being placed opposite to each other, the up platform is situated some fifty yards south of the disembarking place of the passengers from Crewe. There is no means of exit from the company's premises for persons coming by up trains but by crossing the line between the two platforms to the footgate on the downside, and therefore passengers wanting to travel from Chelford to any station south have also to cross the line. The pathway over the line is wide and is rendered as convenient as it possibly can be under the circumstances, but then the trains are so frequent that it is always necessary to keep a good look out. There is only one waiting room and that is on the down line adjoining the booking office. This, perhaps, is not of much importance in summertime, because it is as pleasant to be in the open air as under cover; but in severe weather, such as it has been lately and last week in particular, persons can only be expected to remain before a cheerful fire until the latest moment. They then have to run across the line to the imminent danger of life and limb.

The victim on Thursday seems to have been so anxious about her train that she paid no attention to friendly warnings given her by those who gave evidence at the inquest. She was told by one that she had not time to cross without the train being upon her, and by another that the approaching train was a goods train and not the one she required. Heedless, she went forward and on passing over the second metal on the down line, she stumbled and fell across the 'six foot', her head and shoulders coming over the near metal on which the engine of destruction was about to pass. What followed is too terrible to describe: suffice it to say, that at some fifty yards up the line, her remains were found strewed about – a portion of her head and face here, a leg there, and numberless fragments in all directions.

The inquest took place at the Dixon's Arms on Monday, before Mr Dunstan, Cheshire coroner, when Mr Liddell was chosen foreman of the jury.

Edward Norbury, labourer of Withington near Alderley, said on Thursday morning last, he was at Chelford Station, and saw the deceased there and another woman with her. The witness was waiting to meet the train coming from Manchester about 9.30 but it happened to be late that morning. The deceased and the woman with her were stopping in the waiting room upon the down platform warming themselves, the morning being very cold and inclined to be foggy. They had previously crossed from the up (Crewe) platform. The noise of the train was then heard coming from the Manchester direction. On hearing this, the deceased and the woman that was with her rushed out of the room towards the line. The witness, feeling sure that the train was too close, told them it was unsafe to cross the line. They looked towards the coming engine and train and then ran across. When deceased got to the 'six foot' she slipped. The other woman who was in front of her got across. The deceased endeavoured to recover herself and scrambled as well she could towards the up line, when the guard that hangs down in front of the engine wheel struck her forward. The witness was so shocked that he turned his head away and did not see what followed. When she fell across the 'six foot' her head and shoulders were across the metals of the up 'four foot'. The engine was close upon her when she fell. The driver of the Knutsford mail was standing at the footgate at the Knutsford side, by the side of the witness when the accident happened. There were several persons on the platform, and the ground was very slippery. The train was one that did not stop at Chelford Station. The driver whistled before the train got to the station, and before the witness warned the deceased: and he gave the 'pop' whistle on passing the station just before the girl fell.

John Holland, driver of the Knutsford mail, said he was with the last witness at the time. He told the deceased when she was in the waiting room that the train she heard coming was not her train. The deceased was also warned by the last witness. She hesitated a little and then rushed across after her companion. Her foot appeared to catch the off metal, where she fell upon her stomach, and then tried to get up again and go across the rest of the way. The force of the engine took the deceased half-way up the up platform, some 50 or 60 yards, and then the whole train passed over her. The witness went up to her immediately afterwards. She was quite dead and her body mangled and much cut up. Part of her head was gone: her bowels torn open and one of her legs laid across the metals. The remains, as soon as they could be collected together, were taken across to the Dixon's Arms Hotel.

Charles Jervis, station master at Chelford, said the deceased, Sarah Ann Hall, was a dressmaker, residing at Over Peover. The train was a goods train not timed to stop at Chelford and travelling at about 35 miles per hour. The witness heard the whistle as it was approaching. The passenger train expected was the 8.50 a.m. out of Manchester, due at Chelford at 9.35 a.m. The accident took place at 10.08 a.m. The crossing had been cindered the night before. There was no porter with the witness at the time, but he had an acting porter with him not in livery.

The Jury found a verdict of 'Accidental Death' but a long conversation took place among them as to the means of ingress and egress to and from the up platform and the best means of improving it. Some of the Jury held that a footbridge should be erected over the line as the only method of securing safety. It appeared to be the general opinion that convenient waiting rooms should be attached to each platform: and that there was not sufficient persons employed that the amount of business required. Mr Jervis, the station master, was questioned by some of the Jury as to his opinion of the views that they had expressed, when he stated that, while he believed a communication to the road from the up line would prove a vast improvement at the station, he did not think any benefit was to be gained by the erection of a footbridge over the line. Regarding the station being under handed, one of the company's servants was absent at the time of the accident in consequence of illness, and his place was being temporarily filled by a plate layer.

Friday 2 May 1890
Chelford v Snelson – cricket

This match came off at Chelford on Saturday and was won by Snelson mainly through the batting of Messrs F H Farbridge (who scored 46), W Gledhill (18) and Kay (16). On the losing side W Gouldern batted well for 20 and also bowled successfully. Messrs R C Farbridge and Brown bowled very effectively for Snelson. Both teams were entertained to tea at the Hotel Chelford, thanks to the kindness of Mrs Farbridge.

Friday 25 July 1890
Assault at Chelford

At the Wilmslow Police Court on Tuesday William Dykes, gardener, was summoned by John Clarke, wheelwright, for assault at Chelford on the 12th inst. – defendant admitted the assault and pleaded provocation – Complainant said he was on the road near to Mr Boulderstone's shop about 10 o'clock on the night in question when Dykes and another man 'lay in wait' for him. Dykes came up and asked if complainant could 'do it now' and he (complainant) replied that he could do it, but that he was not going to do it then. They then had a little talk and then Dykes struck him over the left eye. The eye was very much swollen next morning. The Bench ordered the defendant to pay the costs.

26 September 1890
Collapse of Barn at Chelford

An alarming incident occurred the other day on the Yew Tree Farm, Chelford, which is in the occupation of Mr Moss. It appears the barn which adjoins the road was roofed with flags and the whole of the roofing suddenly gave way and fell with a crash. Fortunately none of the farm workers or any cattle were near at the time or somebody would have been seriously hurt, if not killed on the spot. The building is a very old one and it is said this mishap is due to the rotten condition of the woodwork.

3 October 1890

We are asked to give notice that the public vaccinator will attend at Chelford School on the third and fourth Wednesday in October and April at three o'clock.

21 November 1890
Letter to the Editor - Chelford Station

Sir

I was very pleased to see in your last edition that some one has pointed out a few of the dangers attending the above station but your correspondent has omitted that which a regular passenger or contractor has to contend with daily.

In the first instance, the milk carts, which should on dark mornings and evenings carry a light, are often sent to the station in a hurry, and driven by lads, who, in the absence of their masters, race and pass one another regardless of anyone on foot. You can easily see the difference when the farmer brings his own as some do. Anyone going to Manchester by the 7.24 a.m. train must get to the platform as best he can, after finding his way through about a dozen milk carts and a chance of being knocked down by a tankard. The railway officials are in no way to blame. They do their utmost to cope with the increasing traffic. Why not have the milk loaded in a siding apart from the ordinary passenger traffic?

As yet we have no footbridge to cross the line. It is the rule not the exception for two trains to be at Chelford at once. In that case you must scramble across the metals as best you can. Other stations along the line have a bridge across. Every station between Crewe and Stockport has one, except Chelford.

Yours etc., A Daily Passenger.

21 November 1890
Riding Without Reins

At the Macclesfield County Sessions on Tuesday, Joseph Stanley, carter, was summoned for riding without reins at Lower Withington on the 8th inst. PC Bowyer proved the case and a fine of 2s.6d and the costs was inflicted.

19 December 1890
None Attendance of Son at Withington School

At the Macclesfield County Sessions on Tuesday, John Bailey, labourer of Withington, was summoned for neglecting to comply with an order to send his child regularly to school at Withington. This case was before the court a month ago when certain statements were made by the father respecting his son's treatment at school and the Bench adjourned the case upon Col. Dixon promising to make enquiries. On Tuesday Col. Dixon said he had made inquiry, and he found that the character of the boy was a very bad one. He had seen the schoolmaster and another person who was interested in the school, and had learnt that the boy had been corrected in school, not severely, but simply in the ordinary way. The statement which the boy's father made in that court a month ago, that the boy came home from school 'black and blue' was perfectly untrue so far as he (Col. Dixon) could hear. He had learnt also that the home of the boy was not altogether of a satisfactory nature and he thought it would be better for him to be sent to an industrial school. Bailey said his lad was now going to Swettenham School and he thought he would go on all right. He did not want him to leave home and he would, in future, see that he went to school. The Bench conferred and ultimately the Chairman said they had decided not to make an order for his removal to an industrial school but they wished to give warning that if again he misbehaved himself and was expelled from school they should commit him to an industrial school. Defendant however, must pay the usual fine of 6d and 4s.6d costs.

CRICKET – OVER PEOVER v. CHELFORD

The following report has been extracted from a 1986 publication of 'The Guardian Book of Cricket' edited by Matthew Engel and has been reproduced by permission of the publishers, Pavilion Books Ltd.

NORMAN SHRAPNEL   27 June 1955

If village cricket is not what it was, it has certainly not lost its modesty. What club, entitled to call itself Peover Superior, would otherwise be content, as this one is, with the colloquial Over Peover? Yet the traditional pattern has certainly been shaken up a little, as was evident at the local Derby in Cheshire on Saturday.

Beneath the ass-head banner of the Mainwarings, who, lived here for close on a thousand years, on a field where General Patton was watching his boys play baseball not so long ago, the village team was beaten by its great rivals from Chelford. A chauffeur led the home side. The visitors, aiming fantastically higher in distance and speed, were captained by a distinguished radio astronomer. The Mainwaring ass-head might have been thought to droop a little, and the family motto ('Devant si je puis') to hide itself in a fold, at the sight of this lithe expert in cosmic rays looking, in his striped cap, like a highly senior member of a Science Sixth, thoroughly capable of hitting scientific sixes.

What Chelford won by was not, as it turned out, astronomical: a mere 46 runs, and in the last five minutes. 'We'd have slaughtered 'em on the old ground,' an elderly spectator was saying; he referred to the one that was ploughed up in the war, about the time the bomb fell on the farm where the club's equipment was stored.

The present ground would seem to have compensating virtues. It is beautiful; it is rent-free; it is even – to the surprise, no doubt, of all properly trained in the lore of English village cricket – flat. It would take more than a war, more even than General Patton's baseball boys, to kill cricket in Over Peover. An old army hut was bought for a song, a veranda made of sawn-up railway sleepers and abandoned telegraph poles was nailed on the front, a small kitchen and some water were provided for the ladies' tea committee, and the new age was born.

Much, today, was as it had always been. Ringed by the vast circle of mown hay, over which cows gazed, were the scarlet caps of crouching fielders like poppies among the daisies. The creaking birds, the rumbling lorries, and now the screaming jet-planes; the rhythm to this counterpoint was provided by George the score-boy, clashing his numbered plates as he hung them on their nails. The fast bowler – a scowl, seven strides, and a leap. The slow bowler – two walking and four trotting paces, a hop, and a cunning look suggesting that his mind was on something else. The fielding eager with overthrows. A short boundary on one side bringing four for a tap; so distant a one on the other that the lustiest clout was lucky to get there.

Much was obviously different. The spectators, for the most passionate match of the year, were a mere handful. This could not be wondered at, when the humblest and most remote cottager is able to twist a knob and bring Evans leaping or Trueman pounding before him. Making ends meet – with costs always rising, and vice-presidents admitting to no increase in wealth – must be a painful problem for most village clubs.

Here they are resourceful in the way of special efforts and unconventional attractions like the six-a-side tournament, which has its final on Wednesday. This knocks tradition right out of the ground. Each player except the wicketkeeper bowls one over, and the winner is the team scoring most runs in the five overs, irrespective of the number of wickets lost.

Sixteen local clubs are taking part. A match last about forty minutes, and three can be got into an evening's play. The impatient villagers, avid for sensationalism, like it. They even pay. A collecting-box is circulated, and, according to the treasurer, an evening of six-a-side can be 'quite a nice money-raiser'.

But today we were back in the older cricketing world of morals, manners, and Mainwarings, which meant something a good deal less than 50 runs an hour. The distinguished radio astronomer – whose side, unlike the more strictly local Over Peoverites, was buttressed with foreigners from places as far afield as Didsbury, Jodrell Bank, and Australia – looked serenely at George's creeping arithmetic and confessed that Chelford were usually happy if they had 120 on the board. A wicket fell. Sometimes, added the distinguished radio astronomer less serenely, one was able to win with as little as 80 on the board.

Chelford's chief hitter, reputed to have made sixty in twenty minutes the other day, peeled off his sweater, hit a brisk two, and at the next ball was marvelling at his fallen bails. Four more wickets fell for the subsequent seven runs. The radio astronomer assumed a cosmic expression and strode off to put on his pads. But then there was a stand that carried the afternoon to tea and declaration, so that he did not bat after all.

The distinguished radio astronomer referred to in this article was Bernard Lovell, now Sir Bernard Lovell, of Jodrell Bank Telescope who was at one time captain of Chelford Cricket Club.

CHELFORD EVACUEES

During the Second World War Chelford was host to a number of children evacuated from Gorton, Manchester and East London, the children ranging in age from 5 to 12.

By utilising information taken from the School Log Book it was possible to locate a number of these evacuees and a reunion was held in the new school on Saturday 15th July 2000. Present day members of the village who had connections with the evacuees were also invited to the reunion. In attendance for the event, and the village summer fair which followed the reunion, were Mr Martin Bell, MP for Tatton and the Mayor and Mayoress of Macclesfield, Mr and Mrs Walter Wright.

A full programme of events was arranged including a presentation of handbell ringing and the singing of war-time songs performed by the present school children.

The school itself was 'decked out' with Union Jacks, war-time posters, gas masks and other war-time memorabilia including an air raid siren.

Many of the evacuees had not seen each other since their schooldays nor had they, in many instances, seen the people of Chelford with whom they stayed or remembered from school.

The event had considerable coverage in the local press, the following report by Lauren Cumming appeared on Wednesday 2nd August 2000 in the Macclesfield Express.

Their memories of the time they spent in Chelford are varied – some happy, some desperate to return to their mums and dads.

Peter Barber, 66, had the clearest memory of how they arrived in the village. "My memories are as clear now as they were then," *he said. He remembers taking the evacuation consent form home for his parents to sign and marching down to Belle Vue train station with his fellow pupils from Old Hall Drive School in Gorton.* "We all had little green haversacks, luggage labels tagged on to our coats and I think we were given an apple and an orange."

A bus took them from Macclesfield station to Chelford. "The first place we were taken to was Lady Boddington's. We were given a sack and told to fill it with straw. We slept in a long room above the stables".

Later they would be taken to the village hall where villagers came and chose which evacuees they were going to take in. Despite being the last to be picked, Peter feels he struck lucky because he stayed with a couple who ran the village newsagents and toffee shop. "My stay with the Drew family was very, very pleasant, they were so kind. I had a smashing time there," he said.

But Audrey Iball now 68, remembers it being a difficult time for her. She was chosen to live at the Grange in Chelford. "I came from what I would call a humble home with a loving mum and dad and I was chosen by the lady of the house to stay with them. She said 'I'll have her' – I will never forget those words.

"They had no children and really it was the servants that I lived with, so I was very lonely. It was a very difficult period for me." Audrey eventually persuaded her parents to take her home. "Unfortunately, coming from an ordinary working class home I was out of my depth and longed to be at home with Mum and Dad," she said.

Many went to Chelford with their siblings and ended up being separated.

Vera Peterkin and her younger brother, Frank Galliford, were both at the reunion. They were ten and six when they were evacuated to Chelford. At first they were put together but were later moved to different houses. "We were taken to the Grange first. Then Frank was moved. I wasn't particularly happy about being split up from him and asked my father if I could be moved. I stayed with a family who lived in a cottage near the railway where I settled quite happily," Vera said.

Hilda Manning, who was the only one of the group from East London to be traced, was also separated from her two younger brothers. "Mum told me to look after them but no-one wanted to take three children. I told them there was no way I was going to leave them but they persuaded me that they would just be down the road," she said. Hilda stayed at Bank House and her brothers, Ray and Ron, went to a farm a little way out of the village. She remembers visiting them at the weekends with her friend, Violet Schofield, and always arriving with muddy hands and knees from climbing trees and jumping brooks on the way. Her abiding memory of going to the village school was all the knitting they did. "Our teacher, Mrs Cash, had asthma and when she left the room because she was having an attack she used to tell us to carry on with our knitting. We used to knit like mad. In fact we knitted the most mittens and balaclavas for the troops out of all the schools in Cheshire. I was very pleased with that at the time," she said.

Sisters Eunice Cooper, 73, and Frances Thompson, 69, were evacuated with another sister, Rosemary, and their little brother, John. As the oldest, Eunice stayed with John and they lived in the Manor House. "We had a fantastic time there. They really made us feel part of the family," she said. For two children from Gorton, living at the Manor House was the lap of luxury. "We were made to feel really important. The maid used to bring our letters on a silver tray," she remembered.

Frances enjoyed her stay so much that she kept in touch with the family for years. Frances and her sister, Rosemary, lived with a Mr and Mrs Walsh and their two daughters, Audrey and Gwenifer. "We were happy there, they really looked after us. We had to call them Mr and Miss and I still did so until the last one died last year," she said.

One thing they all seem to remember is the weather. Jack Fovargue, 67, who now lives in Bollington, said: "The thing that did strike me was the depth of the snow. It was the deepest snow I had known."

Jean Routledge, 70, who spent some of her stay in Chelford with Lady Dixon, said: "I remember during the winter being given tin trays to sit on and slide down the snowy slopes in the garden."

Frank recalled being taken to school on a tractor when it snowed. "The farm lane was blocked by a snowdrift. I usually had to walk. The farmer dropped me off at the roundabout and the wind blew my bag out of my hand and my sandwiches fell in the snow," he said.

The evacuees were taken on a tour of the village with a special stop at the old school which they all attended during their time in Chelford.

Back at the new school, they were each presented with a painting of the village and a booklet containing old pictures, their reminiscences and pages from the school log book kept during the war.

All the evacuees were full of praise for the reunion organisers.

Audrey said: "The whole day has been wonderful, it is something I will always remember."

Peter agreed: "Everybody really appreciates what they have done for us. We would really like to thank them."

EVACUEES OUTSIDE OLD SCHOOL

Left to right with ages when they were living in Chelford. Jean Routledge (nee Faulkner) 9, Peter Barber 7, Frances Thompson (nee Foley) 8, Hilda Manning (nee Punshon) 10, Vera Peterkin (nee Galliford) 10, Frank Galliford 6, Eunice Cooper (nee Foley) 12, John Lowe 7, Jack Fovargue 7, Audrey Iball (nee Brown) 6.

CHELFORD SCHOOL HANDBELL RINGERS

Left to right: - Lauren Goldstraw, Charlotte Heywood, Karen Swindells, Scot Jackson, Camilla Sheridan, Michael Bottomley, Liam Sullivan, John Gresham, Matthew Swindlehurst.

CHELFORD SCHOOL SINGERS

Left to right back row: - Maisie Norbury, Liam Sullivan, Michael Bottomley, Lauren Goldstraw, Scot Jackson, Charlotte Heywood, Karen Swindells, Matthew Swindlehurst, Camilla Sheridan, Jack Baskerville.

Left to right front row: - Hallam Sullivan, Jonathan Sparks, Sophie Williamson, Georgia Hammond, John Gresham, Hannah Wilcock, Ben Barron, Nicholas Boon, Laurence Wardell.

Evacuees with Martin Bell and Keith Plant (organiser) sounding the 'all clear' – Mayor and Mayoress of Macclesfield in rear of group.

A separate book about the reunion containing all the evacuees' memories, extracts from the School Log Book for the war-time period and the programme of events is available from the publishers.

One of the other children at Old Hall Drive School, Gorton was Joe Hughes who wasn't evacuated to Chelford with all his friends. He has recalled his memories of that period and with his permission his story is repeated below.

THE ONES LEFT BEHIND BY JOE HUGHES

September the first 1939

No school today. War was virtually inevitable if Germany invaded Poland, and most of my friends were going to a safer place, away from the expected bombing of our major cities.

I was not going with them, nor was my sister, Edie. My dad, who had been shot in the leg when only 17 years old and finished the First World War in hospital blue, was a bit philosophical about it all. "....all going together" wasn't what a nine year old wanted to hear, but as everyone knew the war would be over by Christmas.

So there I was, stood on the footbridge overlooking Belle Vue station with a hive of activity below me. I looked eagerly to see a familiar face, but they were so much alike. The boys in short trousers and little jackets, with an oversized luggage label in their lapel, and a little cardboard box hanging from a loop of string on their shoulders.

I felt an outsider; my friends and I had always shared our lives together up to this moment.

The carriage doors started banging, a green flag waved, a whistle blew and the L.N.E.R. tank engine chugged away.

I stood looking down on the empty platform. I had nothing else to do. There was no school, no pals, so I went home.

Mothers always know what to do at times like that. A jam butty.

"Go and see who else is still at home, and don't go near any water," rang in my ears as I left.

Joe Hedley was coming out of number 66 where he lived. At least I had one pal. He was off to see his grandma who lived in West Gorton, so I joined him on the two mile walk as my grandparents also lived off Birch Street. My grandma's front door was wide open. It always was. Another jam butty and I was fortified to find Joe and make our way home.

Life wasn't so bad after all, and for a few weeks we passed the days in similar fashion. Exploring.

Germany did invade Poland, the allotments overlooked by Old Hall Drive school were turfed, and a barrage balloon rose above it, to protect us from German dive bombers. Naval guns were installed on Mellands playing fields nearby to shower our houses with shrapnel whenever the Jerries approached.

My dad had a set of cigarette cards "Air Raid Precautions," and he set about protecting our house with a criss-cross of brown sticky paper on all the windows, black-out material joined the curtains across the windows.

The authorities decided our gas masks were inadequate for the latest chemical cocktails and we had to have an additional green filter taped over the nose piece. My aunt Jessie, who was a shirt machinist, made a more substantial case for it out of the leatherette material. The cardboard box had got tatty anyway.

The days got shorter and a cold winter set in. The few of us who had not been evacuated were summoned to school. To conserve energy on the school's heating, our small number gathered into the hall and somehow the teachers managed to educate several classes simultaneously. The milk arrived daily in one third pint bottles with a cardboard top with a push-in hole for the straws. Teacher, in her wisdom, would heat the milk by putting the crate near the radiator which gave the milk a horrible taste. We suffered in silence, for that is what we were supposed to do in those disciplined days.

We knew the evacuees were also experiencing a cold winter for, in the school corridors, framed photographs were hung showing my friends playing in the snow.

The black-out was so effective our mothers armed us with little torches, which contained U2 batteries that had a very short life and we usually arrived home with a light so dim as to be near useless. Mothers always know what to do and we were encouraged to eat raw carrots so we could see in the dark.

One day I visited my aunt Lizzie who lived in Droylsden. It wasn't until my mother and I returned home that evening that I realised I had left my gas mask at my aunties. My mother and father tried to reassure me that everything would be all right. After all, there had, as yet, not been any air raids.

Fate decided to intervene and in the late evening came the rising and falling wail of the air raid sirens.

Convinced I was going to be gassed at any moment I stood in the coal place under the stairs with my mam, dad and sister until the steady tone signalled the all clear.

Standing under the stairs was an unpleasant way of spending the evening. Thankfully, soon afterwards, a team of men dug a hole in our garden and erected an Anderson Shelter, which my father covered with soil and grass camouflage.

It wasn't long before the shelter had two foot of water in it, and my first job on arriving home from school was to bale out the water. We had a large zinc bath (my father was of coal mining stock), which I dragged to the entrance of the shelter and put as much water into it as I could drag back to the drain.

The few young people who were left on the estate "copped for" a disproportionate amount of running errands;. a regular trip to the coke yard included. All right if you had an old pram, but we didn't and a quarter hundred weight was all I could carry in a little hessian sack, which doubled the journeys to Belle Vue sidings.

There was a lot of responsibility put on young shoulders, and there were some hazardous jobs, like going to Wellington Street with the wireless battery for recharging, so dad could listen to the news, Lord Haw Haw, and ITMA.

Empty glass bottles were at a premium and you had to take one to the shop next to Berry's on Ryder Brow Road to be refilled with Lanry bleach. Poor Joe fell and broke the bottle he was carrying and took the colour out of the front of his jacket.

The day I remember best of all was when my mother asked me to see if our neighbour at number 30, Mrs Faulkner, wanted me to run an errand. Imagine my surprise when stood in the living room was her son John, home from Chelford.

We stood for ages looking at each other, grinning like Cheshire cats. This was the start of the homecomings, but to show how much he loved Chelford, John took me one day to the farm where he and his sister, Jean, had been living.

Soon after, all my pals were home, and on the dark nights, I would gaze up to the skies to watch the searchlights fanning and searching for the enemy. We soon recognised the drone of the German bombers and still remember the stick of bombs that fell on Betts Farm, Old Hall Drive, and Lindeth Avenue.

Defiantly, at five foot nothing, we formed our group of Commandos, scaling walls, jumping streams and climbing ropes, for as Churchill said, "We will fight them in the streets".

THE DIAMOND JUBILEE OF QUEEN VICTORIA
Tuesday 22 June 1897

To commemorate the above event and to record how Cheshire towns and villages celebrated the Diamond Jubilee, a book was compiled by John H Cook[1]. Extracts from this publication covering Chelford, Snelson and Lower Withington are detailed below: -

Parish of Chelford (Macclesfield Union)

Names of Councillors and officials in office on Jubilee Day 1897.

Parish Council

Col. George Dixon JP CC Astle Hall Chelford
    (Chairman Parish Council and Cheshire County Council)
Dale, John (Vice Chairman) Astle Farm, Chelford
Basford, Thomas – Astle Farm, Chelford
Gledhill, Thomas Heald – Dixon Arms, Chelford
Ballachey, H.H. Esq. – Chelford
Haigh, John D – Post Office, Chelford
Cooke, Wm H Esq. – The Grange, Chelford
Moss, George – Smithy, Chelford

Officials

Page, Elijah – Clerk Chelford

Rural District Councillor

Callwood, James – Roadside Farm, Chelford

Jubilee Celebration at Chelford

Chelford had a general holiday in Col. Dixon's park with a free tea, paid for by voluntary subscriptions, and each school child had a medal.

---

[1] Alderley Research Centre of the Family History Society of Cheshire – Ref. CRO1 (On loan from Cheshire Record Office)

Parish of Snelson (Macclesfield Union)

Names of Councillors and officials in office on Jubilee Day 1897

Callwood, James – Roadside Farm, Chelford
        Guardian and Rural District Councillor for Snelson and Chelford.

Parish Council

Higham, Robert – (Chairman)
Barber, Edward
Bucktrout, Samuel Whitlow
Gibson, John Hope
Gleave, Josiah
Pierpoint, William

Officials

Bell, Thomas – Overseer
Blackshaw, Charles
Clarke, Samuel – Assistant Overseer and Clerk to the Parish Council

Jubilee Celebrations at Snelson

One part of Snelson is in the ecclesiastical parish of Higher Peover and the other part in the parish of Chelford.

Those inhabitants who belonged to the parish of Chelford were given a free tea in Astle Park, the seat of Col. Dixon JP, Chairman of the Cheshire County Council.

There were athletic sports in the Park, after which tea was served in a large tent, the caterer being Mr T H Gledhill, hotel proprietor, Chelford. The Macclesfield Band played during the afternoon and after tea, for dancing, up to 10 o'clock, after which fireworks were discharged.

Those belonging to Peover parish went to the Jubilee at Peover Hall, where sports were the order of the day. Tea could be had anytime during the afternoon.

The Cross Town Band, Knutsford, played selections during the afternoon and in the evening for dancing. It turned out a very wet afternoon.

Parish of Lower Withington (Macclesfield Union)

Names of Councillors and officials in office on Jubilee Day 1897

Parish Council

Leigh, Captain Egerton (Chairman) JP, Jodrell Hall
Gilbert, Edwin (Vice Chairman) – Daisy Bank, Chemist
Bower, John – Broade Hall, Farmer
Bloor, Richard – Dicklow Bank, Farmer
Bailey, James – Withington, Farmer
Kennerley, B John (Treasurer) – Shelmore Farm, Farmer
Venables, Thomas – Well Trough Hall, Farmer

Rural District Councillor

Venables, Thomas

Officials

Cheetham, Henry – School House, Schoolmaster
        Assistant Overseer and Clerk to the Parish Council
Cheetham, Mrs J E Margaret – School House, Assistant Mistress
Cheetham, Miss E Verona – School House, Organist
Schwabe-Thackeray, H – Withington House, Overseer
Massey, James – Broade Hall, Overseer
Atkinson, D Augustus – Parsonage, Curate-in-charge
Gilbert, Edwin – Daisy Bank, Churchwarden
Bower, John – Broade Hall, Churchwarden
Tomlinson, George – Brook House Field, Postman

Jubilee celebrations at Withington Lower

The Queen's Diamond Jubilee was celebrated in this parish on Jubilee Day. Some time previously a small committee had been appointed, with Revd. A D Atkinson as Chairman, Mr Edwin Gilbert as Treasurer and Mr Henry Cheetham as Secretary. Subscriptions were invited, so that the proceedings should be social, pleasant and joyful. As a result a respectable sum was subscribed, and all subscribers' families – whatever the amount – were invited to attend and participate in the event. In addition to these, all the scholars at the National Day and Sunday Schools, the Church Choir and Officials, together with the Wesleyan Sunday School Scholars, Teachers, Choir, and Officials, the Scholars, Teachers, and Choir of the Primitive

Methodist Chapel were present, and the widows, old and infirm people were not forgotten. Early in the afternoon a most appropriate service was held in the Church, after which all proceeded to a field in which sports, games, &c., were indulged in until teatime. After partaking of an excellent tea in the National School, games were again resumed until about 8 o'clock, when the children were dismissed and presented with medals, prizes, oranges and buns. The adults remained and enjoyed themselves by a pleasant dance in the School till late in the evening. The whole proceedings passed off with so much real pleasure and enjoyment that the historical importance of the day will never be effaced from the hearts and minds of all who were privileged to take part in the festivities.

Though not within the remit of this book, it is interesting to recall 'The Sports', which formed part of the celebrations at Peover Superior.

Assembling at the Schools at 1.30, the children were marched in procession with flags flying to the park, where, after a short interval, their sports commenced. The greater part of these were got over before tea time, and consisted of Flat Races for boys and for girls of various ages, Three Legged Race, Potato Gathering Race, Egg and Spoon Race, Sack Race and Umbrella and Bun Race. The Needle-Threading competition had to be abandoned in consequence of rain. The Tug of War between 10 boys and 15 girls was a very exciting affair, the boys in the end proving victorious. But so well did the girls acquit themselves that the committee decided to give them a second prize.

The adults' sports commenced soon after 3 o'clock, and most of the events were well contested, and attracted great interest on the part of the spectators. The Flat Races brought out a good many competitors, that for "men of 50 years" showing that some of the old birds are "strong on the wing" still. The Smoking and Sack Races caused much amusement. The two fast Bicycle Races were capital contests, and the slow ditto was a marvellous exhibition of balancing skill on the part of the winner. The Hammer Throwing competition was also a great attraction. There were a large number of entries, and an excellent performance was the result. Three events, especially reserved for the ladies, showed that the sterner sex cannot altogether claim a monopoly of speed and skill, but must allow some credit, even in athletics, to their fair and gentle sisters. The last item put down on the programme – the Tug of War, married v single men – was a grand event, and called forth the greatest excitement. The tape didn't stir more than an inch or so for the first few minutes, but in the end, after about 12 minutes' hard tugging, the married men pulled their rivals over the mark. Bravo matrimony!

An extra race, "150 yards Flat Race for the Band, each man playing his own instrument and his own tune," elicited roars of applause, and ended, we believe, in a victory for the Trombone, though Big Drum gave a good account of himself. We had music for once in the afternoon, at least; it might have been a Comic Opera! Messrs. Crankshaw and Davenport kindly acted as starters and handicappers for the adult events, and Messrs N Dale and J Dale for the children's races, while the judges were Messrs. Worth and Lea. We were sorry that Mr Kinsey, who was to have officiated at the sports, was unable to be present, he had to do a bit of judging of a different kind – on a special jury at Chester Assizes.

OVER 60'S PARTY AT CHELFORD

December 1971

A full and festive start to Christmas for some 112 members of Chelford and Lower Withington Thursday Club. On Saturday night, after a sherry, the members sat down to Christmas dinner, organised by the Club's Committee. After the meal they were entertained by Mr J Scott (conjurer), Mrs Russell (clog dance) and Miss D Wheeldon who played the organ and led the community singing. Before leaving, each members was presented with a Christmas pudding donated by Mrs J Simpson.

CHELFORD SENIORS FOOTBALL TEAM c 1895

They were that good they played with ten men. Which one is David Beckham's Grandfather? Answers to the authors.

CHELFORD FELLOWSHIP DINES AT THE ANGEL

The Advertiser 22 January 1971

Included in the above newpaper picture are Jose Parfit, Edith Dyer, Mrs Boon?, Nora Blomfield, David Lowe? Mrs Henry, Mr Arthur Schofield, Rev Henry and Mrs Bessie Massey.

Knutsford's Angel Hotel was the venue on Wednesday, last week, for the Chelford Women's Fellowship annual dinner. Twenty-seven members and their husbands attended.

Grace was said by the Vicar of Chelford, the Rev. M J B Henry, who thanked the fellowship leader, Mrs H J B Day, for her hard work during the year. In reply, Mrs Day thanked her committee for their work and the vicar and Mrs Henry for allowing the group to meet in the vicarage.

Later, the vicar presented Mrs Day with a bouquet of spring flowers.

After dinner, games and dancing were organised by Mr John Ryder.

MOTHER AND TODDLERS AT CHELFORD
Taken from
The Advertiser, 9th December 1976

Included in the above picture are Julia Slater, Charlotte Slater, Robert Barber, Pam Barber, Alan Slater, Ann Boyling, Sue Couling, Joan Barber and Andrew Barber.

Crackers and balloons added to the festive spirit at Chelford mother and baby club Christmas party last Thursday.

Ten toddlers and their mothers attended the annual party at Chelford vicarage. Party games and a tea ensured the event was a success. Many of the mothers competed in "A home made cracker" competition. Mrs J Slater won first prize and Mrs A Boyling came second. Mrs Durrington judged the competition. The party was organised by Mrs Joan Mottershead and Mrs M J B Henry.

CHRISTMAS 1973
(Taken from The Advertiser, 27ʰ December 1973)

Margaret Brown (seated extreme right), one of the organisers, with another organiser, Mrs Betty Holland (third from right front row).

Also included in the above picture are Susan Bradley, Luke Holland, Irene Hamilton and many others.

More than 120 attended the Chelford Parish dance held at the Parish Hall on Friday. The dance realised more that £30 for local charities.

The entertainment was provided by the Hawaiian Sound Band and the dance was organised by Yvonne Newton, Margaret Brown and Betty Holland.

CHRISTMAS FAIR – DATE UNKNOWN

Tinsel and fairy lights were the order of the day at Chelford Village Hall on Saturday when Chelford Parish Church held their annual Christmas Fair. Our photographer found this happy group during the afternoon. They are, back: (left to right), Fay Kerrigan, Margaret Brown, Janet Crimes and, front, (left to right) Karen Newton, 7, Steven Boyling, 3, Mrs Yvonne Newton, Steven Newton, 6, and Dawn Boyling, 5.

CONFIRMATION AT CHELFORD 1975

Included in above picture are Rev. Henry, Julia Massey, Janice Brown, Margaret Brown, Susan Barber, Jill Hartwell, Ann Williamson, Fay Kerrigan, David Irlam, Christine Pimlott and Judith Pimlott.

GARDEN PARTY 1970
(Taken from the Express, 2 July 1970

A garden party with a difference took place at Chelford on Saturday. It should have been held in the Vicarage gardens, but owing to the bad weather, had to be inside the Vicarage. It proved successful for £70 was raised for church funds. The house was crowded with visitors who very quickly emptied the various stalls. There was an exhibition of dolls and dolls clothing, organised by Miss A Walsh, and of brass rubbings arranged by Miss C Wilson, the Vicar's step daughter. A few stalwarts played bowls on the lawn and there were a few tables of whist in the Vicarage. Bowls winners were Mr A Barber and Mrs J Camm and whist winners were Miss K Gough and Mrs Henry. Competition winners were Mrs Stanier, Mrs J Camm, Miss A Walsh and the Vicar, the Rev. M J B Henry. Winners of the children's flower arrangement competition were Carole Bradley and Ralph Robertson.

GARDEN PARTY 1970

NEW YEAR'S EVE 1973
(The Advertiser 10 January 1974)

During the past year Mrs Margaret Brown, Mrs Betty Holland and Mrs Yvonne Newton formed the Chelford Dance Committee and since then they have realised £150 for Chelford organisations.

On New Year's Eve they held a dance in the Parish Hall to thank everyone who has helped and attended their money realising efforts in the village. About 90 people were there and music was provided by Gary William's Disco. Mrs Gweneth Shemilt decorated the hall and Mrs Irene Hamilton served refreshments.

OPEN DAY AT CHELFORD SCHOOL 1975

Included in the above picture are Antony Brown, Peter Shemilt, Alison Shemilt, Bruce Watts, ?? Watts, Richard Griffin, Andrew Griffin, Linda Hamilton, Sharon Mayers, Mrs Marjorie Halman, Mrs Beryl Lofthouse, Mrs Rita Worthington Samantha Andrew and Nickola ?

VISITING SANTA AT CHELFORD
(The Advertiser 6 December 1979)

Three-years-old Hazel Shenton enjoys a magic moment at Chelford parish Hall Christmas Fair on Saturday as she sits on Santa Claus's lap with his attendants and other visitors looking on. The fair drew a large crowd and among those present were the Deputy Mayor of Macclesfield, Councillor E Coppock and Canon Henry.

In addition to Hazel Shenton and Santa Claus the picture above includes Janice Brown, Emma Boyling, Philip Hornby and Karen Newton.

SANTA AT CHELFORD 1975

Children with Father Christmas, looking on are Mr Nicholas Winterton, MP, for Macclesfield (middle) and the Rev. M J B Henry.

(The Advertiser 11th December 1975)

Father Christmas with his helpers were the main attraction at Chelford Parish Church annual fair on Saturday.

Mr Nicholas Winterton, MP for the Macclesfield Constituency, introduced Father Christmas to the hundreds of people who attended the event in the parish hall. Misses Vicky Hallam and Rachel Bailey were dressed as fairies to help Father Christmas. Mr and Mrs Winterton were presented with buttonholes by Dawn Boyling and Alison Shemlit on behalf of the Sunday School.

Numerous stallholders were kept busy throughout the afternoon and the many people who helped to make the event a success included Mrs T Newton, (produce), Mrs A Turnock, (Christmas presents), Mrs M J B Henry, (bric-a-brac), Mrs A Henshall, (plants), Mrs L Curfoot, (competition), Mrs A Sutcliffe, (cakes), Mrs J Hugle, (good-as-new), Mrs B Michell, (competition), Mrs J Walsh, (sweets), Mrs D Brown, (toys), Mrs A Hornby, (refreshments), Misses L Tickle and C Wilson, (Competition). The event realised more that £500 for church funds.

SUNDAY SCHOOL 1967

Included in the above are: - Richard Okill, Les Boon, Philip Okill, John Camm, David Williamson, Helen Okill, Susan Kitching, Andrea Kitching, Margaret Okill, Carol Bradley, Susan Okill, Allan Oliver, Shena Burgess, Judith Pimlott, Gail Burgess, Ann Williamson, John Provust, Nigel Kerrigan, Sandra Dingle, Robert Brown, Sally Newton, Janice Brown, Andrew Dingle, Sandra Hamilton, Faye Kerrigan, Janet Crimes.

Women's Bowling at Dixon Arms
(Newspaper article with no date)

An inter-club match for the Fitzsimmons Shield was played at Chelford and District Women's Bowling Club at the Dixon Arms. The shield, (centre) held by Mrs Freda Turnock, club secretary, was won by Mrs Freda Kerrigan (right) with the Turnock Rose Bowl which she also won recently. Also pictured (left to right) are Mrs Margaret Brown, winner of Ladies Cup, and Mrs Elsie Plant, Mrs Betty Bradley and Mrs Barbara Camm, all semi-finalists.

COMMERCIAL DIRECTORIES

The first trade directory in Britain was produced in 1677 to list all London merchants. However, it was another 100 years before directories started to appear in other major cities like Birmingham (1763), Manchester (1772) and Sheffield (1774).

By the 1850's there were editions for almost the whole of the country including small market towns and rural districts. New volumes were produced at regular intervals throughout the 19th century and into the 20th century until they were replaced by telephone directories.

Early directories concentrated on prominent members of the community and, usually included extensive information about the town or village, its population, size, schools, history, rail and coach links, churches, non-comformist chapels and charities etc.

Many local libraries have copies of the directories relating to their particular district, with County Record Offices and large central libraries holding copies covering more extensive areas.

The best known of these directories are Bagshaw's, Kelly's, Piggot's, Morris's and White's. White's directory of 1860 included the following information concerning Chelford, Lower Withington, Snelson and Old Withington.

CHELFORD 1860

Chelford is a small well-built village, township, and chapelry in the Macclesfield Hundred, 7 miles West from Macclesfield, contains 1,150 acres of land, and in 1851 had 39 houses and 263[1] inhabitants, of whom 129 were males and 134 females. Rateable value £2,435, of which sums the railway is rated at £540. John Dixon Esq., owns the whole of the township except the Manor House farm and the farm occupied by Mr Nichols, which is the property of Mr Bent, a minor. About the year 1264 the manor was given to the Abbot of Chester by Robert Pigot, on the condition of furnishing a chaplain to say mass for the repose of his soul, such service to take place in Chelford Chapel three days in the week, and the remaining four days before the altar of St Nicholas in Prestbury Church. In the 22nd year of Elizabeth it was held by Henry Mainwaring Esq., of Kermincham, and subsequently passed to the Mainwaring of Peover. This township is intersected by the London and North-Western Railway, and there is a neat station from whence there are eleven passenger each way daily except on Sunday, when there are only four. Mr John Wilkinson is

---

[1] The census returns for 1851 give a total population of 260 of which 131 were males and 129 female.

the station master. Adjoining the station is an extensive coal wharf belonging to Lord Vernon. The Dixon's Arms Railway, Commercial, and Posting Hotel is also situated close to the station. The house is fitted up with every comfort and convenience for visitors. Post horses and carriages may be had on the shortest notice by application to the proprietor, Mr William Adams.

Astle Hall is a neat stuccoed mansion surrounded by a finely wooded park, the picturesque scenery of which is much improved by the artificial lake which empties itself into a brook called Peover Eye. It is now the seat and property of John Dixon Esq., who succeeded to the estate on the death of Colonel Dixon, the latter having purchased it from the trustees of Colonel Parker. At a very early period the estate was held by the Order of St John of Jerusalem, and the Asthulle family.

The Chapel is a small brick edifice with a belfry, situated on the Middlewich road, and was consecrated in 1776. There was a chapel here as early as 1264, the chaplain of which had a salary of £4.6s.8d from Chester Abbey. The living, a perpetual curacy, value £100, has been augmented with £600 benefactions, and £600 parliamentary grant. John Dixon Esq., is patron, and the Rev. D Paterson, B.A., incumbent. The parsonage is an ancient residence mantled with ivy, situated at the cross of roads a little north of the church. It was purchased with a sum of £250 obtained from Queen Anne's bounty, and £150 left by Dame Dorothy Jodrell. There are ten acres of glebe land.

Free School - The school was built by John Parker, and was endowed in 1754, with £100 given by Samuel Brooke, £100 by Thomas Moss, and £50 by the said John Parker. A further sum of £200 was bequeathed by Robert Salisbury Brooke in 1806 for the same object. The sum of £10 on account of Brooke's Charity is paid to the schoolmaster every Christmas, and £9. 4s at Midsummer by Colonel Parker's trustees. Children from Chelford, Withington and Nether Alderley, both boys and girls, are eligible for this school. The Parliamentary returns of 1786 state that a sum of £54 left by various donors, was laid out in the purchase of three dwellings under one roof, from the rents of which the Parish officers pay a yearly sum of £2 6s. 1½d for charitable purposes. The poor have a yearly sum of 6s bequeathed by Roger Holland and charged upon lands in Mottram St. Andrew.

Mr R S Brooke, who died in 1814, during his lifetime paid £10 per annum to the poor, on account of two legacies of £100, given or intended to be given by the wills of Samuel Brooke and Catherine Brooke. The amount was paid to 1832 inclusive by Colonel Parker. In the spring of 1833 Mr Parker's affairs were placed in the hands of Charles Cholmondeley and John Drummond, Esqs., under a deed of trust, and by them the £10 is still paid. Samuel Hardy, by will of 1834, gave to the minister and churchwardens the sum of £50, the interest thereof to be applied towards the benefit of the poor of the townships. The sum of £45 was received as the amount of this legacy (after deducting legacy duty), which has been placed in the Macclesfield bank. These several bequests produce a yearly sum of £12.12s.1½d., which is distributed in sums varying from 8s to £2 among poor and aged persons and widows who receive no relief from the poor rate.

Post Office - James Jackson Gledhill's. Letter arrive from Congleton at 7.0 a.m. and are dispatched at 6.15 p.m.

Residences

William Adams, victualler, Dixon's Arms and Railway, Commercial and Posting Hotel
Samuel Dale   blacksmith
Richard David   farm bailiff
Joseph Dingle   joiner
John Dixon Esq.   Astle Hall
James Jackson Gledhill   shopkeeper
Joseph Holford   coal agent, Chelford station
Margaret Kennerley   victualler, Archer Inn
Rev. David Paterson, B.A.,   Parsonage
Samuel Roylance   blacksmith
Peter Whalley   schoolmaster
John Wilkinson   station master

Farmers etc.

Richard Billington   farmer
Thomas Beech, Manor House   farmer
John Dale, Astle   farmer
Charles Fisher   farmer
Margaret Kennerley   farmer
Timothy Lockett   farmer
Thomas Mellor   farmer
Edward Moss   farmer
Charles Nichols   bridge master and surveyor
                                      for the county of Chester
Samuel Norbury, Astle   farmer
Wm., Rushworth, Astle   farmer

Chelford Station (London and North Western Railway). There are 11 passenger trains each way daily, Sunday excepted, when there are 4. John Wilkinson, station master.

Omnibuses From the Dixon's Arms & Railway Hotel. (Wm Adams, proprietor). To Knutsford at 9.0 a.m., 2.30 a.m. and 6.0 p.m. daily (except on Sunday, when it leaves at 10.20 a.m.) to meet the trains at the above mentioned times to forward passengers to Knutsford. To Macclesfield, Tuesday and Saturday, at 9.0 a.m. and returns at 4 p.m.

LOWER WITHINGTON 1860

Lower Withington is a small scattered village and township in the Macclesfield Hundred, 6 ½ miles N.N.W. from Congleton, intersected by the Manchester and Birmingham Railway, contains 2,125 acres of land, a great portion of which is light fertile soil. In 1851 there were 113 houses and 570 inhabitants of whom 280 were males and 281 females[2]. Rateable value £3,400, of which sum the railway is rated at £163,12s.8d. The principal landowners are John B Glegg Esq., Egerton Leigh Esq., Edward Foden Esq., Mr John Snelson, Mr Isaac Bayley, Mr John Cooper, Mr Thomas Stubbs, Mr Richard Bratt and Mr Joseph Baguley. Randle de Blundeville gave this township, together with 20s rent from the Mill at Macclesfield, to Robert the son of Salmon, on the render of a pair of gilt spurs, in return for which gift Robert quit-claimed to the Earl all the lands which his father held in Normandy. The manor was subsequently held by the Mainwarings, Davenports, and Parkers, and on the death of the late Colonel Parker, was devised to trustees for sale. The singular elevation in this township, called Tunstead Hill, is supposed to have been the site of a village anterior to the Saxon era.

Welltrough Hall, an ancient timbered mansion, was formerly the seat of the Davenports, from whom descended the Davenports of Bramhall, Henbury and Woodford. The Wesleyan and the Primitive Methodists have each a chapel in the village.

The Red Lion Inn, in this township, has been occupied by the family of Foden for upwards of 200 years. The Black Swan, now more commonly called the Trap Inn, received its latter appellation about 50 years ago. A man named John Peak who was employed in the erection of two cottages close by, was accustomed to visit the Black Swan to dine. On one occasion, there being rather more company than usual, he was induced to delay his departure, and stayed the remainder of the day. From this

---

[2] The 1851 census gives the figures as 283 males and 287 females.

circumstance he named it the Trap Inn, but fully made up his mind that it should never *trap* him again.

Charities - Thomas Boden's gift. The legacy duty of £48 has been paid on this bequest, and the remaining sum of £432 has been invested in the purchase of a house and about 1 ½ acres of Cheshire land, which is let for £22. 10s., per annum of which £10 a year are paid for the liquidation of the chapel debt, £10 to the township school, £1 to the Sunday school and 30s., are kept in hand for incidental expenses. The poor have a small sum yearly from Roger Holland's gift, noticed with Prestbury, and £1 a year from John Foden's charity.

Residences

Michael Baker, schoolmaster
John Buckley, blacksmith
Samuel Norbury, tailor
Peter Slack,
Thos. Street, bricklayer

Inns and taverns

John Bower, Cheshire Hunt
Joseph Foden, Red Lion
Charles Slack, Trap Inn

Farmers

Samuel Appleton
John Baguley
Joseph Baguley
Geo. Barber
Thos Barber
Robert Basford
Isaac Bayley
Noah Bennett
Thos. Harrison
Wm. Jepson
John Kennerley
John Lea
John Massey
Wm. Partington
James Pimlott

Joseph Slack
Cyrus Slater, Welltrough Hall
Geo. Slater
Thos. Street
Thos. Stubbs
Wm. Summerville
Geo. Thorley
John Wainwright
John Walkely

Shoemakers

John Barlow
John Coppack
John Foden
Geo. Hurstfield

Shopkeepers

Peter Burgess
Thos. Coppack
Ralph Hall
John Kennerley
Frances & Sarah Lowe
James Nixon
Sarah Staley

Wheelwright

Wm Cooper
Samuel Norbury (& maker of all kinds of agricultural implements)

Joseph Slack

SNELSON

Snelson is a small village and township in the Macclesfield Hundred, 5½ miles S.E. from Knutsford, contains 369 acres of land, and in 1851 had 39 houses and 169 inhabitants, of whom 93 were males and 73 females[3]. Rateable value £920, of which the Manchester and Birmingham Railway is rated at £400. The principal land owners are John Dixon, Esq., Mr Richard Knowles, Mr Thomas Norbury, Mrs Hannah Whitlow, Trustees of Peover School, and the executors of the late Mr Joseph Gleave. There are also a few other small proprietors. The principal estate in this township was anciently held by the Mainwarings. On the marriage of Henry de Aldithley to Bertra, daughter of Ralph Mainwaring, she had the township given her as a dowry. The township subsequently became divided, and a family settled here which assumed the local name, and possessed a great portion of the property. They continued here several generations, and about 1640 the heiress married Mr Parker, of Astle, in whose descendant the principal estate in the township is vested. There are no manorial rights exercised. The Wesleyan and New Connection Methodists have each a chapel here, in connection with which are Sunday Schools.

Directory: -

George B Horsley, hop merchant.
Elizabeth Norbury, shopkéeper.
Mr Thomas Norbury, Snelson Cottage.
James Reade, boot and shoe maker.
Robert P Willcock, wine merchant.

Farmers: -

Thomas Barber
Thomas Basford
Thomas Bradford
Job Hobson
James Johnson
George Potts
Hannah Whitlow
William Woolfe,

---

[3] The 1851 Census gives this figure as 76 females.

OLD WITHINGTON

Old Withington is a small township pleasantly situated in a fertile part of the county, in the Macclesfield Hundred, 8½ miles W.W. by S. from Macclesfield. The township contains 1,600 acres of land, and in 1851 had 29 houses and 189 inhabitants, of whom 92 were males and 97 females. Rateable value £1,066. John B Glegg, Esq., is Lord of the manor and principal owner. The manor of Old Withington was among the earliest possessions of the Ardernes of Aldford, and was held under them by the Camvilles of Staffordshire. In the reign of Henry III Walkelyne de Arderne granted to Robert de Camville release of all homages or rents due to him in Old Withington, in reward of the services rendered by him in the wars in Gascony. This Robert afterwards, granted to Oliver Fitton and John de Baskervyle about 1266, the manor in moieties. The whole eventually became vested in the Baskervyles, and is now the property of his lineal descendant, John Baskervyle Glegg, Esq., whose ancestor assumed that name on suceeding to the estates of the Gleggs of Gayton. Withington Hall, a handsome stuccoed mansion, pleasantly situated in an extensive and well-wooded park, is the seat and property of John B Glegg, Esq. The poor of this township are entitled to a yearly sum of 3s., bequeathed by Roger Holland, and charged upon lands in the township of Mottram St. Andrew.

Directory

John Baskervyle Glegg, Esq., Withington Hall
Charles Alen, gardener
George Brown, gamekeeper
Ralph Hall, Shopkeeper
Edward Lea, agent to J B Glegg, Esq.
John Roylance, clog maker
Thomas Roylands, blacksmith and agricultural implement maker Dingle Smithy

Farmers

Mary Arrowsmith
David Bloor
Peter Bloor
James Davenport
Thomas Hulme
George Jackson
James Roylance
Ann Slater
Wm Snelson

FALLOWS HALL – NETHER ALDERLEY

Situated on the Chelford to Monks Heath road, set back off the road on the right hand side, approximately 800 yards from the present Monks Heath crossroads.

FALLOWS HALL IN 1947

The Fallows Hall estate was originally called LeFalwitz, an Anglo-Norman spelling for Falwis meaning the ploughed lands.

It was granted by Robert de Aldford, about the time of King John (1199-1216), to his younger brother, Henry de Ffalwiz who in turn passed it on to his son Thomas.

A Thomas de Ffalwiz was living in 1339 and another of the same name in 1385.

The name continued to occur from time to time either as party to or in connection with local deeds, for instance among the Davenport deeds, where one of the witnesses in a proof of age in June 1399 was Thomas de Ffalghes 'aged 50 years and more', who had a son, Thomas, born at 'les Ffalges' on 3 May 1378.

A John Fallows was, according to the Heralds Visitation, living in 1435/6 and Thomas Fallows, his son, had an exemption from serving on juries in 1512[4]. Oliver Fallows, the son of Thomas, was living in 1549, the estate passing from him to his son John who in turn was succeeded by his son, William Fallows, living in 1613 and buried at Alderley on 18 July 1629.

The estate then appears to have been passed to John Fallows, William's nephew (the eldest son of William's younger brother, Roger), John, who had married Anne daughter of Henry Bradshawe[5] of Marple, died c 1650. John's son, William[6], was born c 1625 and is entered at the Cheshire Visitation of 1663-4[7] as:

Fallows of Fallows in Alderley Parish

William who had married Alice, daughter of Hugh Hollinshead, died in 1677 and was buried at Alderley. His son, also named William, was baptised at Alderley on 28 November 1667 and died intestate in 1694 leaving a son, then two years of age, as heir to the estate.

In 1697 an Act of Parliament was obtained to enable William, as an infant, to sell the estate to pay debts due on the death of his father, and the following agreement[8] was drawn up.

John Bradshawe - England's first president 1649-1653

4	Cheshire Recognisance Rolls Cheshire Record Office
5	The Henry Bradshawe mentioned above was the father of John Bradshawe who was born in Marple in 1602 and baptised at St Mary's Church Stockport. It was John Bradshawe who, as Lord President of the High Court of Justice, tried and sentenced King Charles I to death in 1649. He then became president of the Council of State, effectively England's Chief Executive between 1649 and 1653 and during this time his signature, John Bradshawe President, was on the orders of the Government of England and can be said to have been the first, and only, President of England. Whether he ever visited his sister, Anne, at Fallows Hall is not known. The chances are that at some stage he will have done, linking Nether Alderley/Chelford to the highest power in the land at that time.
6	One of William's sisters was Elizabeth who married Ralph Furnival of the Milne House, Chelford and was bewitched to death in 1654 by the three witches of Chelford.
7	Visit made by Heralds from the College of Arms to inspect the authority by which they bore arms and proof of their estate.
8	Astle Estate Document, Box No. 1, Bundle No. 1, John Rylands University of Manchester Library Bradshaw and others to John Parker.

First part	Agreement between Henry Bradshaw (son of Henry Bradshaw of Marple Esq. Thomas Hollinshead of Heywood, Gentleman Frances Hobson of Pastur? And
Second part	Mary Fallows, widow, (Relict of William Fallows late of Fallows Hall in Nether Alderley), gentleman deceased. William Fallows, infant son and heir of William Fallows And
Third part	John Parker of Astle, gentleman.

By Indre 13 July 1697 The persons named as First Part plus Thomas Statham of Tideswell, Co., Derby, Gent and Mary Fallows, convey to John Parker of Astle, gent., the capital messuage or demesne house in Nether Alderley called Fallows Hall in holding of John Bradshaw, gent., and Mary Fallows.

The Fallows family then moved to Heywood Hall, Nether Alderley and subsequently into Derbyshire. A branch of the Fallows family still had connections in Snelson, the name appearing in an Assignment of Lease in 1741 and a lease of mortgaged property in 1743.

24 June 1741　　　Assignment of Lease

(1) George Fallows of Sandbach, yeoman
(2) Wm Shaw of the same, gent

(1) has for several years rented a farm in Sandbach from (2) and owes him £76.9s.7d rent. For better securing this sum (1) assigns to (2) the lease of a messuage in SNELSON, co. Chester, which he holds from John Lowndes.

17 May 1743　　　Lease of mortgaged property

(1) George Fallows of Snelson, yeoman
(2) Wm Lowndes of Deers Green in Smallwood, gent
(3) Nathaniel Fallows, son and heir apparent of (1)

(1) has a lease for three lives from John Lowndes, deceased brother of (2) of the messuage etc., in SNELSON, and being indebted to him in £150 mortgaged the lease to him. (2) has since lent (1) £20 on bond, and this

also is to be charged on the leasehold premises. (1) and (2) now lease the premises to (3) at a rent of £20 a year payable to (2) for 7 years.

The Parkers, who now owned the estate, were to become the most prominent family in the area throughout the 18th century and until 1834 when the whole of the Astle estate was sold to Henry Dixon[9].

Whether the Parkers lived at the Hall is not clear and probably quite unlikely. A tithe dispute of 1771 involving reversionary annual payments in lieu of Tythe Hay in kind contains the following statement: -

> "The Revd. John Parker, Clerk for Fallows Hall and Demesne now in the Tenure of Nathaniel Walley – Four Pence."

Included in the 1771 Tithe Dispute is the following statement: -

> 'There is also a private way in the Township of Nether Alderley which begins at the Town Field Gate and leads through Clays Lane, part of the Demesne of Heywood, and also along to Fallows Hall in which the Rectors successively for Time out of Mind have had a Right Tithe Property and Interest and may de Jure ride and lead their Tithe and other Things through the same Way without leave or lett of any person whatsoever.'

A little later, in 1775/6 Thomas Parker and John Parker are mentioned in a Deed of Allotment or Award of Enclosure to Mr Gaskell[10], relative to the Title of Thomas Parker to an estate called Fallows Hall.

Included in this deed is an award to allot, amongst other allotments, unto John Parker his heirs and assigns: -

> "One piece or parcel of common or waste ground lying on Monks Heath marked No 3 in the map of the plan annexed to the said award containing 2 acres 1 rood and 35 perches of statute measure or thereabouts adjoining on the north west side to ancient enclosed lands of the said John Parker on the south east of Chelford road and Northeast to the road leading to Sandle with directions to make and maintain the fences thereto.

---

9 Further details in Chelford A Cheshire Village published 1999.
10 Astle Estate Documents, Box No. 2, Abstract No. 8, John Rylands University of Manchester Library.

Also one other piece or parcel of common or waste ground lying on Monks Heath aforesaid marked in the said map or plan No 6 containing 2 acres 3 roods and 17 perches of like measure or thereabouts adjoining on the Northeast end of Chelford road on the Northeast side is to allotment on the same Heath No. 7 on the south end to Knutsford Turnpike Road on the west side to ancient enclosed lands of aforesaid J T Stanley and to the allotment on the Heath No. 5 with like directions to make and maintain fences but: the same as the Chelford Road and the allotment No. 7.

Also one other piece or parcel of common or waste ground lying on Sandle Heath marked on said Map on plan No. 1 containing 3 acres and 2 roods of like measure or thereabouts on the north side to Sandle Heath Road east end to ancient enclosure of Wm. Fallows south side to ancient enclosure of John Parker south west end to the road on the Heath leading to Fallows Hall.

Also one other piece or parcel of common or waste ground lying on Sandle Heath aforesaid marked in the said map or plan No 4 containing 13 acres and 4 perches of like measure or thereabouts adjoining on the north side to Sandle Heath road, east enclosure and leading to Fallows Hall, south side of the ancient enclosure of John Parker on the west end to ancient enclosure of J T Stanley of Sandle Heath Road with like directions to make and maintain fences of last mentioned allotments.

Note – sorry this seems confusing, but that is how it is described in the document.

In 1802 and also in 1810 the Land Tax Assessments for Nether Alderley show Thomas Parker as Proprietor of Fallows Hall and Samuel Blackshaw as occupier.

The Census of 1811 taken on the 27th May list Samuel Blackshaw aged 50, his wife Mary age 46, eleven children, seven boys and four girls, and three servants.

The hall and estate appears in a 1817 Mortgage[11] from Thomas Parker to Thomas Gaskell for 1000 years for securing the repayment of £5000 and interest.

Included in this latter document is the following extract: -

"All that capital messauge farm or tenant with the appurtenances of him the said Thomas Parker situate lying and being in Nether Alderley in the said county of Chester and commonly called by the name of Fallows Hall together with the several fields, closed or parcels of land thereunto

---

| 11 | Astle Estate Documents, Box No. 1, Bundle No. 1 John Rylands University of Manchester Library. |

belonging commonly called or known by the several names of the Little Stubble the Hollin Knowle the Great Stubble the Little New Hey the Great New Hey, the Greater Bridgefield the Little Bridgefield, the German Ground the Greene, the Middle Shaw, the Middle Shaw Meadow, the Bottom Meadow, the Great Moss Field, the Little Moss Field, the Moss the Brick Field the Brickfield Meadow, the Cross Flatts, the nearer Cross Flatts, the Great Sand Field, the Lesser Sand Field, the Least Sand Field and the Brook Meadow or by whatsoever other name or names the same or any of them have or have been called or known containing by estimation eighty seven acres and thirty three perches of land of statute measure.

Samuel Blackshawe and his family were still resident in 1821 but by 1831 he does not appear in the census return. The head of the family appears to be Samuel's son, also named Samuel, who was listed together with his mother, Mary, and his sister, Alice, and brother, Edward.

The Tithe Map of the 1840's shows that the Hall was now owned by John Dixon Esq., presumably purchased as part of the Astle Estate in 1833 and occupied by James Hague.

The apportionment accompanying the map is shown below: -

Landowner	Occupiers	No	Name & Description	State of Cultivation	A	R	P
John Dixon Esq.	James Hague[12]	123	Homestead	Pasture	2	-	38
		112	Heath pasture	Pasture			
		115	Far + New Hey	Arable	7	1	25
		117	Little Bridge Field	Arable	5	1	16
		114	Great Hey	Pasture	9	2	32
		118	Middle Shaw + Meadow		5	3	15
		120	Middle Shaw Field	Meadow	6	-	28
		121	Green Field	Pasture	7	2	16
		122	Fish Pond Field	Meadow	6	-	12
		124	Hollin Knowle	Pasture	10	3	22
		125	Great New Hey	Arable	13	-	23

---

12   It must be noted that at least two families of Hagues' were resident in Nether Alderley in 1831, the Census showing James Hague age 48, his wife, Mary age 52, together with their family and Thomas Hague age 56 and family.

126	Great New Hey		9	2	34
136	Moss	Pasture	6	1	84
137	Part of Moss	Meadow	4	1	-
138	Part of Moss	Meadow	2	2	25
139	Near Sand Field	Meadow	17	2	20
140	Further Sand Field	Pasture	14	-	30
147	Middle Sand Field	Arable	7	2	27

James Hague was still the occupier at the time of the 1851 Census, the record covering Fallows Hall being as follows: -

PLACE	OCCUPIER	RELATIONSHIP	STATUS	AGE	OCCUPATION	WHERE BORN
Fallows Hall	James Hague	Head	M	46	Farmer of 141 acres employing 2 labourers	Great Warford
	Jane Hague	Wife	M	40		Nether Alderley
	John Hague	Son	U	19		Nether Alderley
	Mary Hague	Dau	U	15		Lower Withington
	William Hague	Son	U	14		Lower Withington
	Margaret Hague	Dau		12	Scholar	Lower Withington
	Joseph Hague	Son		10	Scholar	Lower Withington
	Jane Hague	Dau		8	Scholar	Lower Withington
	James Hague	Son		6	Scholar	Nether Alderley
	Hannah Hague	Dau		4		Nether Alderley
	Anne Hague	Dau		1		Nether Alderley

246

Mary Kennerley	M.I.L	Widow	77	Retired farmer	Nether Alderley
Sarah Mellor	Niece	U	16	Milliner	Chelford
Elizabeth Ward	Serv.	U	27	House servant	Henbury
Joseph Massey	Serv.	U	24	Farm Labourer	Nether Alderley
Isaac Gooling	Serv.	U	20	Farm Labourer	Macclesfield
William Earlam	Serv.	U	17	Farm Labourer	Snelson

It would appear from the above that James Hague and his family moved from Lower Withington to Fallows Hall in 1843/4.

James Hague and his wife, Jane, were still living at the Hall in 1881, the census record for that year showing him as a retired farmer and a Lodger (Head). Also recorded as an occupier of the Hall is Samuel Worthington, a farmer of 141 acres employing 4 labourers. Samuel's wife, aged 32, was named Anne, and, as the 1851 Census records, Anne, daughter of James Hague, aged 1, it is reasonable to assume that they are one and the same and that Samuel Worthington was James Hague's son-in-law.

Ten years later, in 1891, Thomas Wilson was the occupier. Thomas was born in Scotland. It is interesting that his wife's name is Anne, born 1851 in Nether Alderley, and that with them on the night of the census was Thomas Wilson's niece, Emily Hague. There was obviously some connection with the previous owner, James Hague. Possibly Samuel Worthington, recorded in the 1881 census, had died and his widow, Anne, had remarried Thomas Wilson. A study of the Parish Registers would resolve this possibility.

According to the Commercial Directories for the early period of the 20th century, Thomas Wilson was resident at the Hall in 1910 but by 1923 and again in 1934 a James Wilson is listed.

The Hall was owned by the Dixon family from 1833 until it was sold to Sir Edwin Holt (the founder of Holt Radium Institute, Manchester) in 1947. The Hall was again sold in 1967 by Lady Holt to George Roberts and twelve months later was purchased by the present owner, Dr Patten.

Following the Wilson's tenancy of the Hall, the tenants, until the purchase by Dr Patten, were the Barlow family.

The Hall itself has been extensively altered over the years but parts of the building are reputed to date from the 17th century.

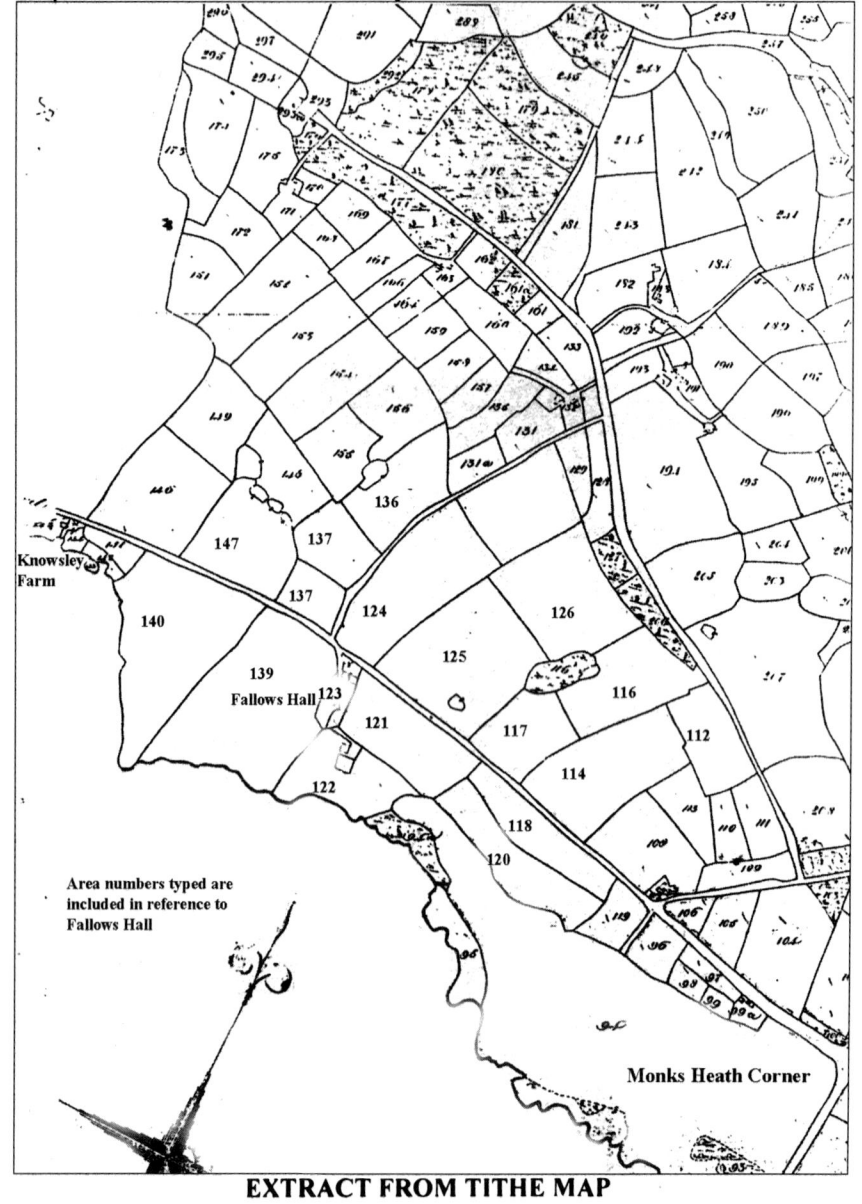

Knowsley Farm

Fallows Hall

Area numbers typed are included in reference to Fallows Hall

Monks Heath Corner

EXTRACT FROM TITHE MAP

248

MONKS HEATH

Monks Heath, as its name implies, was part of the estates of the Abbey of Dieulacres near Leek in Staffordshire. After the dissolution of the monasteries, all the lands in Alderley parish belonging to the abbey were sold in 1544 by the Crown to William and Francis Sheldon of Weston, Warwickshire. Later in the same year all the lands in Alderley were purchased by Ralph and Thomas Greene who in turn sold Monks Heath to William Ward, the then tenant, whilst retaining their own tenement for themselves.

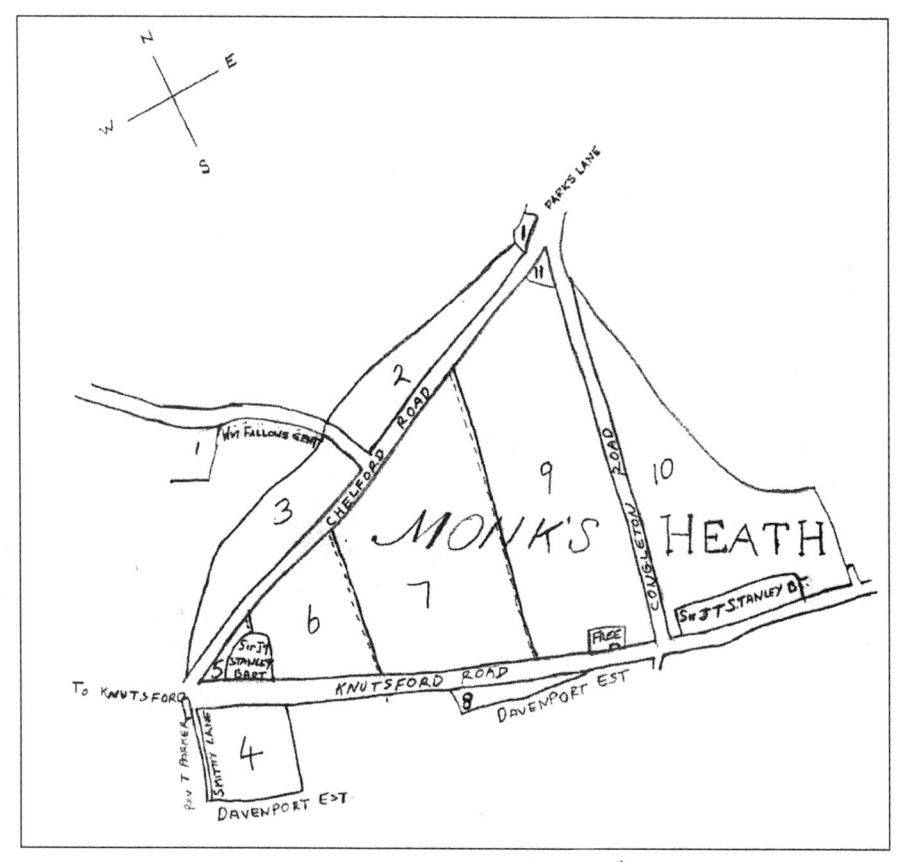

Part copy covering Monks Heath[1].

---

[1] Map attached to Allotment of Commons in Nether Alderley 13 December 1776. The document accompanying the map was signed and sealed by Edward Stelfox, Richard Orford and John Hayes in the presence of Jos Ceake and David Moors.

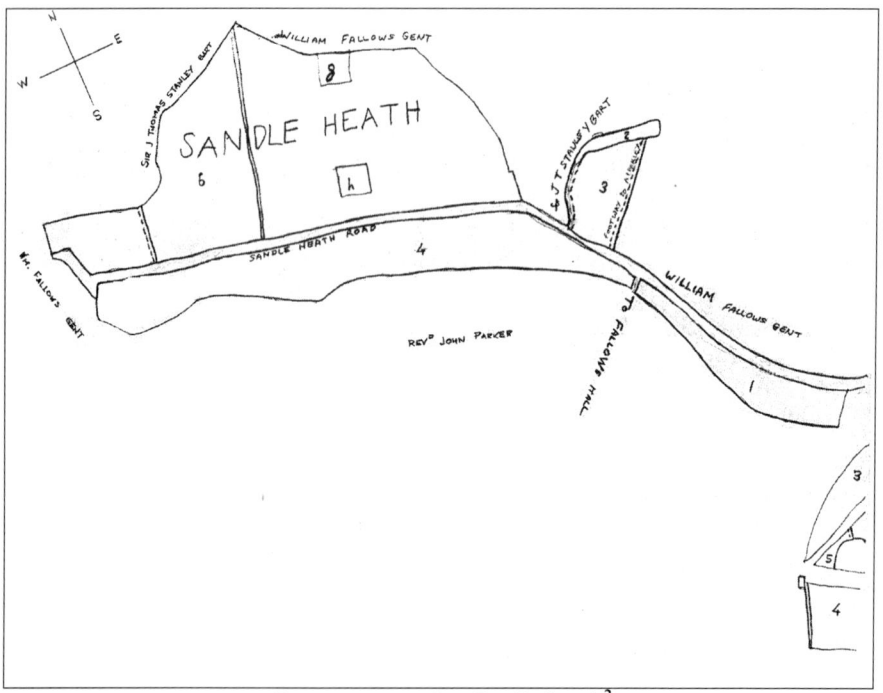

Part copy covering Sandle heath[2]

By a deed dated 18 January 1566, William Ward settled his messuage and lands in Nether Alderley in trust for his son and heir, Henry Ward and in 1571 he was a party to the marriage settlement of his grandson, John Ward.

The Ward family continued to live at Monks Heath until 1648 when it was first mortgaged and then sold to Philip Antrobus, who lived there for some years. He died c 1657 leaving six daughters as co-heiresses. The house and lands were subsequently re-purchased by John Ward in 1720 for £1500.

The 1771 Tithe Dispute (for details see chapter on Soss Moss Hall) lists a Stephen Palfreyman as tenant at the Hall and the 1802 Land Tax Assessments show John Ward as the occupier, Davis Davenport as the proprietor and Thomas Davenport as the owner.

---

2   Map attached to Allotment of Commons in Nether Alderley 13 December 1776. The document accompanying the map was signed and sealed by Edward Stelfox, Richard Orford and John Hayes in the presence of Jos Ceake and David Moors.

Later in the 19th century the Tithe Map of 1842 shows that the occupier was (William) Rogers and Edward Davis Davenport as the landowner.

The Tithe Map for the Monks Heath area is shown later, the associated Apportionment List containing the following information: -

LANDOWNER	OCCUPIER	NO	NAME + DESCRIPTION	STATE OF CULTIVATION	A	R	P
Edward Davis Davenport	Rogers	93	Four acres	Wood	2	-	19
		94	Wavering Hill	Pasture	54	3	15
		94a	Wood		2	-	-
		95	Thistles Clough	Pasture	2	1	8
		96	Smithy Bank	Pasture	2	-	14
		91	Homestead		2	-	33
		88	Barn Field	Pasture	3	-	10
		89	Barn Field Meadow	Meadow	3	2	39
		90	Barn Field	Arable	5	2	10
		92	Marl Field	Pasture	11	1	20
		87	Hill Field	½ Arable ½ Pasture	9	1	10
		84	Stables Meadow	Meadow	5	2	9
		104	Common Piece	Arable	7	1	16
Lord Stanley of Alderley	Henry Henshaw & others	82	Three cottages + Gardens		-	3	2
" "	Rebecca Bratt	100	Homestead		-	-	25
	Rebecca Bratt	83	Garden		-	-	33

Areas 80 + 81 + 78 + 79 + 101 + 102 are described as Common.

Ten years later the 1851 Census gives the following information relative to Monks Heath Hall.

Monks Heath Hall	William Rogers	Head	M	59	Farmer of 168 acres	Leek, Staffordshire
	Sarah Rogers	Wife	M	47		Leek, Staffordshire
	Elizabeth Rogers	Dau	U	15		North Rode, Cheshire
	John Rogers	Son	U	13		North Rode, Cheshire
	Thomas Rogers	Son		11	Scholar	North Rode,
	Sarah Anne Rogers	Dau		9	Scholar	Higher Peover
	Hannah Rogers	Dau		7	Scholar	Higher Peover
	Joseph Rogers	Son		3	Scholar	Higher Peover
	John Rogers	Nephew	U	19	Farm Labourer	Congleton
	Frances Woodward	Serv.	U	40	Farm Labourer	Rushton, Staffs
	Joseph Thornyhough	Serv	U	22	Farm Labourer	Leek, Staffs
	John Hanney	Serv	U	20	Farm Labourer	Ireland
	Martha Bloor	Serv	U	24	House Servant	Withington

According to the 1881 Census a total of nine families were living in the Monks Heath area.

Monks Heath Hall	Daniel Bostock	Head	M	58	Farmer of 160 acres	Odd Rode
	Mary Bostock	Wife	M	52		Swettenham
	John Bostock	Son	U	32	Farmer's son	Swettenham
	Henry Bostock	Son	U	26	Farmer's son	Swettenham
	Martha Bostock	Dau	U	21		Swettenham
	Daniel Bostock	Son	U	18		Alderley

	Jessie Bostock	Dau		7		Alderley
	Caesar J Foden	Serv	U	17	Farm Servant	Alderley
	Amelia Potter	Serv	U	17	Farm Domestic	Macclesfield
Monks Heath	Hugh Bailey	Head	M	66	Coal Agent	Norton, Staffs.
	Harriet Bailey	Wife	M	61		Rocester, Staffs.
	Lillian A Bailey	Gran-dau		10	Scholar	Macclesfield
	Elizabeth H Southeron	Gran-dau		4		Macclesfield
Monks Heath	James H Biddulph	Head	M	26	Gardener	Rushton, Staffs.
	Harriet Buddulph	Wife	M	23		Flash, Staffs.
	Thomas Biddulph	Son		2		Rushton, Staffs.
	James Biddulph	Son		1		Alderley
Monks Heath	Joseph Foden[3]	Head	M	52	Joiner	Alderley
	Margaret Foden	Wife	M	40		Carlisle D..., Cumberland
	William Foden	Son	U	19	Wheelwright	Alderley
	Ellen Foden	Dau		12	Scholar	Alderley
	Margaret Foden	Dau		10	Scholar	Alderley
	Jane Foden	Dau		9	Scholar	Alderley
	Nathan Foden	Son		7	Scholar	Alderley
	Edith Foden	Dau		5	Scholar	Alderley
	Henry Foden	Son		4	Scholar	Alderley
	Ethel Foden	Dau		3		Alderley
	Esther Foden	Dau		2		Alderley
Monks Heath	William Foden	Head	M	40	Farm labourer	Goostrey
	Jane Foden	Wife	M	36		Ollerton
	John E Foden	Son		8	Scholar	Peover

---

3   Joseph Foden carried out a lot of the wooden restoration work in St. Mary's Church, Nether Alderley.

Location	Name	Relation	Status	Age	Occupation	Birthplace
	Margaret Foden	Dau		6	Scholar	Peover
	James Foden	Son		3		Peover
	John Foden	Brother	U	38	Postman Letter Carrier	Alderley
Monks Heath	Peter Slater	Head	M	52	Agricultural Labourer	Siddington
	Mary Slater	Wife	M	55		Rushton, Staffs
	Ann Slater	Dau	U	20	Dressmaker	Henbury
Monks Heath	Charles Slater	Head	M	21	Farm Labourer	Alderley
	Mary E Slater	Wife	M	18		Snelson
	Samuel Slater	Son		1		Snelson
Monks Heath	Samuel Worthington	Head	M	24	Farm Labourer	Alderley
	Sarah A Worthington	Wife	M	26		Alderley
	Arthur H Worthington	Son		2		Alderley
Iron Gate Inn	William Higginbotham	Head	W	63	Farmer of 20 acres and Publican 1 Ser Man	Henbury
	Frank Higginbotham	Son	M	24	Farmer's son	Alderley
	Kate Higginbotham	D.I.L	M	22	Dairymaid (Agr. Lab.)	Ireland
	Jane Pennington	Serv	U	19	General Servant	Ollerton
	Joseph Bowers	Serv	U	21	Farm Servant Indoors	Withington

The Iron Gate Inn was situated on the corner of Monks Heath crossroads and was at one time a coaching inn. The Liverpool Mail Coach, which passed through Wilmslow and Congleton, changed horses at this point. The earliest reference to the Iron Gate as an Alehouse occurs in the list of licensees of 1762 when Richard Leather is listed followed by John Thorley in 1765-6, Cecil Gibbon 1774, Sarah Gibbon 1784-88, Thomas Lowe 1789-1804 and John Bratt 1805-28.

Around 1828 the Inn closed as a coaching house, probably due to the decline of coach travel, though it continued as an Inn for some considerable time.

The Apportionment List with the 1842 Tithe Map shows, against area plan 100 (i.e., on the corner of the crossroads), the occupier as Rebecca Bratt. Perhaps she was the widow of John Bratt who was given the licence for the selling of ale between 1805 and 1828.

The final census of the 19th century taken in 1891, shows that Daniel Bostock and his family were still resident at the Hall. He was a farmer of 160 acres, employing five servants.

Within the 20th century the records show that in 1910 Thos. Ward and George Webb, both farmers, lived at the Hall, followed by Walter Moores in 1923 and Albert Dawson in 1934.

The original hall was demolished in the 19th century and replaced by a new one on the original site.

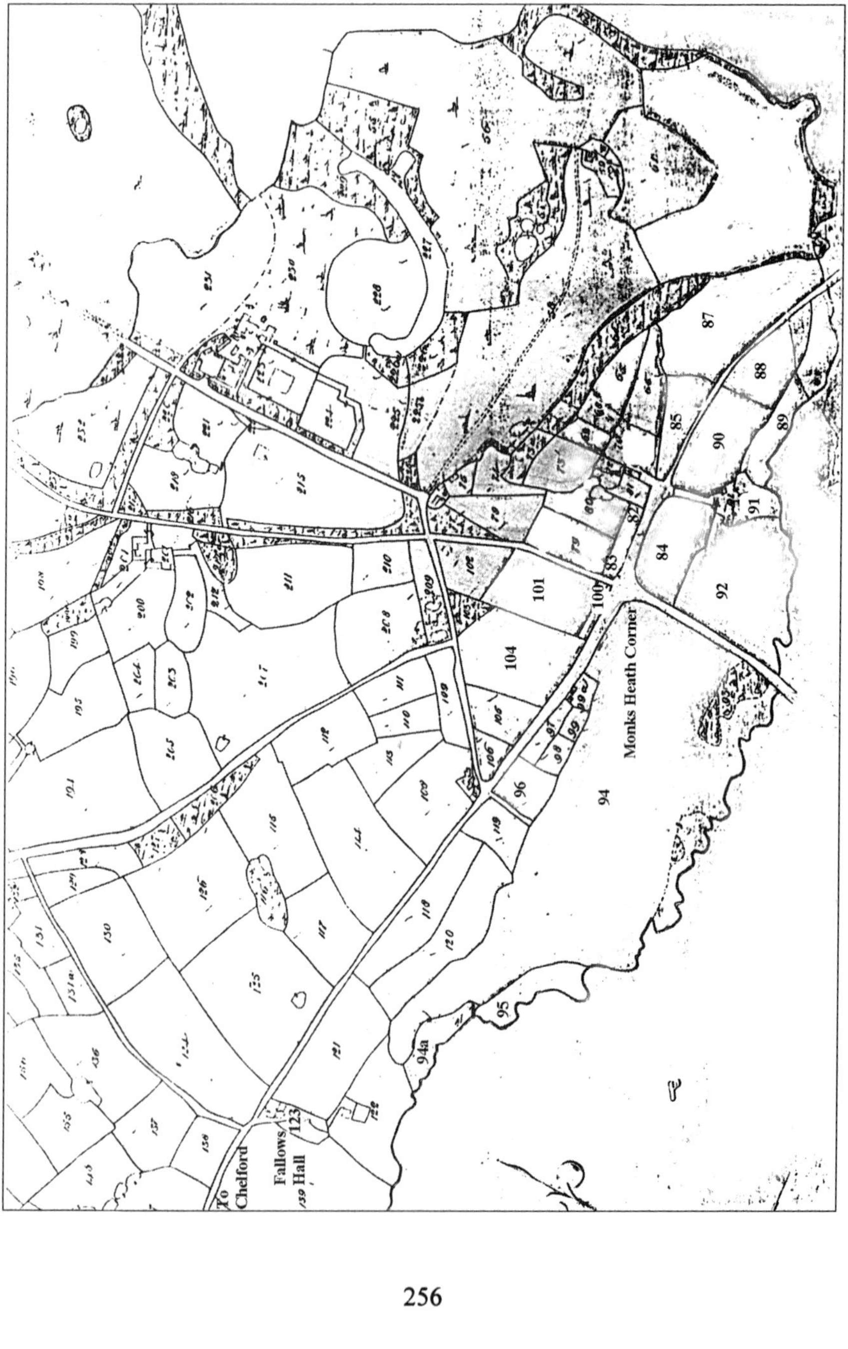
To Chelford
Fallows Hall
123
Monks Heath Corner
94
94a
95
96
100
101
104
84
85
87
88
89
90
91
92
83
82

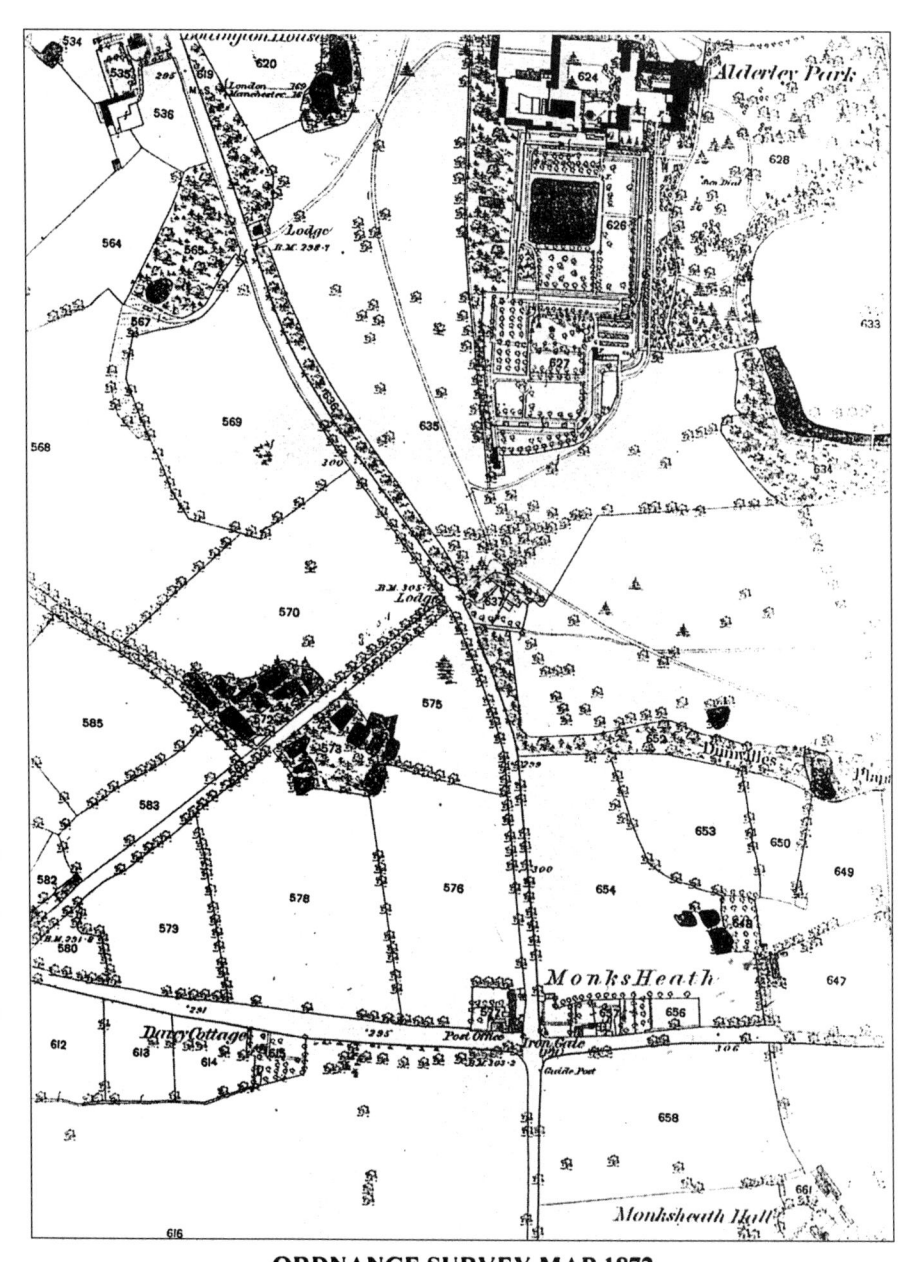

ORDNANCE SURVEY MAP 1872
Part extract from Cheshire County Record Office ref: OS 36.5

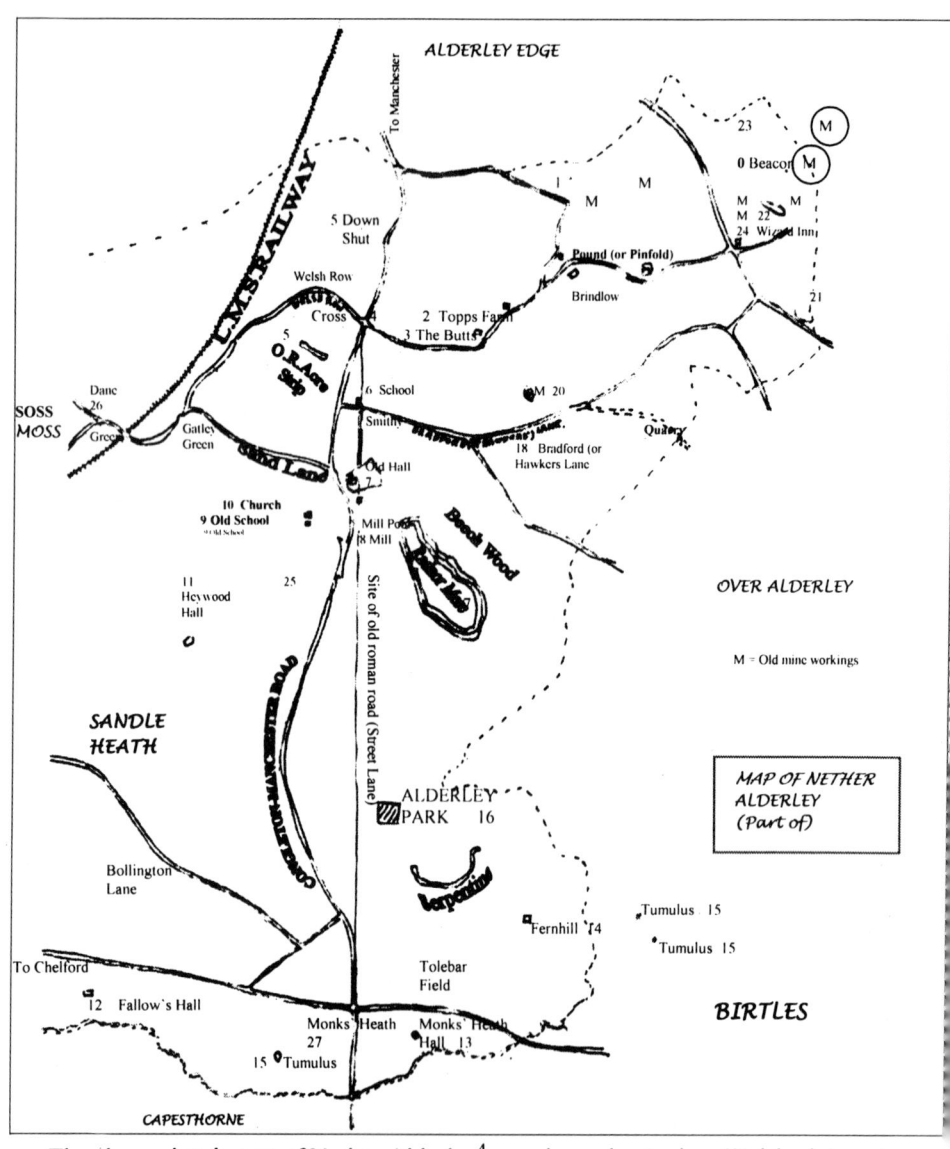

The above sketch map of Nether Alderley[4] was drawn by Audrey Walsh, date not known. The identification details have been typed on by the authors. For identification details see next page.

---

4. Cheshire County Record Office – Frances Crompton collection Ref: D5453 Box 5

IDENTIFICATION DETAILS OF NETHER ALDERLEY MAP – (previous page)

1. Stone Hammer found here.
2. Previously Pinfold farm.
3. Archery Butts.
4. Possibly site of market.
5. Remnants of open field farming.
6. Built 1822.
7. Old Manor House.
8. 14th or 15th century mill.
9. Built 1623.
10. First record 1329.
11. Heywood/Hollinshead/Fallows family.
12. Originally belonging to Abbey of Dieulacres.
13. "   "   "   "   "
14. "   "   "   "   "
15. Round Barrows.
16. Once known as the park or Park House.
17. Artificial ornamental mere.
18. Named from sport of hawking.
19. Now little used.
20. Large heap of slag from iron bloomery.
21. Site of British fort.
22. Engine vein. Ancient surface workings.
23. Beacon.
24. Once known as Miners Arms.
25. Site of old brick yard.
26. From Anglo Saxib Daen – a feeding place for pigs.
27. Alderley Fair held here.

SOSS MOSS HALL- NETHER ALDERLEY

In his book on Cheshire Place Names, J P McN Dodgson refers to Soss Moss with its Hall and wood as meaning a wet, sloppy moss, soaking on the bounds of Chelford and Snelson. The earliest known spelling appears to be Sostemosse in 1389 when the area, plus 5 acres in Monks Heath, was held by Margarita, daughter and heiress of Petri (Peter) de Arderne[5] deceased.

SOSS MOSS HALL IN NETHER ALDERLEY C 1850

The Hall was built in 1583, twenty-five years after the accession of Elizabeth I. For many years the property was the residence of a family named Wyche who had originally settled at Davenham, but who, on the marriage of Thomas Wyche of Davenham, gent to Margaret, daughter and sole heiress of William Barnes, of Nether Alderley, came to live in this township. It is possible that the estate had previously belonged to the Barnes', but from the name and date, T Wyche 1583, on a stone in the large chimney-stack of the building, it is clear that he was either the builder or rebuilder of the Hall. Thomas's brother, Richard Wyche, was the father of Sir Peter

---

[5] The Arderne family were, at that time, Patrons of Alderley parish. A Margarita, widow of Jon de Arderne, being patron of the Rector living in 1410 when the rector was Robertus de Legh in. Maybe the same Margarita.

Wyche who was, for twelve years, Ambassador to Constantinople and knighted by Charles I.

Thomas Wyche died on 27 January 1615/6 and his Inquisition post mortem[6] was taken at Middlewich in 1619 before Hugh Maynwaring Esq., and Henry Delves, by the oaths of a number of local inhabitants. The document refers to one capital messuage, one cottage, 15 acres of land, 10 acres of meadow, 15 acres of pasture and 2 acres of wood in Bromley in Nether Alderley, plus other property and lands in Davenham, Leftwich, Bostock and Rushton, Staffordshire. His son and heir, Richard Wyche, was stated to be 38 years of age at the date of the taking of this Inquisition.

It appears from the Wyche pedigree[7] that the family lived at the Hall until 1751 when it was sold together with the estate to Sir Edward Stanley and it remained part of the Stanley estate until it was broken up in the late 1930's.

In 1771a survey of the hamlets in the parish of Alderley was drawn up as part of a tithe dispute[8] with the local rector. This survey contains the following reference: -

> "The following sums are payable at Easter as Modums on Reversionary annual payments in lieu of Tythe Hay in kind.
>
> Henry Clarke as Tenant to the same for a Tenement called Soss Moss House.   One Penny."

It is interesting to note that in 1771 at the time of this tithe dispute, a William Wyche was listed as the proprietor of Soss Moss House and the 1802 and 1810 Land Tax Assessments also show a William Wyche as proprietor. Additionally, the Land Tax Assessments for these years also list Edward Wyche and William Woodall as occupiers. Therefore the Wyche family must have remained in the area for some years after the Hall was sold to Sir Edward Stanley, probably as farmers.

The 1811 Census taken on 27th May contains the following information relative to the families of Edward Wyche and William Woodall[9].

6	Cheshire Record Office.
7	East Cheshire Vol. 2 by J P Earwaker.
8	Included in the Parish Registers of Alderley Parish – Cheshire Record Office or Alderley Centre of the Family History Society of Cheshire.
9	Records retained in the Alderley Edge Research Centre of the Family History Society of Cheshire and W Keith Plant's private papers.

Master of Families	Other Persons	Age	Occupation
Wyche Edward		46	Farmer
	William Wyche	16	
	John Wyche	13	
	Samuel Wyche	10	Children
	James Wyche	8	
	Thomas Wyche	8	
	Richard Wyche	6	
	Ann Bryatt	46	Servant
Woodall William		66	Farmer
	Sally Woodall	36	Daughter
	Ann Woodall	19	Daughter
	William Woodall	27	Son
	Ann Woodall	24	Wife
	Eliz. Woodall	2	Child

Edward Wyche and William Woodall are again listed in the 1821 Census but in the case of Edward Wyche, this time his wife (presumably) Hannah, age 64, is added and the William Woodall listed is the son of the William listed in the 1811 Census. The 1831 Census lists Edward and Hannah Wyche age 66 and 74 respectively. There is, however, no reference to William Woodall, the head of the family is shown as Ann Woodall. So what happened to William – had he died sometime between 1821 and 1831? There is a record in the Parish Registers showing the burial in 1825 of Wm. Woodall of Nether Alderley age 42. What the 1831 Census does show is a connection between the Woodall and the Wyche family. Ann's daughter age 20 is called Hannah Wyche, so she must have married one of the Wyche family. Also shown in the record for Ann Woodall is a William Wyche, presumably Hannah's child.

The Tithe Map, see later and Apportionment List (see below) drawn up in the 1840's show the Landowner as Lord Stanley and the Occupier as Randle Baskerville.

Landowner	Occupiers	No	Name & Description	State of Cultivation	A	R	P
Lord Stanley of Alderley	Randle Baskerville	307	Homestead Lane & Pits		2	2	23

259	Bradley	Arable	7	3	23
260	Bradley	Arable	6	1	38
262	Long Colley Hay	Meadow	7	1	50
263	Little Colley Hay	Arable	6	-	4
281a	Great field	Pasture	2	2	23
281	Great Wheat Field	Meadow	3	1	21
280	Far Burnt Field	Arable	4	1	17
282	Horse Close	Arable	2	2	12
283	Wheat Field	Pasture	8	3	23
305	Orchard	Meadow	-	1	31
306	Hemp Yard		1	1	30
308	Gorsey Croft	Meadow	4	1	39
310	Rough		1	-	13
313	? Lands	Pasture	8	-	25
314/315}	Middlefield & Pitsleads	Pasture	2	-	33
316	Pitsleads	Pasture	1	3	9
317	Grow Croft	Pasture	2	-	10
318	Near Moss Field	Arable	5	-	39
320	Far Moss field	Arable	5	1	2
323	Intake	Pasture	-	3	30
382	Part of Burnt Field	Arable	2	-	39
381	Yew Lane	Pasture	5	3	19

Randle Baskerville was still living at the Hall at the time of the 1851 Census, the full entry being as follows: -

						BORN
Soss Moss Hall	Randle Baskerville	Head	M	55	Farmer of 90 acres	Over Alderley
	Margaret Baskerville	Wife	M	54		Bold, Lancashire
	James Baskerville	Son	U	26		Little Warford
	John Baskerville	Son	U	21		Nether Alderley

Samuel Baskerville	Son	U	18		Nether Alderley
Thomas Baskerville	Son	U	15		Nether Alderley
Hannah Leigh	Serv	U	24	House Servant	Cranage

The 1881 Census shows that Randle's eldest son, James, had taken over the farm and was living at the Hall with his wife, Ruth, and three of their children, Fred, Walter and Harry, together with three servants.

One of Randle's other sons, Thomas, was still resident in the Soss Moss area farming 85 acres. At the time of the 1881 Census he was living with his wife, Betsy, seven children and four servants.

1872 Ordnance Survey Map

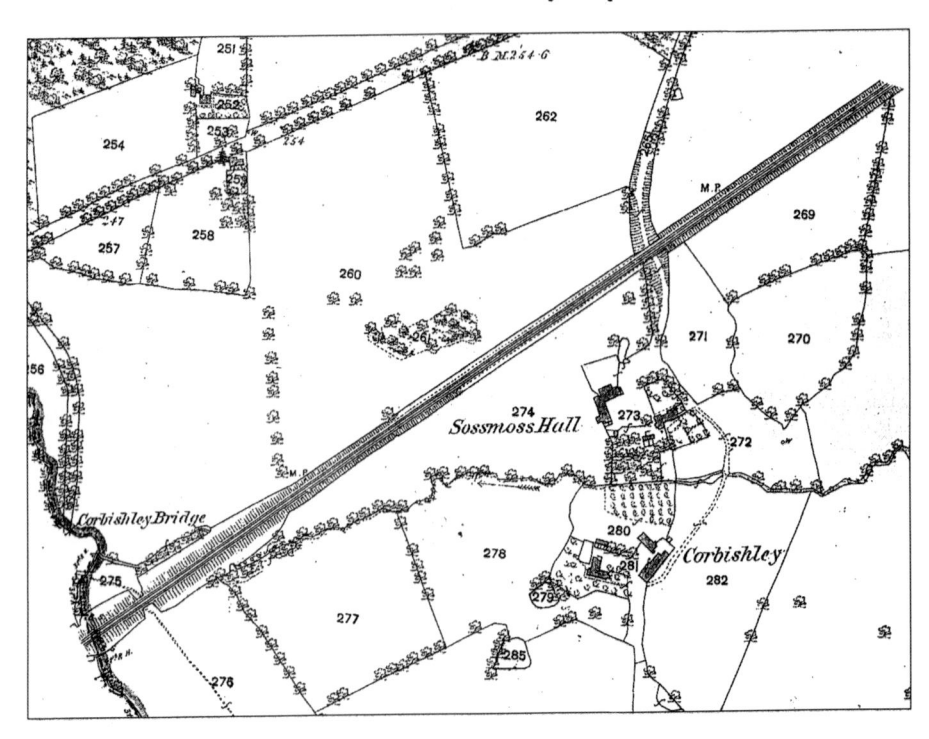

264

Ten years later, in 1891, James and Ruth Baskerville were still living at the Hall with their children, Walter, Ellen, (not listed in the 1881 Census) and Harry.

Within the 20th century, the resident in 1910 was John Dawson, in 1923 Albert Dawson and in 1934 Wilfred Proudlove, all listed in the Commercial Directories as Farmers.

The kitchen of the Hall once served as a meeting place for Methodists. A plaque over the fireplace reads *"Nether Alderley Chapel 1835 - 1940"*. The plaque was placed there to commemorate the room having been set apart as a Methodist Meeting Place of Worship incorporated into the Macclesfield Circuit; also to record the gratitude of the worshippers to the members of the Baskerville and Webb families, who were for upwards of one hundred years actively associated with the cause.

The interior of the house displays a number of heavy oak beams and a 'huge-walk' in type fireplace with a niche set into the wall at the side of the fireplace, this niche being used to keep salt dry. In 1847, when making some alterations to one of the rooms near the chimney, a curious wall-painting was discovered. It was described by the tenant at that time, Randle Baskerville, as showing small figures of men and women in long dresses of different colours, some wearing curiously shaped hats. Unfortunately it was covered up before an investigation could be made to establish its origin.

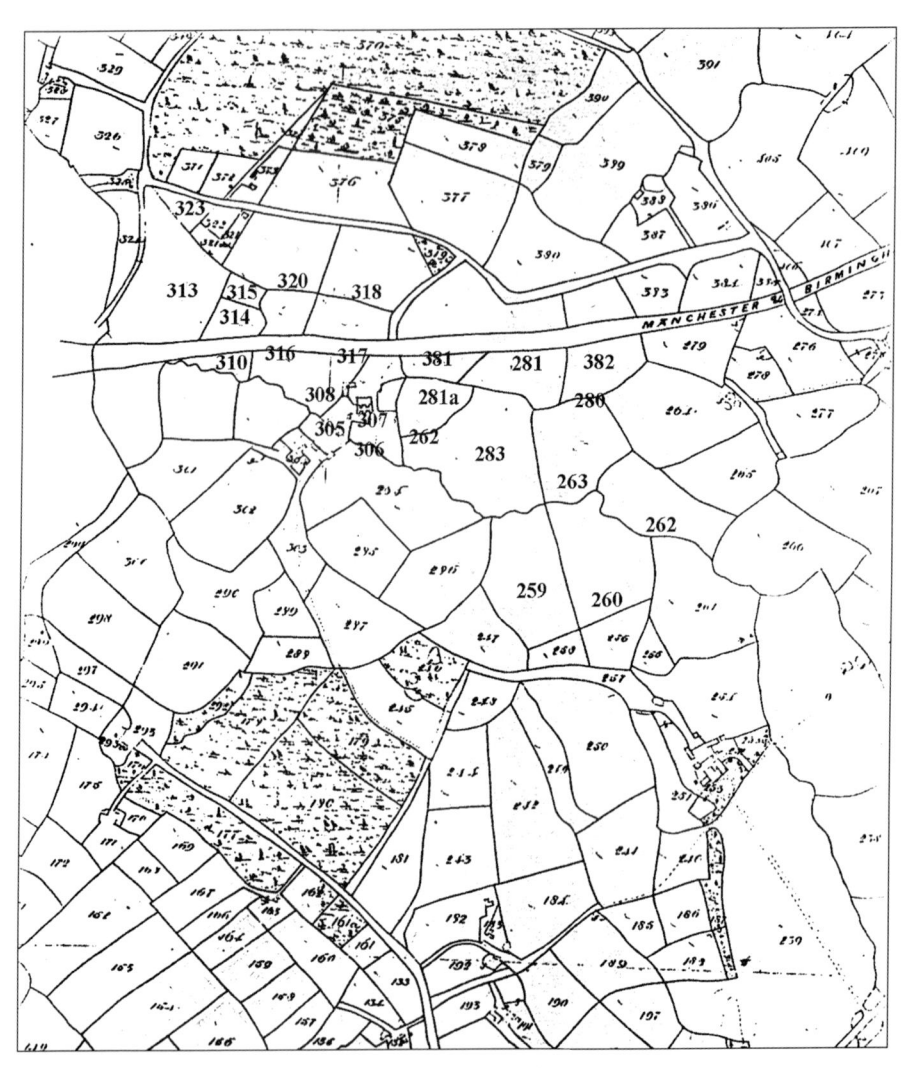

EXTRACT FROM TITHE MAP

Areas in circles are included in reference to Soss Moss Hall.

LITTLE WARFORD

According to some scholars Warford had Roman connections but to what extent is not known. Certainly by the Anglo-Saxon period it appears to have been of higher status than the settlements at Chelford, Lower Withington and Snelson.

Warford, following the Norman Conquest was held by Ranulph (Randle), the entry in the 1086 Domesday Book being as follows:

> *Wareford* (Warford)
>
> *Ranulph himself holds Warford and Godgyth [holds] of him. She held it herself and was free. There is a half a hide paying geld. There is land for 1 plough. There she has 2 oxen and 4 slaves and 2 female slaves. It is worth 3s. It was waste.*

Based on the above and the fact that the area was stated to have a value (compared to most of the surrounding areas which were designated as waste) Godgyth must have been of some importance in the area. Earl Hugh's barons, the more important men in terms of their landholdings in Cheshire, (one of whom was the said Ranulph de Masnilwarin above), had under tenants of their own, in some cases of English origin. Such was the case in Cheshire where Ranulph succeeded the English lady Godgyth at several estates. She herself survived at least to 1086 as his tenant, probably living at Warford, where the female slaves recorded in the Domesday Book were perhaps her attendants.

Sometime later, the village was divided into two, Great Warford and Little Warford, both within Bucklow hundred. Early in the 14th century the division of hundreds was amended with Great Warford allocated to the Macclesfield hundred and Little Warford remaining in the Bucklow hundred.

The hamlet of Little Warford (the little part of Warford), was, around the year 1200, given by Roger Mainwaring of Warmincham to Robert Vernon.

During the 13th century various documents refer to Old Warford, an area now little known. It probably lay west of Little Warford in the southern area of Marthall Township. Moat Hall may be the site of a mediaeval manor house in Old Warford. According to J.P. McN Dodgson in his "Place Names of Cheshire".

> *Near Glovers Cross is a detached portion of Little Warford, with which manor that of Old Warford is much confused in the records. There is evidence that the mill belonging to Great Warford was on a stream*

bounding upon Ollerton. The southern part of the present day Marthall Township formerly consisted of Warford territory and is probably the original site of Warford and the settlement controlled by Godgyth referred to in the Domesday Survey.

In 1562, the 4th year of Elizabeth 1st's reign, Gilbert Lea of Middleton in Yorkshire, Esquire, sold Little Warford to John Millington and Henry Hough and later, in 1573, the same Henry Hough settles his land for his own use and on his death, to his nephew, Thomas Antrobus of Lincoln-Inn and his heirs. Two years later the lands in Little Warford were divided between John Millington and Thomas Antrobus.

Subsequently, in 1615 Thomas Antrobus and Elizabeth, his wife, passed all their lands in Little Warford to Thomas Colthurst and his heirs, this Thomas Colthurst[10], in turn, selling the land in 1618 to Stephen Smith. One year later the lands were sold to Randle Mainwaring of Over Peover whose heirs in 1666 still possessed this one division of the original estate.

The other division, which belonged to John Millington, was, in 1666, in the possession of Millington Colthurst, possibly as a result of marriage between members of the Millington and Colthurst families.

In 1620 William Bayly purchased from Sir Randle Mainwaring the freehold of land of inheritance in Little Warford, the Bayly family (subsequently spelt Bealey) residing in the area for at least 100 years.

The Will of William Bealey in 1706 included the following inventory:

An Inventory of the Goods, Cattells and Chattells of William Bealey the elder, late of Little Warford in the County of Chester, yeoman, apprized, viewed and valued by Peter Colthurst of Little Warford aforesaid and John Lowe of Chelford in the County of Chester, Gent, the ffifth day of April Anno Dom 1706.

	£	s	d
One pair of bedsteads with its furniture	01	08	04
Shifts and new cloath	00	05	00
One riding coat	00	08	00
ffour doz and ½ of Silver buttons	01	16	00
ffour doz and ½ more of Silver buttons	01	16	00
One cloath coat	00	05	00

---

10   The mill in Little Warford was at this time referred to as Colthurst Mill.

One stuff? Coat and wascoat	00	03	04
Three doz. and eliven of brass buttons tipt with silver	00	02	00
Three doz. and ten of brass buttons tipt with silver	00	01	11
One coat and horn buttons	00	04	06
Two wascoats	00	04	06
One cloath coat	00	06	00
One pair of ? coloured breeches	00	03	00
One pair of breeches and one pair of lining	00	03	00
One old pair of breeches and a pair of lining	00	01	00
Three pair of stockens and a pair of socks	00	03	00
Two pair of shoes a pair of spittboots and a pair of clogs	00	06	06
Three caps	00	01	00
ffour pair of gloves	00	00	10
Bands handkerchiefs and caps	00	01	06
Three hatts	00	04	00
Saddle bridle and one whip	00	02	06
One pair of silver buttons for breeches	00	01	06
One great bible and other bookes	00	09	00
One cloak	00	03	06
One coffer and box within it	00	03	00
Two chairs and two cushions	00	01	06
One dial a pike staff and square staff	00	01	06
Some tools	00	09	00
In ready money bonds and specialties	90	02	03
TOTAL	99	18	02

Apprized by us

Peter Colthurst, John Lowe

The 1723 Oath of Allegiance contains the following names as resident in Marthall and Little Warford.

Acton John	-	Marthall	Colthurst John	-	Little Warford
Acton William	-	Marthall	Colthurst Peter	-	Marthall
Baguley Ralph	-	Marthall	Colthurst Thomas	-	Little Warford
Bailey Elizabeth	-	Little Warford	Cooper Joseph	-	Marthall
Barrow Jonathan	-	Marthall	Cragg Richard	-	Marthall
Burgess Robert	-	Warford	Dutton Mary	-	Marthall
Burgess Samuel	-	Warford	Glover Jonathan	-	Marthall
Casm Edward	-	Warford	Glover Randle	-	Marthall

Gresty Thomas	-	Warford		Pickering Ralph	-	Warford
Henshaw Peter	-	Warford		Plant Frances	-	Warford
Henshaw Samuel	-	Marthall		Pownall Mary	-	Warford
Hooley John	-	Warford		Pownall Samuel	-	Warford
Leigh Thomas	-	Marthall		Roe Jane	-	Warford
Longworth Peter	-	Marthall		Rylance William	-	Marthall
Mainwaring Elizabeth		Warford		Shepley Charles	-	Warford
Moston Thomas	-	Marthall		Wilson George	-	Warford
Okell William	-	Marthall		Wood Nathaniel	-	Marthall
Palden John	-	Warford		Worthington Samuel		Marthall
Perkin Thomas	-	Warford				

Note – not including Great Warford.

The manor of Marthall with Little Warford was purchased in 1745 by Samuel Egerton from Sir Peter Warburton of Arley.

Bagshaws Commercial Directory of 1850 contains the following information relative to Little Warford: -

> "Little Warford is a hamlet in this township situated 4 miles east South East from Knutsford, the inhabitants of which are exempt from paying to the highways, and from duty, but in all other respects is annexed to Marthall. This place was part of the ancient inheritance of the Mainwaring's. Gilbert Lee, Esq., being possessed of this estate in the reign of Queen Elizabeth, conveyed it to John Millington and William Hough. Millington's moiety, in 1666, passed to Millington Coulhurst; three-fourths of the estate, which was subsequently inherited by Samuel Holland, and is now the property of Peter Holland, Esq. Lord Stanley, Joshua Siddeley Esq., and Richard Brooks Esq., are also proprietors. Mr William Mason's farm is a detached portion of the hamlet[11], surrounded by the land in Marthall, and situated some distance from the rest of the hamlet.

The 1850 Directory lists the following people as residents of Little Warford: -

---

11   From Bryant's map of 1831 it appears that this piece of land is the present area north and east of the cross roads near Marthall Church and directly opposite the Church.

Brown William, farm bailiff to P. Holland Esq.
Dale Samuel, blacksmith
Jennings John, wheelwright
Rawlins Thomas, corn miller
Callwood James, farmer
Mason William, farmer
Summerfield John, farmer

It would appear from the above list of the prominent residents that in 1850 Little Warford extended northwards from the western end of Carter Lane and included the Sandle Bridge area, which housed the smithy and the corn mill. It also includes the small area directly apposite the present Church (see note 11). Little Warford did not include Moat Hall or the Church, which were in Marthall.

The Browns, Dales, Jennings and Rawlins were still resident a year later - the 1851 Census[12] containing the following information: -

Name	Relation to Head	Condition	Age	Occupation	Where Born
William Brown	Head	M	53	Bailiff (farm)	Knutsford
Mary Brown	Wife	M	57		Knutsford
Note: the above lived at Sandle Bridge Farm					
Samuel Dale	Head	M	60	Blacksmith employing 2 men	Marthall
Mary Dale	Wife	M	57		Great Warford
William Dale	Son	U	29	Blacksmith	Little Warford
Samuel Dale	Son	U	18	Blacksmith	Little Warford
Eliz Harries	Serv	U	15	Servant	Peover
Joseph Acton	Lodger	U	71	Pauper Agricultural labourer	Withington
John Jennings	Head	M	72	Wheelwright	Mottram St Andrew
Elizabeth Jennings	Wife	M	68		Little Warford
William Jennings	Son	U	47		Little Warford
Thomas Jennings	Son	U	43	Silk weaver	Little Warford
Samuel Jennings	Son	M	30	Wheelwright's son	Little Warford
Margaret Jennings	Wife	M	26	Wheelwright's son's wife	Great Warford
John Jennings	Son		4		Little Warford
Ann Jennings	Lodger		1		Little Warford

---

12   Cheshire County Record Office Ref: HO 107/2163 mf 2/19.

Ann Dale	Granddau	U		16	Servant	Great Warford
William Wych	Servant	Widower		56	Journeyman	Alderley
William Hoad?	Lodger	U		40	Labourer	Great Warford
Thomas Rawlins	Head	M		65	Miller	? Derbyshire
Elizabeth Rawlins	Wife	M		54		Over Peover
William Rawlins	Son			13	Scholar	Marthall
Elizabeth Grime?	Serv	U		18	House servant	Endbury [Henbury]
Joseph Cheetham	Serv	U		13	Journeyman Miller	Little Warford

By 1864 Edward Bowden, living in Sandle Bridge had taken over from William Brown as farm bailiff, William Dale (presumably the son of Samuel Dale) was the blacksmith[13], John Jennings was still the wheelwright and a William Rawlins was a miller at Coltier's mill. Of the farmers listed in 1850 James Callwood and John Summerfield were still there in 1864 but William Mason had been superseded by either James or John Mason.

Moving forward to 1878, no changes had occurred since 1864.

Three years later the 1881 Census returns show complete family details for the Bowdon, Dale, Jennings and Rawlins. All as shown below.

Edward Bowden, age 60, born Surlock was the head of the family, a farmer of 177 acres. He was a widower and living with him were five of his children, Frederick age 28, John age 24, Ada Annie age 17, Alice age 14 and Emily age 11, all born Marthall apart from Frederick who had been born at Gorstage.

William Dale, the blacksmith, age 59 born Marthall, lived with his wife, Hannah age 57, and William his son age 22 whose occupation was given as Clerk Bookkeeper and Traveller in Iron. They had one servant, Hester Steele age 54 and born Lower Peover.

The wheelwrights were father and son, Samuel and John Jennings, Samuel age 60, living on the night of the census with his wife, Margaret age 58, and Alfred Jennings, his grandson age 11. John was age 34, born Withington, married to Eliza aged 31, born Mottram St Andrew. They had four sons, William age 9, John Henry age 5, Frank age 2 and Walter age 11 months, together with one daughter, Elizabeth age 7, living with them on the night of the census.

---

13 The Dale family had been the village blacksmiths as far back as 1798 (see list of Little Warford wills).

Coming now to William Rawlins. The census shows William as a Corn Miller, the head of the family, born Marthall and aged 43. He was married to Pheobe and with them on the night of the census were their children, John Hogg Rowlins age 22, William age 20, Arthur H age 28 and Sarah Anne age 11. All children were born in Marthall.

Of the above Wm Dale, John Jennings and William Rawlins are mentioned in the 1901 Directory. There is no reference to Edward Bowden. However, there is a reference to a Samuel Wilson, not mentioned in previous directories but listed as a farmer in Little Warford.

Kelly's Directory of 1928 contains the following information relative to Little Warford.

Wm M Burgess	-	Miller	Colthurst mill
Walter Callwood	-	Farmer	Fir Tree Farm
John Oliver Clark	-	Farmer	Peck Mill Farm
Wm Dale & sons -	-	Agricultural Implement Makers and Dealers, Engineers and Blacksmiths.	
Charles Hamnett	-	Head gardener to the David Lewis Manchester Epileptic Colony.	
John Jennings & son	-	Wheelwright	
James W Parry	-	Farm bailiff to the David Lewis Manchester Epileptic Colony.	
Walter Preston	-	Engineer to the David Lewis Manchester Epileptic Colony.	
Wm Slater	-	Shopkeeper	

Apart from Herbert Davies, who had taken over Peck Mill Farm, H Groves and sons, who now had Colthurst Mill and James St Clair, Robert Goostrey and Frederick Pratt, who were gardeners, farm bailiff and engineer, respectively for the David Lewis Centre, all the residents listed in the 1928 directory were still there in 1939.

It is now thought that Carter Lane, which forms the boundary between Chelford and Little Warford, and Pepper Street, formerly called King Street, which leads from Dixon Drive to Snelson, may be the remains of an ancient route from Alderley Edge, crossing Peover Superior by a direct line of lanes and paths by Parkgate, Peover Hall and Longlane Farm to Cross Lanes Farm in Allostock. This route would have been the middle section of the medieval route between Macclesfield and Northwich[14].

The following wills relating to residents of Little Warford can be viewed at the County Record Office, Chester.

1576	William Blackshall		Will and Inventory
1580	James Baxter		Will and Inventory
1603	Hugh Blackshaw		Inventory only
1665	Ann Davenport		Will and Admon.
1677	Ann Pott	Widow	Will and Inventory
1684	Hugh Grasty	Yeoman	Will
1708	William Bealey	Yeoman	Will and Inventory
1723	William Bealey	Yeoman	Will
1727	Richard Cragg	Yeoman	Will and Inventory
1728	John Findlow	Yeoman	Will
1780	Edward Corner		Admon.
1798	John Dale	Blacksmith	Will
1810	Daniel Burgess		Will
1813	William Dale	Blacksmith	Will
1818	William Dale	Smith	Will
1828	William Wych	Yeoman	Will
1838	John Cheetham	Miller	Admon.
1886	Peter Hope	Farmer	Will
1896	George Bickerton		Will

The 1842 Ordnance Survey map shows a Davenport Hall situated on Carter Lane some way north east of Mere Hill (now the corner of Dixon Drive and the Chelford to Knutsford Road) and where a road or bridle way runs off to Peck Mill. No other records have been found relative to this Hall. However, it must have existed, otherwise it would not have been shown on the O.S. map. It has also been said that when Seddon's were building the new houses in this area early 1980's they came across some foundations in this area. Whether they were the remains of Davenport Hall is not known and unless one of the existing villagers has any information, perhaps we shall never know.

---

14 The course of the medieval routes between Macclesfield and Broken Cross and between Cross Lanes, Allostock and Northwich are fairly well established. The middle course between Broken Cross and Cross Lanes could have been one of three possible different routes or possibly three middle sections may have been in use. Of the other two middle sections, one appears to have run through Chelford and the other, Siddington and Lower Withington before connecting to Cross Lanes.

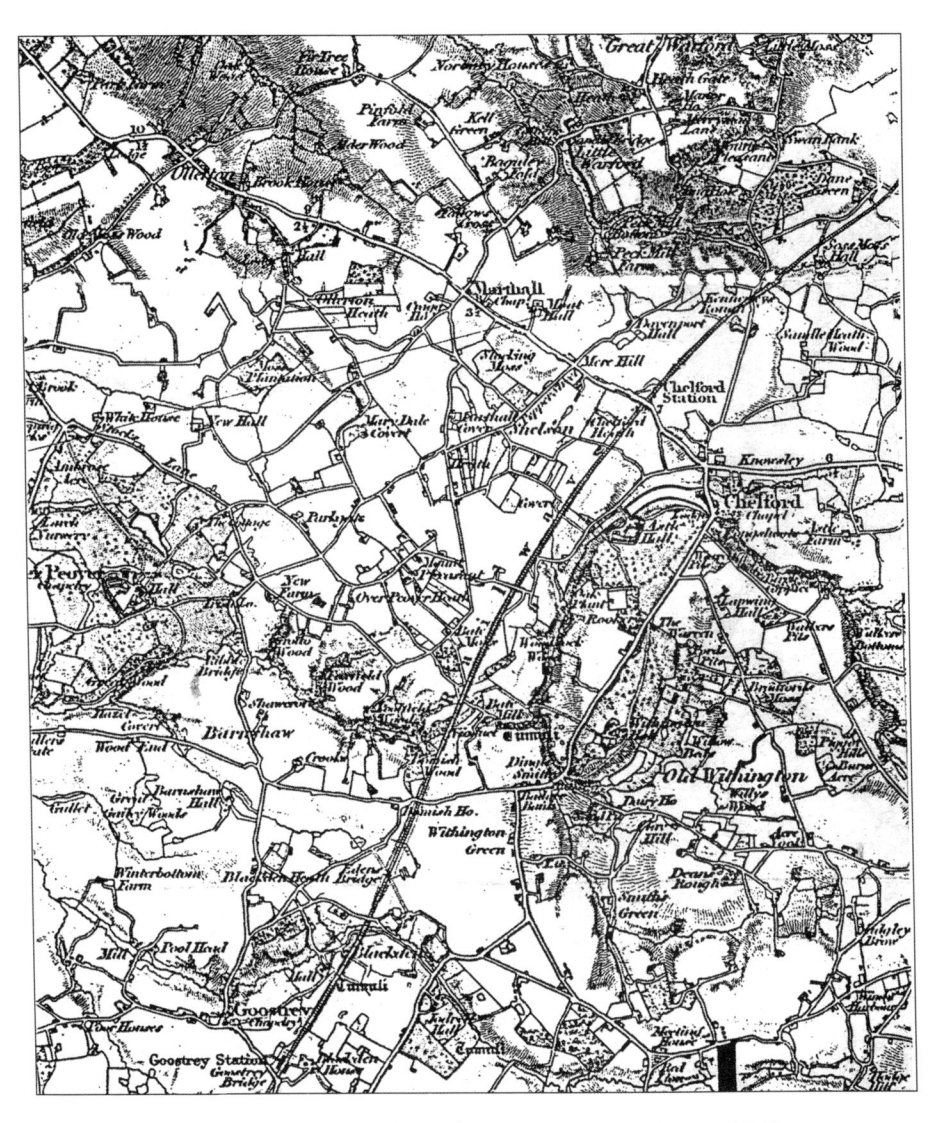

**First Edition of One-inch Ordnance Survey Map – 1842
Showing Davenport Hall on Carter Lane**

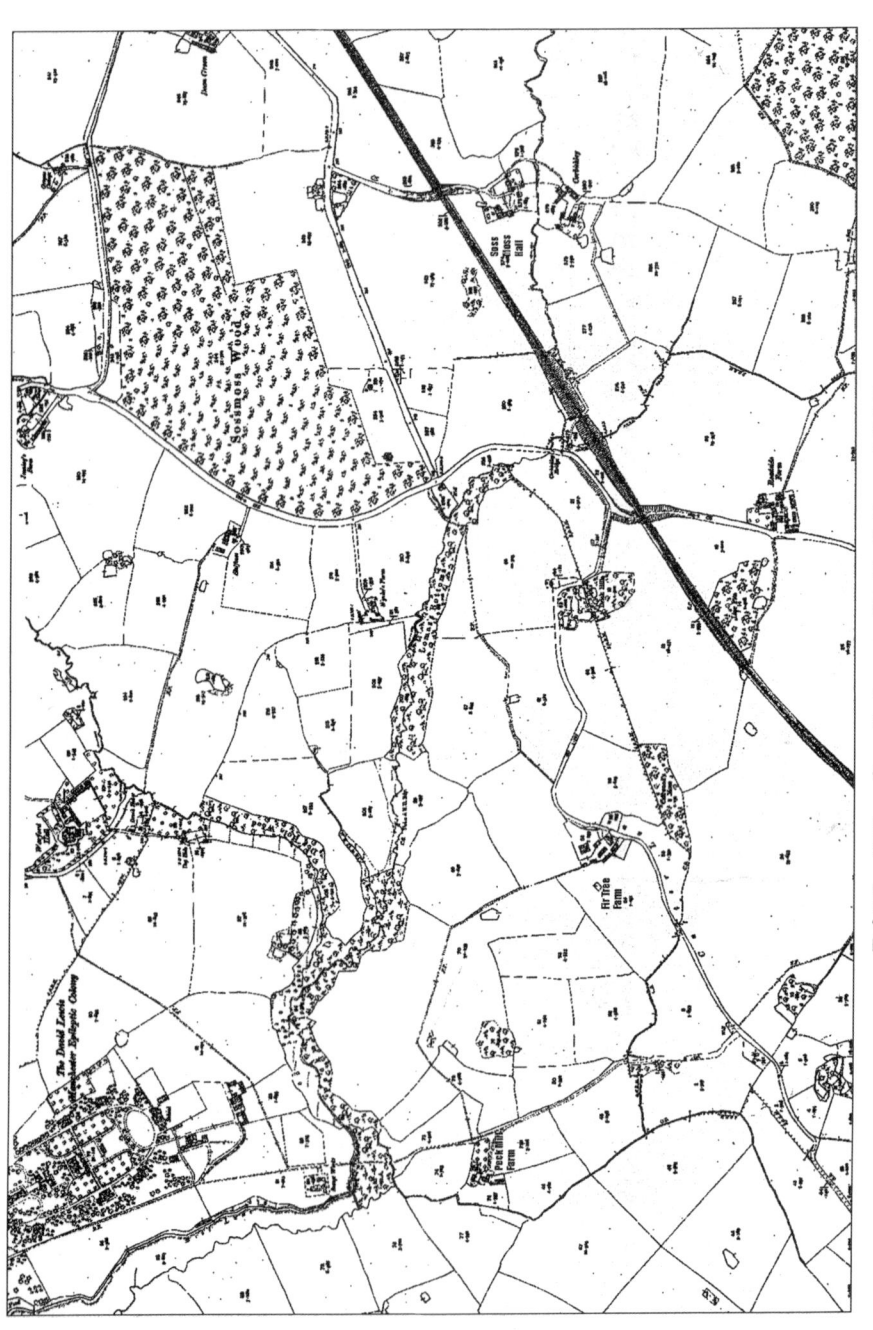

Little Warford Area O.S. Map 1909

PECK MILL FARM – LITTLE WARFORD

The Farmhouse at Peck Mill Farm was extended in 1794 when R + M Brook built the larger left-hand side of the building. The much smaller cottage to the right of the present doorway probably dates from a much earlier period, maybe early 17th century.

Near the area of the farm is Peckmill Bottoms (bottom of Peck Mill), the name possibly referring to a type of mill with a 'pecking' movement, or to the capacity of the grinding stones the medieval word peck referring to a measure.

By using the Land Tax Assessment records it is possible to establish that in 1780 the farm was owned and occupied by George Cragg[1] and the sum assessed at £1.5s.0d. The records show that by 1784 the farm was owned by Ann Hayes and occupied by William Stodard, Ann Hayes continuing as the proprietor owner until 1815, though the occupiers changed in 1793, when Richard Pool is listed, in 1794 when Widow Pool is shown, and in 1815 when Wm. Wych took over the farm.

Richard Brooke appears to have purchased the estate about 1816 and it is possible that the ancient map in the hands of the present owner's dates from this period – see next page.

The Land Tax Assessment records seem to indicate that Richard Brooke became the owner in 1816. There is, however, a stone built into the front wall of the farmhouse with the date of 1794 and the names R + M Brooke. Perhaps the Brooke's extended the property in 1794 for the then owner, Ann Hayes eventually purchasing it at a later date.

---

[1] The Cragg family were long time residents in Little Warford, a Richard Cragg (yeoman) filing a will in 1726. The inventory attached to this will contains a reference to Findlow field, this field also being named on the ancient estate map shown on next page. The Cragg family must therefor have been resident at Peck Mill farm from at least the early part of the 18th century.

MAP OF PECK MILL ESTATE C 1800

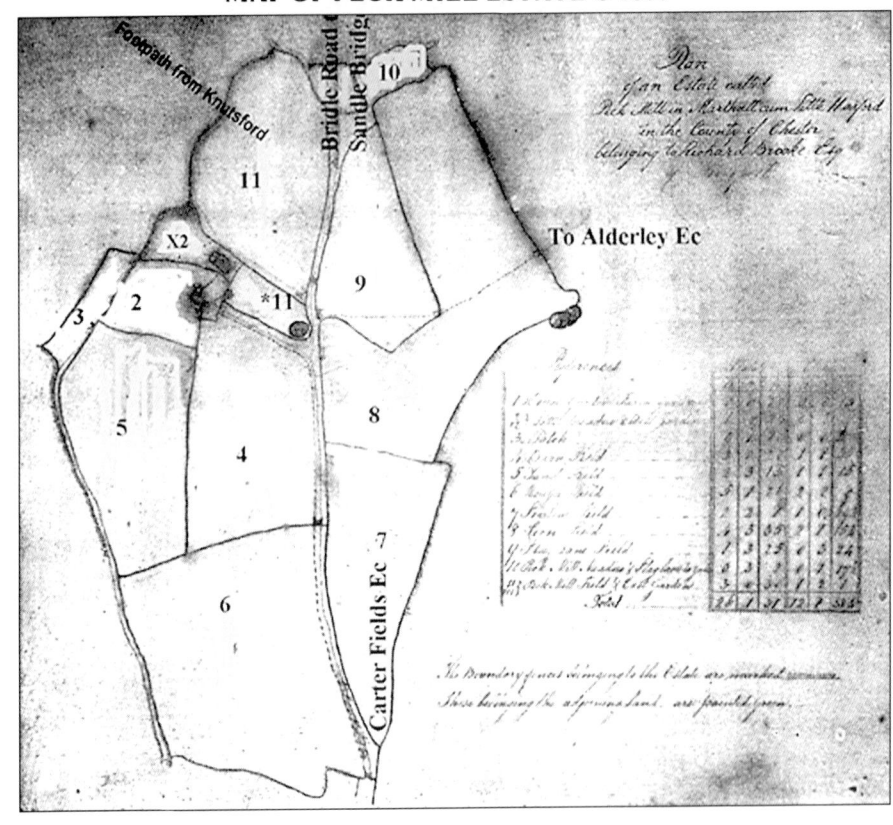

DETAILS OF MAP OF PECK MILL AREA

Top left hand corner	=	Footpath from Knutsford
Top left centre	=	Bridle road to Sandle Bridge
Right hand side	=	To Alderley Ec.
Bottom centre	=	Carters fields Ec.

Top right words are:

Plan
Of an Estate called
Peck Mill in Marthall cum Little Warford
In the County of Chester
Belonging to Richard Brooke Esq.
Of Stourport?

Bottom right words are *The Boundary fences belonging to the Estate are marked* " ". *Those belonging to adjoining land are painted green.*

References		Statute			Cheshire		
		a	r	p	a	r	p
1	House Garden Farmyard Ec.	0	0	28	0	0	13
2 ⎫ X2 ⎭	Little Meadow and West Garden	1	0	24	0	2	
3	Patch	0	1	25	0	0	31½
4	Barn field	3	0	20	1	1	36
5	Land field	2	3	15	1	1	15
6	Houghe field	5	1	26	2	2	9
7	Finlow field	2	2	1	1	0	29½
8	Loon field	4	3	35	2	1	15¾
9	Flag Lane field	1	3	25	0	3	24
10	Peck Mill Meadow and Flag Lane to Gate	0	3	2	0	1	17½
11 ⎫ *11 ⎭	Peck Mill Field and East Garden	3	0	30	1	2	1
	Total	26	1	31	12	1	38¼

WILL OF WILLIAM WYCH

IN THE NAME OF GOD AMEN I William Wych of Little Warford in the County of Chester Yeoman do make and publish this my last will and Testament this ninth day of May in the year of our Lord One thousand eight hundred and nineteen FIRST I will and direct that all my just Debts funeral expenses and the charge of the probate of this my Will be paid and discharged I give devise and bequeath all that my messuage lands and promises with the appurtenances situate lying and being in Great Warford in the County of Chester unto Samuel Dale of Little Warford aforesaid Blacksmith To hold to him/hers Executors Administrators and assigns upon the trusts and to and for the intents and purposes hereinafter mentioned expressed and declared (that is to say) Upon Trust to pay the rents issues and profits thereof into the proper hands of my dear wife Elizabeth Wych or otherwise shall and do permit and suffer her my said wife to waive and take the same to and for her own use and benefit for and during the term of her natural life and from and immediately after her decease upon trust to pay and apply the yearly rents issues and proceeds thereof for and towards the maintenance education and bringing up of all and every the child and children which I may have at the time of my decease until they shall respectively attain the age of twenty one years (or such other period as they shall in the opinion of my said Trustee his Executors or Administrators be able to maintain themselves respectively) as my said Trustees his executors or Administrators may deem proper and subject as aforesaid I give and devise my said messuage lands and premises unto my son Samuel Wych his heirs and assigns for ever but in case my said son Samuel shall happen to die under the age of twenty one years without leaving lawful issue or born in due time afterwards or leaving such issue all of them should happen to die under the age of twenty one years without leaving lawful issue then I give and devise all my said premises unto my son Jool/Joel Wych his heirs and assigns for ever in like manner and in case my said son Jool/Joel shall happen to depart this life under the age of twenty one years without leaving lawful issue as aforesaid then I give and devise the same premises unto my son William Wych his heirs and assigns for ever in like manner and in case my said son William shall happen to die under the age of twenty one years without leaving lawful issue as aforesaid then I give and devise the same premises unto my daughters Elizabeth Wych and Fanny Wych equally between then share and share alike as tenants in common and not as joint tenants their heirs and assigns for ever with remainder to my own right heirs for ever and as to for and concerning all and singular my personal estate and effects whatsoever and wheresoever and of what nature or kind so ever I give and bequeath the same unto my Executors hereinafter named their Executors and Administrators upon trust to permit and suffer my said wife Elizabeth Wych to have hold and enjoy the same and to waive and take the interest and yearly proceeds thereof for and during the term of her natural life for the maintenance and education and bringing up of all and every my said children until they shall be enabled and qualified to maintain and support themselves respectively in the opinion of my said Executors and the survivor of them his Executors or Administrators and from and after the decease of my said wife I give and bequeath the same unto and equally amongst all and every my said children (save and except my son Samuel and such other son or sons as shall become possessed of my said messuage lands and premises so devised to or in Trust for them as aforesaid share and share alike and if any of my said children (except as aforesaid) shall happen to die under the age of twenty one years leaving lawful issue such issue to take his her or their parent or parent's share only the same to become vested in each such child at the age of twenty one years or marriage which should first happen share and share alike and in case all or any of said last mentioned child or children happen to due under the age of twenty one years without having been married then the share or shares of such of them so dying to go to the survivor and survivors of them and the lawful issues of such survivors such issue to take his her or their parent or parent's share only and to become vested in him her or them at the age of twenty one years or marriage which shall first happen And I hereby direct that my said Executors and the survivor of them his executors and administrators shall reimburse himself herself and themselves all such costs charges and expenses which they shall be put unto in and about the execution of the Trusts of this my will or anywise relating thereto and I hereby appoint the said Samuel Dale and my said wife Elizabeth Wych and my son Samuel Wych executors and executrix of this my will and hereby revoking all former will and wills by me at any time heretofore made I do publish and declare this to be my last will and testament IN WITNESS whereof I the said William Wych the testator have to the two first two sheets of this my will set my hand and to this third and last sheet my hand and seal the day and year aforesaid.

Signed sealed published and declared by the said Testator William Wych as and for his last will and Testament in the presence of us who have hereunto subscribed out names as witnesses thereto at his request and in his presence and in the presence of each other the words "Samuel Dale Little Warford aforesaid Blacksmith".

The twenty-fifth day of November 1828.
Samuel Dale and Elizabeth Wych one of the Executors and the Executrix in this will named were sworn in common form (power being reserved to Samuel Wych the other Executor therein also named to take upon him the Execution of the said Will when he shall lawfully request the same) and they further made Oath that the personal Estate and Effects of the Testator within the Diocese of Chester were under the value of One hundred pounds.
                    Before me
                              Thomas Parker surrogate
The testator died the first day of March 1828.

Personal Estate and Effects
sworn under the value of
One hundred pounds.

Probate issued dated 25 November 1828.

Widow Wych and Richard Brooke are shown as occupier and proprietor respectively in the 1831 Land Tax assessment.

By the time of the Tithe Award 21st August 1847 the occupier was John Summerfield, the apportionment for the tithe being as follows: -

Landowner	Occupiers	No on Plan[2]	Description	Quantities Statute Measure			Rent Charge		
				A	R	P	£	S	d
Brook Richard	Summerfield John	384	House, outbuildings, yard and gardens	1	-	7			
		385		1	-	18	-	2	8
		386		2	3	20	-	6	10
		387		2	3	34	-	6	9
		388		5	1	15	-	11	4
		389		2	2	7	-	6	-
		380		2	3	15	-	6	8

---

[2] The Tithe map showing the Plan numbers is too large to include in this book. It can however be seen at the Cheshire County Record Office, Chester.

381	Plantation and Road	-	3	8			
382		5	-	5	-	12	-
383		<u>1</u>	<u>3</u>	<u>34</u>	<u>-</u>	<u>4</u>	<u>1</u>
		26	2	3	2	17	2

Moving forward three years to 1850 the Bagshaw Commercial Directory for that year listed a John Summerfield as one of three farmers resident in Little Warford. One year later the 1851 Census contains the following information relative to this family.

John Summerfield	Head	M	46	Farmer of 24 acres	born Alderley
Betty Summerfield	Wife	M	40		born Marthall
Ellen Callwood	Mother	Widow	66		born Hale, Lancs.

Note – entry for Ellen Callwood probably incorrect – relationship with head of family should possibly read Mother-in-law.

The 1864 Commercial Directory specifically lists John Summerfield as a farmer resident at Peck Mill as does the 1878 directory.

Three years later the 1881 Census[3] shows the following information.

	Marr	Age	Sex	Birthplace
John Summerfield	M	71	M	Nether Alderley
Rel Head				
Occ Farmer of 12 acres[4]				
Elizabeth Summerfield	M	70	F	Hartford
Rel Wife				
Occ Farmer's wife				
Joseph Callwood[5]	U	55	M	Lymm
Rel Bro-in-law				
Occ Farm labourer				
Sarah Broadhurst	U	16	F	Alderley
Rel Servant				
Occ Domestic Serv.				

3	Cheshire County Record Office – PRO ref: RG11 Piece 3510 Folio 104A page 7.
4	The size of the farm was 26 acres – 12 acres may be enumerator error.
5	Possibly related to John Callwood who was farming at nearby Fir Tree Farm.

By 1896 Peter Slater was farming at Peck Mill Farm. John Oliver Clarke took over the farm some time around 1910 and was listed in the 1923 commercial Directory. Following a two-year period between 1931 and 1933, when a member of the Hewitt family had the farm, the farm was taken over by Herbert Davies, who originated from Shropshire. He ran the farm until 1939 when it was taken over by the present occupiers named Oliver, who in 1942 on the death of the then owner, Mrs Brooke[6] in 1942 purchased the farm and its estate.

The authors would like to thank the present occupier, Mary Oliver, for permission to use various information in this chapter.

---

[6] Mrs Brooke was at the time of her death Head of the Women's Land Army.

RICHARD CRAGG'S INVENTORY, OF LITTLE WARFORD IN THE PARISH OF ROSTHERNE

	£	s	d
Old Cow, little cow	6	12	0
A heifer, great cow	7	2	0
Corn	7	1	6
17 Boards	0	6	0
Hay out of Findlow field	2	2	0
Muck cart and syth	0	12	6
Corn cart	1	1	0
Two short lathers	0	2	0
Another muck hook	0	2	6
1 large ox	0	1	4
Plow	0	7	6
One harrow and shuttle	0	6	0
1 fork and ladder large	0	7	0
Black turfs and hopsacks	0	10	0
? An old shuttle and pan	0	1	2
Brokern timber and rakes and 4 pickills	0	16	0
? And 2 cart saddles	0	4	0
1 pair of hacks and ? hams	0	2	0
Cart rope flag stones	0	6	6
Mare and colt	0	10	0
Paling stones and ladder poles	0	8	6
? ?	0	7	0
Twin trough and lumber about the ?	0	2	0
Flaggs in the orchard and tablestone	0	5	6
Cheese press	0	10	0
Corn and churn chaff	0	4	0
Table in the kitchen	0	4	0
2 little cheese flatts	0	2	0
1 hogs board	0	1	0
One jack with oats in it	0	4	0
Mugs and earthenware	0	1	0
2 mill racks and a little grate	0	1	6
A coffer in the Kitchin	0	2	0
2 pan mugs and 2 black mugs	0	8	0
2 poles and nibling ?	0	4	1
A bed matt board and bolster with balance and curtains	0	6	0
Winnow sheet and cheese tube	0	5	0
Corn in the little ?	0	6	0

Grate, chest	1	0	0
A chair	0	1	0
Pair of sheets, an old pair	0	5	6
Barrell and Kinnele	0	0	4
2 Cover lids and white blankets	0	9	0
A yellow Blanket	0	2	0
Corn on the ground	6	17	0
	43	5	4

Appraised by us this 29th of July 1726 as wittness

        Saml. Henshaw
        Jonathan Cragg the appraiser.

FIR TREE FARM – LITTLE WARFORD

This farm will always be associated with the Callwood family members of this particular family, farming there for nearly 150 years between 1815 and 1949.

The earliest known record relative to the farm is the Land Tax returns for 1780 which lists a Wm. Corner as occupier and the owner as a John Norbury.

However it is fairly certain that the farm is much older than late 18th century and tradition has it that the original farmhouse was built late 17th or early 18th century in what is now the Sand Field, i.e., further down Carter Lane.

Sometime between 1802 and 1811 the farm was purchased by Sir John Stanley, and in 1802 the occupier is stated to be Widow Corner, presumably the relict of Wm. Corner. However, another William Corner, presumably Wm.'s son, was the occupier in 1811. An earlier Corner, Edward Corner, left a will dated 1780 and he may have been the father of Wm. Corner listed in the 1780 returns.

In 1814 Joseph Burchille is listed as the occupier but by 1815 John Callwood had taken over the farm, remaining there at least until 1831 and maybe for some years afterwards.

However, by 1847 the Tithe map of that year shows James Callwood as the occupier and the size of the farm 109 acres.

The full Tithe Award dated 21 August 1847 is as follows:

Landowner	Occupiers	No on Plan[1]	Description	Quantities Statute Measure			Rent Charge		
				A	R	P	£	S	D
Stanley John Thomas Baron	Callwood James	402	House, outbuildings, yard and garden	-	3	-			
		401	Knowl	2	1	11	-	4	11
		400	Barn Hill	7	-	5	-	16	8
		399	Horse Grass Field	4	2	19	-	10	-
		390	Near Chelford Flatt	4	3	27	-	11	8
		391	Further Chelford Flatt	4	3	4	-	11	4
		392	Pingott	-	2	26	-	1	7

---

1   The Tithe map showing the plan numbers is too large to include in this book. It can however be seen at the Cheshire County Record Office, Chester.

393	Blake Field	6	3	27	-	16	5
394	Hubbut Field	5	-	22	-	12	3
396	Wheat Field	9	1	32	1	8	-
397	Big Shay Field	7	2	22	-	18	4
398	Pitfield	4	-	8	-	8	8
404	Calf Croft	-	2	24	-	1	7
403	Bear Croft	-	1	4	-	-	8
405	Moss + Moss Brow	5	1	19	-	11	7
406	Road	1	1	22			
407	Near Shay Field	5	2	31	-	17	4
408	Colley Field	3	2	32	-	9	7
409	Near Friday Flatt	2	1	29	-	5	1
410	Sand Field	6	2	11	-	14	8
411	Old Meadow	2	2	15	-	5	8
412	Moss Bank	5	-	25	-	11	-
413	Pools Moss	6	2	20	-	14	11
414	Further Friday Flatt	2	2	32	-	5	4
526	Curbishley	4	1	20	-	9	4
417	Curbishley Meadow	2	1	23	-	5	1
		109	-	32	12	11	8

James Callwood is included in the 1850 and 1864 Commercial Directories but by 1878 John Callwood is listed, probably taking over from his father, James, when James died in 1877.

The 1881 Census[2] for Marthall cum Warford contains the following information on John Callwood and his family.

	Marr	Age	Sex	Birthplace
John Callwood	M	40	M	Knutsford
Rel: Head				
Occ: Farmer of 104 acres 2 labs. & 1 boy				
Margaret Callwood	M	29	F	Snelson
Rel: Wife				
Occ: Farmers wife				

---

2   Cheshire County Record Office – PRO Ref: RG11 Piece 3510 Folio 1044 Page 7.

Maggie Callwood		4	F	Marthall
Rel: Daur				
Walter Callwood		2	M	Marthall
Rel: Son				
Lorrie Callwood		1	F	Marthall
Rel: Daur				
Henry Webb	U	23	M	Gt. Warford
Rel: Serv				
Occ: Farm labourer				
Joseph Walton	U	16	M	Snelson
Rel: Serv				
Occ: Farm labourer				
Sarah Hobson	U	23	F	Goostry
Rel: Serv				
Occ: Genl. Domestic servant				
Louisa Plant	U	15	F	Peover
Rel: Serv				
Occ: Genl. Domestic servant				

Note - Walter Callwood aged 2.

The same John Callwood is included in the directories of 1896 and 1901 but by 1923 Walter Callwood, John's son, was running the farm, remaining there until 1949 when George Henry Brindley took over. The farm is still in the occupation of the Brindley family and is run by Alan (son of George Henry) and his son John.

When the Stanley estate was sold in 1938 the farm, then 121 acres in size, was purchased by Mrs Pattie Wild of Over Peover.

The authors would like to thank the present occupiers for permission to use various information in this chapter.

REGISTER OF GAMEKEEPERS 1711 – 1868

17 September 1711 - Nathaniel Bartington, Manor of Chelford

19 September 1711 – Peter Wright of Over Peover for Manor of Withington

15 January 1735 – Ralph Kinsey of Ollerton, Gentleman, Gamekeeper of John Baskervyle Esq., for Manor of Old Withington.

17 June 1762 – John Parker of Astle, Clerk Gamekeeper to Sir Henry Mainwaring, Bart., for his Manor of Chelford.

9 Oct 1776 – John Thorley of Old Withington, servant Gamekeeper for John Glegg Esq., for his Manor of Old Withington.

13 September 1791 – Nathaniel Adshead, servant Gamekeeper of Sir Henry Mainwaring Bart., for the Manor of Chelford.

12 August 1791 – John Thorley of Old Withington, labourer Gamekeeper for John Glegg Esq., for his Manors of Old Withington and Blackden.

14 August 1807 – John Bennett of Old Withington, servant Gamekeeper for John Glegg Esq., for Manors of Old Withington and Blackden and lands in Over Peover.

11 June 1838 – Thomas Jones of Old Withington, Yeoman Gamekeeper to John Baskervyle Glegg of Withington for the Manors of Old Withington, Lower Withington and Blackden.

18 September 1844 – Richard Green of High Legh, Labourer to be Gamekeeper to Egerton Leigh of Jodrell Hall, Esquire for the Manor of High Legh and lands in Lower Withington.

29 August 1856 – Joseph Wilson of Old Withington, Yeoman Gamekeeper to John Baskervyle Glegg of Withington Hall, Esquire, Lord of the Manor of Old Withington, Lower Withington and Blackden, to preserve and kill the game within the said Manors.

21 August 1861 – George Brown of Old Withington, Yeoman Gamekeeper to John Baskervyle Glegg of Withington Hall, Lord of the Manors or reputed Manors of Old Withington, Lower Withington and Blackden in the said County of and within the said Manors of Old Withington, Lower Withington and Blackden.

13 July 1867 – John Slater of Old Withington, Yeoman Gamekeeper to John Baskervyle Glegg the younger of Chelford, Esquire, Lord of the Manor of Lower Withington.

24 October 1868 – George Sichcombe of Lower Withington, Yeoman and Peter Sutton of the same place, Yeoman Gamekeepers to John Baskervyle Glegg the younger of Chelford, Esquire, Lord of the Manor of Lower Withington.

The above information was extracted from list of Licensed Tradesmen and Gamekeepers 1629-1844 – Cheshire County Record Office MF96/5.

TITHE AWARD – LOWER WITHINGTON AND SNELSON

By the early 19th century the payment of tithes to the Church had been the established practice for over a thousand years and most villages had 'tithe barns' to stock the grain and root vegetables collected from the inhabitants of each parish. The purpose of the tithe was to support the local clergy and, supposedly, to provide relief for the poor of the village, though in fact this rarely happened.

The tithe equated to one tenth of all the annual produce and was paid by the villagers to the clergy in two kinds: the great tithe and the small tithe. The great tithe was levied on crops, e.g., corn and hay and the small tithe on livestock, wool and non-cereal crops such as turnips. Generally the small tithe was given to the clergy in payment for their services and the great tithe was collected for the maintenance of the chancel of the church and to ensure that the appropriate number of religious services was carried out.

It was the tithe owner's responsibility to collect the great tithe whilst the small tithe was delivered to him by his parishioners.

There were constant disagreements about which items were to be included. For instance, owners of saddle horses did not have to pay a tithe on their animals, but innkeepers were liable for tithes on the grass eaten by their guests' horses.

In order to minimise disputes some tithe holders accepted payment in cash rather than in kind, though this was the exception rather than the rule and subject to change when a new incumbent was inducted.

By the end of the 18th century, the problem of collecting the increasingly bulky tithes meant that there was a growing number of payments made in cash, although the clergy were generally opposed to this, fearing that their income from tithes would decrease if it were not linked to the market value of the produce.

As a result, tithes were a constant source of tension between the clergy and the villagers, which increased during the early period of the 19th century due to the growth of nonconformity and industrialisation.

In 1836 the Whig government of the period made provision for a commutation scheme in statutory law. This scheme allowed for the voluntary commutation of tithes on the basis of a professional land valuation, which had been appraised by a body of commissioners.

To establish a norm as a basis for change, detailed maps were drawn up for each parish in which tithes were payable, showing each residence, garden and field, each being given a reference number. Accompanying the map was an apportionment list detailing against each numbered area the landowner, the occupiers, the state of cultivation (arable, pasture, waste, etc.,) acreage, and the amount of rent payable.

The amount of the tithe was calculated on the basis of the total value of tithes paid over the previous seven years and the rent charges were calculated and checked. Once agreed, the rent charge was then apportioned amongst the landholders depending on the acreage and quality of the land, the latter usually assessed by the state of cultivation of each field.

Between 1838 and 1854 tithe apportionment maps were drawn up for the 11,800 parishes in England and Wales where the tax was still levied.

The tithe award for Lower Withington[3] was carried out in 1848/9. The map and apportionment list, for the purpose of this book are split into four sections, North West, North East, South East and South West. On each map the residence has been highlighted, the accompanying list containing details taken from the apportionment and also, where known, information on occupation taken from the 1841 and 1851 census returns for Lower Withington.

The tithe award for Snelson[4] was carried out in 1847/8, the apportionment list being confirmed on 12 April 1848.

Extracted from the apportionment list are the various places of residence and also, where known, the occupation of the occupier taken from the 1841 and 1851 census returns for Snelson. Also extracted from the Snelson award is the location of various fields used to name the roads on the Seddon estate.

Extracts from the tithe map and apportionment list are reproduced by permission of the Cheshire County Record Office.

A complete summary of the tithe award including places of residence and land within Lower Withington and for Snelson is also shown. This summary includes all land and premises.

---

3   Cheshire County Record Office.
4   Cheshire County Record Office

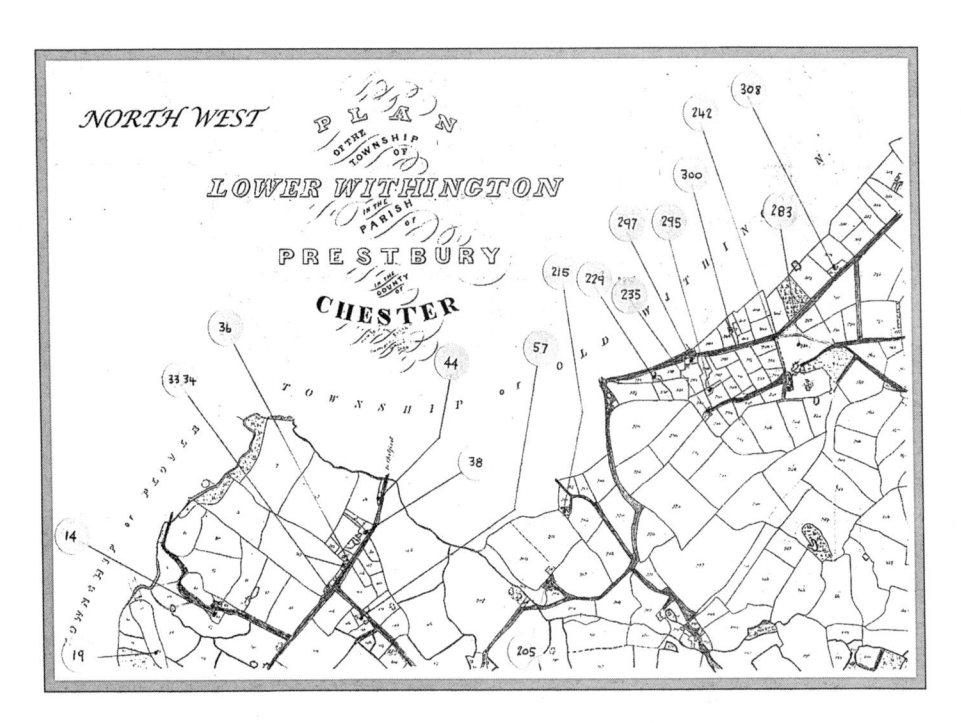

TITHE APPORTIONMENT LIST
North West Lower Withington 9 September 1849

Plan No.	Occupiers	Landowner	Description	Occupation	Quantities in Statute Measure A R P	Rent Charge £ s d
283		Bratt the late Rebecca Devisees Joseph Nightingale and Charles Baguley	Whitcroft Heath		5 2 21	- - -
242	George Barber	John Baskervile Glegg Esq.	Homestead and Garden		- - 30	- - 3
297	Hannah Foden	" " "	Moss House and Gardens		- - 34	- - 6
300	George Booth	" " "	Cottage and Garden		- 1 35	- 1 5
229	William Pennington	" " "	Homestead and Garden	Farm labourer	- - 35	- - 3
295	William Coups	" " "	Homestead and Garden		- - 39	- - 7
308	Peter Hough	" " "	Homestead and Garden	Stonemason	- 2 14	- 1 6
38	Nathaniel Morris	" " "	Homestead and Garden		1 1 5	- 2 10
57	William Beswick	" " "	Public House Buildings	Victualler and Farmer	- 1 16	- 1 -

293

36	Thomas Massey and James Bradley	"	"	"	Two Cottages	Both Farm labourers	-	-	34	-	-	8
205	Sarah Partington	"	"	"	Homestead and Garden	Age 75 no occupation	1	-	34	-	3	8
215	Joseph Norbury Jnr.	"	"	"	House and Garden	Farm labourer	-	-	26	-	-	5
34	James Bradley	"	"	"	Cottage and Garden	Farm labourer	-	1	25	-	1	2
33	Mary Steel	"	"	"	Cottage and Garden	Widow – no occupation	-	1	10	-	1	-
14	Samuel Bloar and Thomas Acton	"	"	"	Cottages and Gardens	Both Farm labourers	-	1	13	-	-	9
235	William Lockett	John Gray, James Lamb and James Hunt Esc., under the will			Homestead	Farm servant	-	1	6	-	-	6
44		Trustees of the road			Toll House and Garden		-	-	24	-	-	-
19		London and North Western Railway Co.			Railway		5	2	23	-	-	-

294

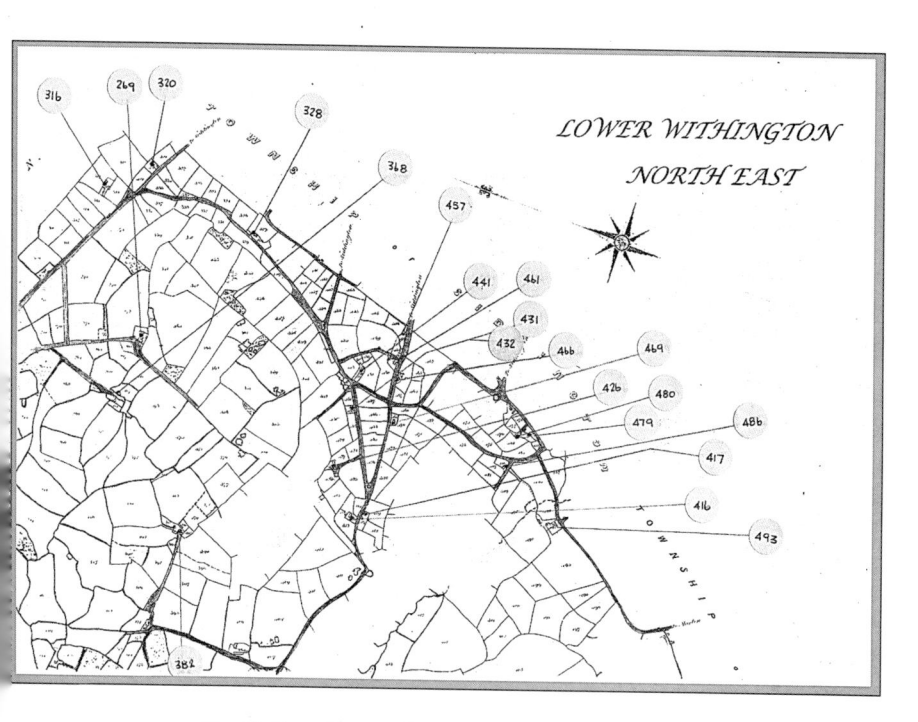

North East Lower Withington 9 September 1849

Plan No.	Occupiers	Landowner	Description	Occupation	Quantities in Statute Measure			Rent Charge	
					A	R	P	£	s	d
368	Noah Bennett	John Baskervile Glegg Esq.	Homestead, Garden and Fold	Farmer	1	-	24	-	1	9
316	Ralph Hall	"	"	"	Homestead and Garden	Shopkeeper	-	1	7	-	-	7
328	Joseph Slater	"	"	"	Cottage, Barn and Garden	Farm labourer	-	2	7	-	1	1
461	James Pimblott	"	"	"	Homestead	Farmer	-	2	32	-	3	8
431	John Upton and Daniel Davenport Junior	"	"	"	Cottage and Garden	Farmer Cow-leach	-	1	-	-	1	2
432	John Upton and Daniel Davenport Junior	"	"	"	Cottage and Garden		-	1	12	-	1	4
426	Samuel Blackshaw	"	"	"	Homestead and Garden		-	1	28	-	1	-
417	Peter Slack	"	"	"	House and Garden	Wheelwright	-	-	23	-	-	2
479	John Wood	"	"	"	Cottage and Garden	Farm labourer	-	-	39	-	-	9

295

480	Henry Johnson	"	"	"	Cottage and Garden	Farm labourer	-	1	2	-	-	10
382	Richard Bloar	"	"	"	Homestead and Garden	Farmer	-	2	10	-	-	6
269	John Deakin	"	"	"	Homestead and Orchard		-	2	6	-	1	8
466	Jane Worth	Joseph Rowbotham, Jane Worth and Hannah Benbow			Homestead and Garden	Widow – no occupation	-	-	28	-	-	-
416	Isaac Bailey	Isaac Bailey			House and Garden		-	1	-	-	-	6
320	John Davies	Samuel Dale			Homestead and Garden	Farm labourer	-	1	14	-	1	-
469	William Kennerley	John Kennerley			House and Garden	Farmer	-	-	29	-	-	8
441	Nathaniel Bradley	CRB Legh Esq.			Homestead and Road	Farm labourer	-	1	1	-	-	11
457	Ellen Potts	James Pimblott			House and Garden	Annuitant	-	1	27	-	1	6
493	John Stubbs	John Stubbs			Homestead and Garden	Farmer	-	2	26	-	1	10
486	John Capper	"	"		House and Garden	Farm labourer	-	1	8	-	1	-

296

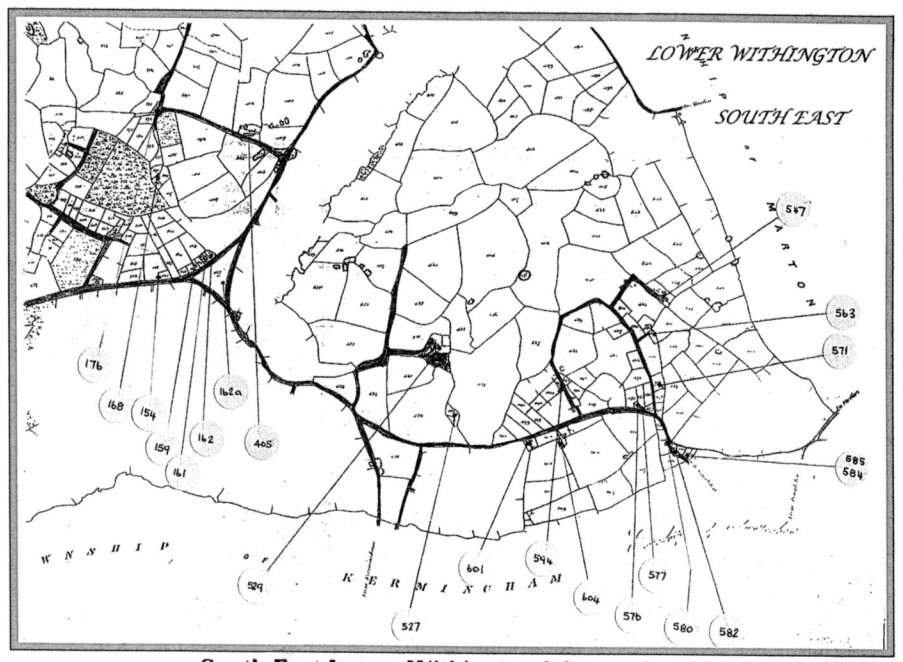

South East Lower Withington 9 September 1849

Plan No.	Occupiers	Landowner	Description	Occupation	Quantities in Statute Measure A R P	Rent Charge £ s d
547	Bradford Yarwood	Bratt the late Rebecca Devisees Joseph Nightingale and Charles Baguley	Homestead and Orchard	Farmer	1 1 -	- 3 -
604	William Eden	" " "	House, Bgs., Gardens and Orchard	Farmer	1 1 9	- 4 6
529			Welltrough Hall Outbuilding and Orchard		1 3 7	- 4 2
527	John Massey	John Baskervile Glegg Esq.	Cottage and Garden	Farmer	- 1 28	- 1 5
601	Charles Snelson	" " "	Homestead and Garden		- - 22	- - 4
594	John Barlow	" " "	House and Garden	Cordwainer	- - 32	- - 6
580	James Lomas	" " "	Homestead and Croft	Farm Labourer	- 2 35	- 2 -
571	Joseph Newton	" " "	Cottage and Garden	Retired Carpenter	- 1 20	- 1 -
176	Josiah Walkeley	" " "	Homestead and Garden		- - 25	- - 6
405	Charles Deakin	" " "	House, Garden and Fold		- -3 12	- 2 6

168	Mary Bradley	" " "	Cottage and garden	Dressmaker	-	- 35	-	-	4
576	Peter Wood	William Gallimore	Cottages and Garden	Farm labourer	-	- 13	-	-	-
577	William Gallimore	" "	Cottages and Garden	Farm labourer	-	- 24	-	-	-
584	Thomas Coppack	Mrs Bickerton	Cottage and Garden	Farm labourer	-	- 25	-	-	-
585	Peter Wood	" "	Cottage and Garden	Farm labourer	-	- 24	-	-	-
154	Joseph Slack	Thomas Hocknell	House and Garden	Wheelwright	-	1	3	-	1	-
582	Charles Slack	George Harrison	Trap Public House and Bgs.	Victualler	-	- 10	-	-	3
563	John Cliff	John Johnstone	Homestead and Garden	Farmer	-	3 12	-	2	3
161	Peter Burgess	Trustees of the Chapel John Foden, Thomas Worth, John Dorcey, Joseph Slack, Thomas Buckley and Richard Foden	House and Buildings	Joiner	-	- 25	-	-	-
162		"	Chapel		-	- 23	-	-	-
159	John Potts	Thomas Birtles executor of the late Peter Taylor	Homestead and Garden		-	-	-	-	-
162a		The Freeholders of the township of Lower Withington	Withington Heath		4	-	7	-	-

298

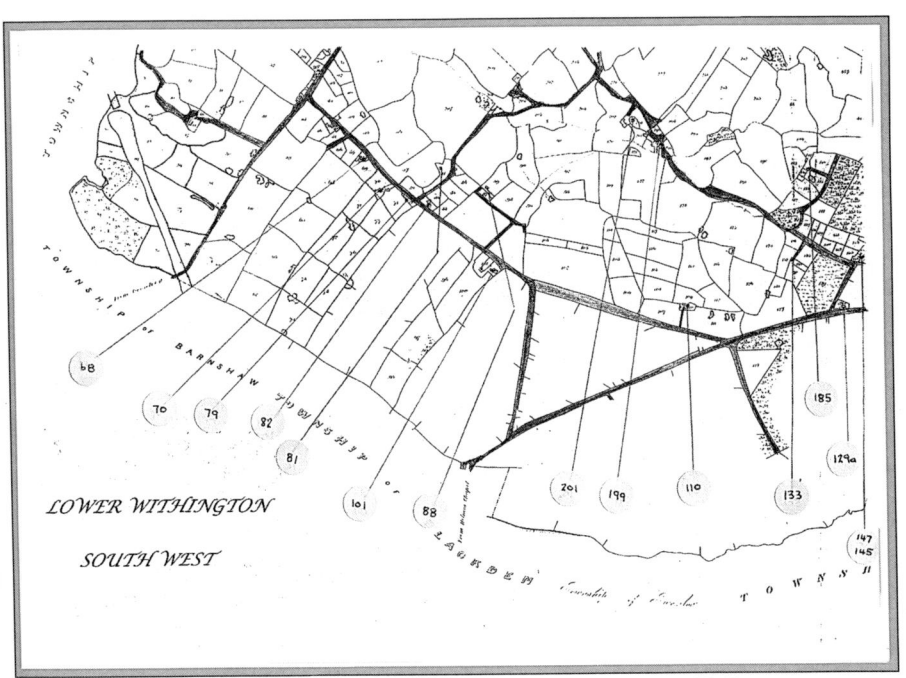

South West Lower Withington 9 September 1849

Plan No.	Occupiers	Landowner	Description	Occupation	Quantities in Statute Measure A R P	Rent Charge £ s d
68	Mark Garner	John Baskervile Glegg Esq.	Cottage and Garden		- - 34	- - -
82	George Hurstfield	" " "	House and Garden	Cordwainer	- - 35	- - 8
110	Jonathan Walkley	" " "	Homestead and Garden		- 1 3	- - 6
88	Joseph Norbury	" " "	Homestead and Garden	Tailor	- - 35	- - 8
201	Samuel Beswick	" " "	Homestead and Garden	Farmer	- 3 20	- 2 3
199	John Carter	" " "	Homestead and Garden	Farmer	- 2 35	- 1 2
81	John Buckley	" " "	Cottage, Garden and Croft	Farm servant	1 - -	- 3 -
133	Lucy Dooley	" " "	Homestead and garden	Farmer	- 1 18	- 1 2
185	James Jones	" " "	House and Garden	Carpenter	- 1 25	- 1 4
101	Thomas Benson and another	" " "	Homestead, Garden and Croft		1 - 34	- 3 8
129a	Daniel Davenport	Daniel Bradley	House and Garden		- 1 29	- 1 6

299

70	John Gilbert	John Gilbert	House, Garden and Orchard	Farmer	1	1	-	-	4	8
79	Samuel Warburton	"	"	Four Cottages and Garden	Cordwainer	-	1	5	-	-	-
147	Thomas Davies	Poor of the Township of Lower Withington	Two cottages and gardens	Farm labourer	-	2	18	-	1	-
145	John Davies	"	"	Cottage and Garden	Farm labourer	-	-	29	-	-	6

SUMMARY OF LOWER WITHINGTON TITHE AWARD

Landowners	Occupiers	Total Quantities A R P	Total Rent Charge payable to Impropriator £ s d	Names of Impropriators
Bratt the late Rebecca Devisees Joseph Nightingale and Charles Baguley	Bradford Yarwood William Eden	43 1 27 27 2 20	4 - - 3 - - 7 - -	The late Rebecca Bratt Devisees, Joseph Nightingale and Charles Baguley
Glegg John Baskervile Esquire	John Massey	222 2 34	22 14 5	John Baskervile Glegg Esquire
" "	Charles Snelson	2 3 24	- 7 -	" "
" "	John Barlow	4 1 3	- 9 11	" "
" "	James Lomas	1 2 12	- 3 9	" "
" "	Joseph Newton	- 1 20	- 1 -	" "
" "	John Gallimore	2 - 6	- 4 4	" "
" "	Josiah Walkeley	4 1 39	- 12 4	" "
" "	Noah Bennett	49 - 33	5 17 3	" "
" "	George Barber	3 2 23	- 6 3	" "
" "	Hannah Foden	- - 34	- - 6	" "
" "	George Booth	6 2 25	- 14 5	" "
" "	William Pennington	7 - 5	- 16 -	" "
" "	William Coups	9 3 20	1 - 6	" "
" "	Peter Hough	12 3 32	1 7 -	" "
" "	Ralph Hall	11 1 38	1 3 8	" "
" "	Joseph Slater	4 - 22	- 8 2	" "
" "	James Pimblott	28 - 16	3 7 1	" "
" "	John Upton and John Davenport	- 2 12	- 2 6	" "
" "	Nathaniel Bradley	2 3 35	- 5 10	" "
" "	Samuel Blackshaw	4 1 18	- 9 8	" "
" "	Peter Slack	6 2 18	1 - 2	" "
" "	John Wood	- - 39	- - 9	" "

301

Landowners	Occupiers	Total Quantities A R P			Total Rent Charge payable to Impropriator £ s d			Names of Impropriators
Glegg John Baskervile Esquire	Henry Johnson	5	3	11	-	16	10	John Baskervile Glegg Esquire
" "	Samuel Jepson	8	1	11	-	19	-	" "
" "	Richard Bloor	79	3	19	8	16	6	" "
" "	Nathaniel Morris	131	-	6	15	17	10	" "
" "	William Beswick	58	-	30	6	-	4	" "
" "	Mark Garner	3	1	19	-	9	-	" "
" "	Thomas Massey and James Bradley	-	-	34	-	-	8	" "
" "	George Hurstfield	3	2	27	-	8	2	" "
" "	Jonathan Walkeley	31	-	5	3	1	8	" "
" "	Sarah Partington	64	3	14	8	-	10	" "
" "	Joseph Norbury	3	3	4	-	9	2	" "
" "	Joseph Norbury Jnr.	2	1	27	-	6	-	" "
" "	Samuel Beswick	83	2	20	10	-	10	" "
" "	John Carter	85	2	28	9	18	10	" "
" "	John Buckley	1	-	-	-	3	-	" "
" "	James Bradley	-	1	25	-	1	2	" "
" "	Mary Steel	-	1	10	-	1	-	" "
" "	Samuel Bloor and Thomas Acton	-	1	13	-	-	9	" "
" "	Lucy Dooley	4	2	30	-	11	8	" "
" "	James Jones	16	1	39	1	-	8	" "
" "	Charles Deakin	47	3	0	5	14	10	" "
" "	John Deakin	112	1	11	12	14	10	" "
" "	Mary Bradley	2	1	20	-	5	-	" "
" "	In hand	134	-	25	7	5	6	" "
" "	Thomas Benson and another	1	-	34	-	3	8	" "
" "	Samuel Hulse	7	3	13	-	15	6	" "

302

Landowners	Occupiers	Total Quantities A R P			Total Rent Charge payable to Impropriator £ s d			Names of Impropriators
Glegg John Baskervile Esquire	Joseph Shaw	5	3	24	-	16	3	John Baskervile Glegg Esquire
" "	Samuel Worthington	7	-	4	-	13	8	" "
" "	Egerton Leigh Esquire	3	-	28	-	5	7	" "
" "	Mary Barber	1	-	-	-	1	9	" "
" "	Ann Bloor	2	1	33	-	7	-	" "
					133	0	0	
" "	Ann Bloor	3	-	-	-	9	6	Egerton Leigh Esquire
Joseph Rowbotham, Worth and Hannah Benbow	Jane Worth	5	0	25	0	77	6	" "
					1	7	-	
Bailey Isaac	In hand	5	3	18	-	17	-	Thomas Driver Esquire
Bickerton Mrs	Thomas Coppock and Peter Wood	-	1	9	-	-	-	" "
Bradley, Daniel	Daniel Davenport	-	1	29	-	1	6	" "
Dale, Samuel	John Davies	5	3	38	-	16	6	" "
Gallimore, William	In hand and Peter Wood	-	-	13	-	-	-	" "
" "	In hand	1	3	11	-	5	6	" "
Gilbert, John	In hand	27	2	35	4	--	-	" "
Gilbert, John	Samuel Warburton	-	1	5	-	-	-	" "
Gray, John	William Cockett	4	3	31	-	11	8	" "
Hocknell, Thomas	Joseph Slack	5	-	25	-	12	4	" "
Harrison, George	Charles Slack	1	-	5	-	3	6	" "
Johnstone, John	John Cliffe	26	-	14	3	5	-	" "
Kennerley, John	William Kennerley	8	-	15	1	4	6	" "
Legh C R B Esquire	Nathaniel Bradley	4	3	37	-	14	2	" "
Poor of the Township of Lower Withington	Joseph Slack	1	2	26	-	3	8	" "
	Thomas Davies	2	-	1	-	4	10	" "

Landowners	Occupiers	Total Quantities A R P			Total Rent Charge payable to Impropriator £ s d			Names of Impropriators
Poor of the Township of Lower Withington	John Davies	1	3	14	-	4	8	Thomas Driver Esquire
Parker Mrs	William Jenkinson	4	1	16	-	11	6	" "
Pimblett, James	Ellen Potts	-	1	27	-	1	6	" "
" "	John Wilkinson	3	3	13	-	11	-	" "
Stubbs, John	In hand	39	-	12	4	11	2	" "
" "	John Capper	-	3	23	-	2	-	" "
Trustees of the Chapel – John Foden, Thos. Worth, John Davies, Joseph Slack, Thos., Buckley and Richard Foden	Peter Burgess	1	3	1	-	5	6	Thomas Driver Esquire MD
" "	Elisha Gibbs In hand	-	1	6	-	-	-	" "
Trustees of Road the late Peter Taylor – Executore Thomas Birtles	In hand	-	-	24	-	-	-	" "
	John Potts	4	2	20	-	12	6	
The Freeholders of the Township of Lower Withington		4	-	7	-	-	-	" "
London and North Western Railway Company	In hand	5	2	23	-	-	-	" "
Public Roads and Waste		65	1	10	-	-	-	" "
		1598	2	12	20	0	0	

James Cawley
Thomas Dyson Firth

Note   Total quantities and rent charge include place of residence and land.

Contained in the archives at Cheshire County Record Office is a document entitled Lower Withington Tithe Assessment Old Arrears[5] but with no date shown. The CRO in their catalogue have given a date of c1813[6]. The document is reproduced as follows. It is interesting to note that the collector is to be allowed six pence in the pound on this assessment and is requested to pay the amount into the bank within 14 days.

LOWER WITHINGTON TITHE ASSESSMENT c1813
Old Arrears

Taken from information in Cheshire County Record Office ref: DDX 269/2

Landlord	Tenants	Landlords Arrears	Tenants Arrears	Received from E Leigh Esq. Balance of account £48.5.0
Egerton Leigh Esq	Jas Bayley	10.13.4		
"	Jas Barber	5.6.8		
"	Chas Harrison	5.0.0		
"	Wm Jackson	18.0.00		
"	Richard Leech	6.5.11		
"	Is. Lea	0.16.0		
"	I Vickers	1.0.0		
"	Thos Wood	0.8.0		
"	Saml Wright	0.16.0		
Thos Parker Esq	Peter Lowe	5.5.0		
"	Edw. Broadhurst	7.10.0		
"	John Clarke	3.5.0		
"	Wm Lowe, Robt Leech	3.5.0		
"	Joseph Stanley	2.10.0		

---

5 Ref: DDX 269/2

6 It is possible, based on the names listed, that the document is in fact later but certainly before 1840 as Thomas Parker, referred to in the document, died in 1840.

Landlord	Tenants	Landlords Arrears	Tenants Arrears	Received from E Leigh Esq. Balance of account £48.5.0
"	Wm Blackshaw	2.5.0		
"	Peter Slack	0.10.0		
"	Henry Dooley (Dean)	0.7.0		
"	Thos Brereton (Dean)	0.4.0		
Thos Foden Do.	Thos Foden	4.10.0		
Mr Hollins	Do. For W Hollins	3.6.8		
" Do.	Do as rent to Do.		1.13.4	
Thos Boden Do.	Thos Boden	0.15.0		
Do.	Thos Foden as tenant		0.7.6	
F Foden Do.	Do. For public house	0.10.0		
Do.	Widow Foden as tenant		0.5.0	
John Partington	John Partington	0.7.6		
Sold up	Geo. Lowe		0.11.0	
	Do. For landlord	1.2.6		
"	Wm Lowe	2.5.0		
Dead	Saml. Lockett	1.0.3		
	Lockett & Firkin	0.4.6		
	Locket & Barlow	0.6.0		
	Jas. Jepson	0.6.9		
Sold up	John Broadhurst		4.17.6	
	Jas. Bayley		5.6.8	
	Do. & Snelson	5.0.0		
	Chas Harrison		1.0.0	

Landlord	Tenants	Landlords Arrears	Tenants Arrears	Received from E Leigh Esq. Balance of account £48.5.0
Dead	Josh. Boden	5.0.0		
"	Do. For tenant		0.2.6	
	Richd. Leech		1.3.6	
"	Josh. Slack		0.4.0	
	Do. For landlord	0.8.0		
Himself	Peter Taylor	0.5.0		
Sold up	Geo Ward		1.15.0	
	Do for landlord	3.10.0		
	Wm Barber		3.0.10	
Dead	Thos. Barnes	0.6.9		
Dead	Kennerley		0.15.6	
"	" his landlord	1.11.6		
"	Chas Lockett		0.2.6	
	" his landlord	0.5.0		
Thos Parker Esq.	Saml. Stanley		2.14.4	
	Josh. Stanley		1.5.0	
Dead	Saml. Gallimore	0.6.9		
"	George Foden		0.6.0	
	" landlord	0.12.0		
E Leigh Esq.	Saml. Wright		0.3.0	*Insane*
	Thos. Davenport		0.8.4	
	" landlord	0.16.8		
Pauper	Wm Snelson		0.3.6	
Thos Parker Esq	Henry Dooley		0.3.6	

Landlord	Tenants	Landlords Arrears	Tenants Arrears	Received from E Leigh Esq. Balance of account £48.5.0
" *Dead*	Peter Lowe		0.7.0	
Himself	John Clarke	6.1.8		
Thos Parker Esq. *Dead*	Edwd. Broadhurst		3.15.0	
Himself	"	1.10.0		
	John Stubbs	1.9.3		
	Geo Worth	0.5.3		
Thos Parker Esq. *Dead*	Thos Brereton		0.5.3	Dead
	Randle Blackshaw	0.2.1		
	Nathl. Bradley	0.2.0		
	Mary Foden	0.5.3		Dead
Never signed	Edwd. Frith		0.19.0	
"	" his landlord	X5.12.6		
C Leigh Esq.	Thos Barber	---	---	
	John Weatherby		0.12.4	
	" landlord	1.5.0		Never Signed?
Dead	Wm Hockenhall	0.3.9		
Sold up.	Jas. Gee for self and landlord	2.5.0		
Dead	Jonah Gallimore	0.16.0		
	Thos. Richardson	---	---	
Thos Parker Esq.	Will. Blackshaw		1.2.6	*Dead*
"	Peter Slack		0.4.0	
Pauper	John Bradley		0.2.0	
	" for landlord	0.4.0		

Landlord	Tenants	Landlords Arrears	Tenants Arrears	Received from E Leigh Esq. Balance of account £48.5.0
Dead	Jasper Brentnall	--	--	
	For self & landlord	1.5.0		
	Geo Nixon		0.3.0	
	" for landlord	0.6.0		
Dead	Sam. Norbury		0.2.9	
Wright	" for landlord	1.0.2		
	Danl. Wakeley		1.5.0	
	" for landlord	9.3.4		
	Wm Mottershead		0.12.0	
	" for landlord	1.7.6		

South Ends

The collector is to be allowed six pence in the pound on this assessment and is requested to pay the amount into the bank within 14 days.

No.	Name	Dr. at % in the pound	Arrears	
49	Edward Broadhurst	1.10.0	1.10.0	*Not signed*
160	Peter Bayley	6.0.0	6.0.0	
29	Josh. Baguley	1.1.9	1.1.9	
8	John Barber	0.6.0	0.6.0	*2/-*
10	John Barlow	0.7.6	0.15.0	*Not signed*
40	John Byron	1.10.0	1.10.0	
100	Isaac Bowers	3.15.0	3.15.0	
12	Isaac Bayley	0.9.0	0.18.0	
10	John Bickerton	0.7.6	0.7.6	
52	Widow Bickerton	1.19.0	2.12.0	
6	Saml. Blackshaw	0.4.6	0.4.6	
84	Stephen Carter	3.3.0	3.13.6	
120	Thos Foden	4.10.0	4.10.0	
36	"	1.7.0	1.7.0	
8	Wm Gallimore	0.6.0	0.6.0	
11	Jas. Jones	0.8.3	0.8.0	
10	Nathl. Bradley	0.7.6	0.7.6	
10	Jas Jepson	0.7.6	0.7.6	
9	"	0.6.9	0.6.9	
24	Saml. Jepson	0.18.0	0.18.0	
27	Saml. Lockett	1.0.3	1.0.3	
360	John Massey	13.10.0	13.10.0	
70	Jas. Hague	2.12.6	2.12.6	
53	John Howard	1.19.9	1.19.9	
3	Thos Oakes	0.2.3	0.4.6	*Pauper*
5	Josh Slack	0.3.9	0.3.9	*Dead*
8	Peter Slack	0.6.0	0.6.0	
50	John Snelson	1.17.6	1.17.6	

No.	Name	Dr. at % in the pound	Arrears	
35	John Stubbs	1.6.3	1.6.3	
4	"	0.3.0	0.3.0	
6	Saml. Stanley	0.4.6	0.4.6	
12	Wm Stayley	0.9.0	0.9.0	
7	Wm Snelson	0.5.3	0.10.6	*Pauper*
7	Peter Taylor	0.5.3	0.5.3	
9	Saml. Taylor	0.6.9	0.9.0	
10	Wm Kennerley	0.7.6	0.7.6	
44	John Kennerley	1.13.0	1.13.0	
7	Jane Worth	0.5.3	0.5.3	
6	Saml Lockett	0.4.6	0.4.6	

SNELSON APPORTIONMENT LIST

Plan No.	Occupiers	Landowner	Description	Occupation	A	R	P
					\multicolumn{3}{c}{Quantities in Statute Measure}
32	James Ashton	James Ashton	House and Garden	Farmer	-	-	33
115	John Carter	Nathaniel Booth	House Building + Garden	Retired Farmer	-	-	30
87	Thomas Thompson	John Dixon Esq.	House + Garden	Cheesefactor	-	1	10
163	Thomas Bradford	" "	House + Garden	Farmer	1	2	12
136	Daniel Henshall	" "	House + Garden	Tailor?	-	-	20
135a	Ann Robinson	" "	Cottage + Garden	Laundress	-	-	16
135	William Wright	" "	Cottage + Garden	Agricultural labourer	-	-	17
46	Charles Coups	" "	Cottage + Garden	Agricultural labourer	-	-	38
45	Isaac Johnson	" "	Cottage + Garden	Agricultural labourer	-	-	38
43	Joseph Buckley	" "	House + Garden	Agricultural labourer	-	-	32
90b	John Roberts	" "	House + Garden	Butler	-	-	24
74b	John Steel and others	" "	Cottages + Garden		-	-	29
37		Freeholders of Snelson	Snelson Common		5	2	33
35a	Enoch Earlam	Joseph Gleave	Cottage + Garden	Hand Loom Weaver	-	-	16
34	Samuel Pearson	" "	Cottage + Garden		-	-	15
33a	John Johnson	" "	Cottage + Garden	Shoemaker	-	-	16
19a	William Gibson	William Gibson	House + Garden		-	-	25
81	Noah Critchley	Joseph Gleave	House Building + Yard	Farmer	-	2	20
133	(Thomas) Basford	Richard W Knowles	House + Garden	Farmer	-	2	30
1	William Wilkinson	Peter Leigh	Cottage + Garden		-	1	12
8	Samuel Forest	" "	Cottage + Garden		-	1	21
9a	Thomas Wood	" "	House + Garden		-	-	25
11	John Tomlinson	" "	Cottage + Garden	Agricultural labourer	-	1	8
10	John Read	" "	House + Garden		-	1	24
146		Manchester + Birmingham Railway Co.	Railway		6	2	0

Plan No.	Occupiers	Landowner	Description	Occupation	Quantities in Statute Measure		
20a		Trustees of Methodist Chapel	Chapel + Yard		-	-	25
69	Thomas Norbury	Thomas Norbury	House + Garden	Retired farmer	-	-	13
137	Peter Shingler	Overseers of the poor of the township of Snelson	Cottage + Garden	Farmer	-	-	14
137a	Peter Shingler	" " "	Cottage + Garden		-	-	14
55	Peter Shingler	" " "	House + Garden		-	3	15
158	James Whitlow	James Whitlow	House + Garden	Land Proprietor and farmer	-	1	4

Plan of the Township of Snelson
In the Parish of Rostherne
In the County of Chester

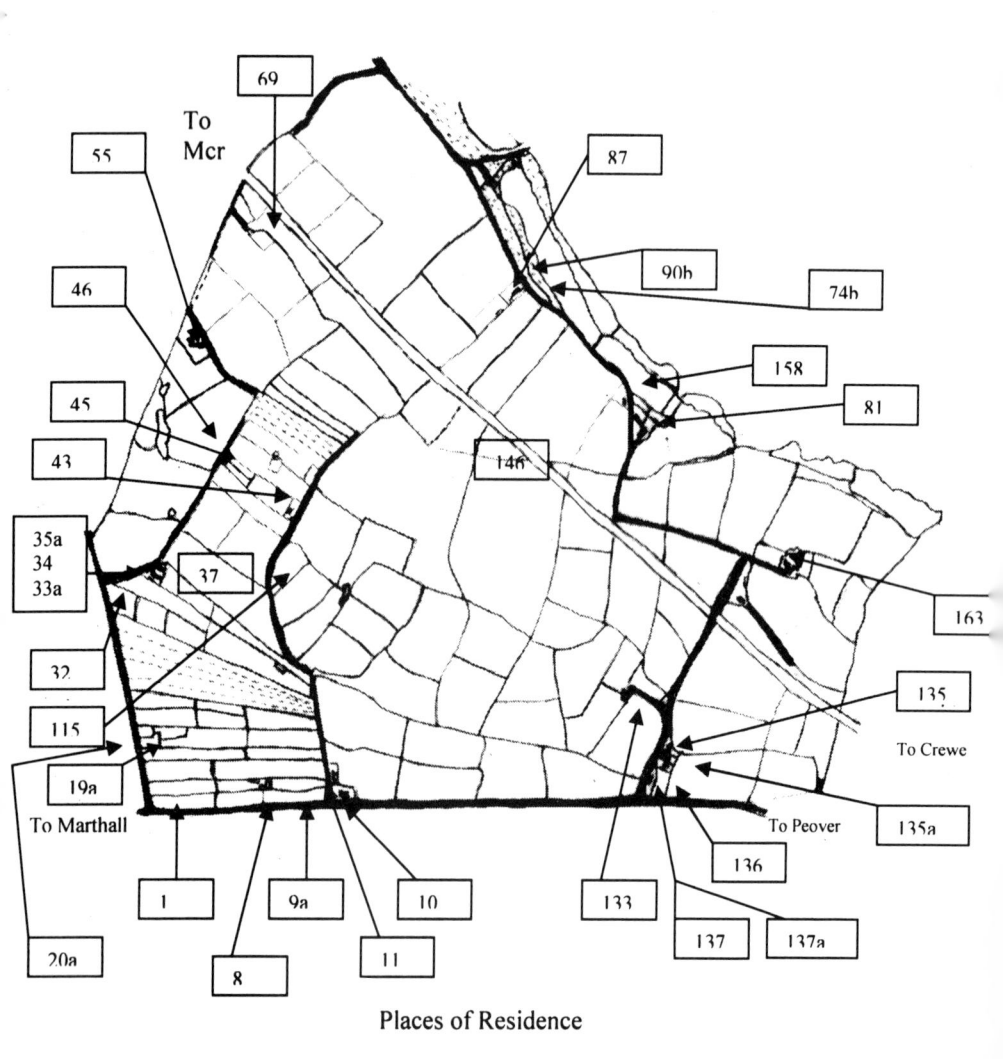

Places of Residence

314

Note - Included in the Snelson Tithe Award were the following references to fields used to name roads on the Seddon Estate, Chelford.

Plan No.	Landowner	Description	State of Cultivation	A	R	P
176	John Dixon Esq.	Drumble Field	Pasture	3	2	17
18	William Gibson	Chapel Croft	Pasture	-	1	23
19	William Gibson	Big Chapel Croft	Pasture	1	-	19
150	Joseph Gleave	Drumble Field	Pasture	2	1	20
130	Richard W Knowles	Barn Field	Meadow	2	2	-
73	Thomas Norbury	Barn Field	Arable	2	3	25
121	James Whitlow	Little Burnt Acre	Arable	4	3	6
120	James Whitlow	Higher Burnt Acre	Pasture	4	-	33
123	James Whitlow	Far Burnt Acre	Arable	3	3	28
122	James Whitlow	Near Burnt Acre	Pasture	3	2	24

Quantities in Statute Measure

Plan of the Township of Snelson
In the Parish of Rostherne
In the County of Chester

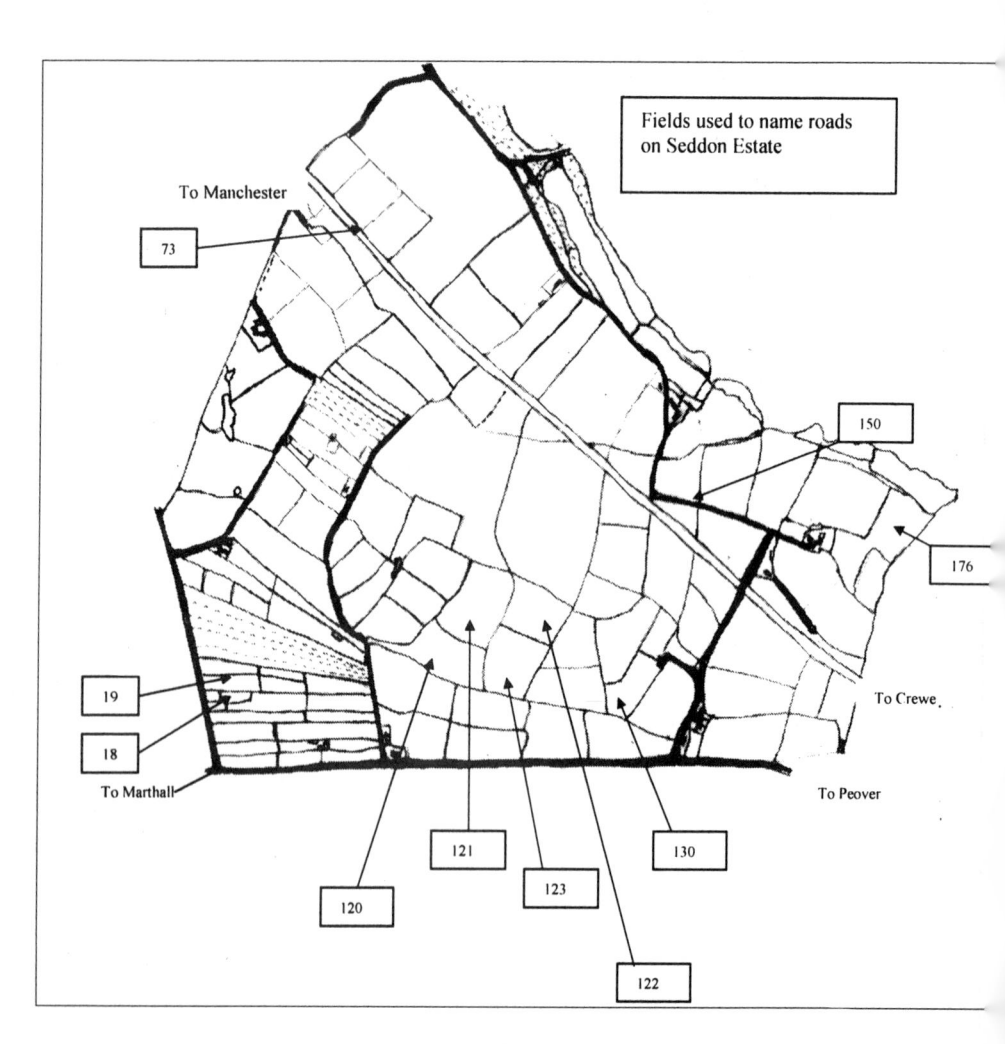

Fields used to name roads on Seddon Estate

To Manchester

73

To Marthall

19

18

150

176

To Crewe

To Peover

120

121

123

122

130

SUMMARY OF SNELSON TITHE AWARD
(Including all land and premises)

Landowners	Occupiers	Total Quantities A	R	P	Total Rent Charge payable to Appropriators £	s	d	Total Rent Charge payable to H Mainwaring – Lessee £	s	d
Ashton James	James Ashton	6	3	8	-	3	-	-	7	6
	Thomas Wood	1	1	37	-	-	9	-	1	-
Booth Nathaniel	John Carter	10	3	35	-	5	6	1	4	9
Dixon John Esquire	John Dixon Esquire	54	3	16	1	7	5	4	7	0
	Thomas Thompson	14	3	2	-	7	2	2	1	7
	James Whitlow	7	1	18	-	3	8	-	17	-
	Thomas Bradford	66	3	34	1	13	6	7	8	5
	Daniel Henshall & others	-	3	9						
	Joseph Buckley	2	2	10	-	1	3	-	5	2
	John Johnson	-	-	25						
	John Carter	3	1	7	-	1	8	-	7	7
	James Ashton	2	1	35	-	1	9	-	4	2
	John Ford	-	2	34	-	-	4	-	-	9
	John Roberts & others	-	1	13						
	Isaac Johnson	-	1	32	-	-	2	-	-	4
	William Rush	5	3	30	-	3	-	-	13	8
Freeholders of Snelson		5	2	33						
Glover Joseph	Enoch Earlam	1	-	34	-	-	7	-	2	6
	Samuel Pearson									
	John Johnson	-	-	31						
Gibson William	William Gibson	3	1	9	-	1	7	-	4	6
Gleave Joseph	Noah Critchley	49	1	20	1	4	8	5	14	5
Knowles Richard W	Basford	35	3	23	-	18	-	3	19	3
Leigh Peter	Peter Leigh	8	-	29	-	4	1	1	-	3
	William Wilkinson	1	1	20	-	-	8	-	2	11
	Samuel Forrest	1	3	1	-	-	10	-	3	-
	Thomas Wood	1	1	3	-	-	7	-	2	5

Landowners	Occupiers	Total Quantities			Total Rent Charge payable to Appropriators			Total Rent Charge payable to H Mainwaring – Lessee		
		A	R	P	£	s	d	£	s	d
	John Tomlinson	-	1	8	-	-	2	-	-	7
	John Read	6	2	31	-	3	4	-	15	3
Manchester and Birmingham Railway Company		6	2	-	-	3	3	-	15	6
Methodist Chapel Trustees of		-	-	25						
Norbury Thomas	Thomas Norbury	32	1	31.	-	16	2	3	4	8
Overseers of the Poor of Snelson	Peter Shingler	-	-	28						
Peover Free School Trustees of	Peter Shingler	28	3	31	-	14	5	3	3	2
Whitlow James	James Whitlow	50	-	8	1	5	0	5	13	8
	John Dixon Esquire	-	3	37	-	1	-	-	2	2
	Public Roads	12	2							
		426	3	27	10	3	6	43	4	-

TITHE AWARD – CHELFORD

Apportionment of the rent charge in lieu of tithes in the Township of Chelford in the Parish of Prestbury in the County of Chester.

Whereas an Award of Rent charge in lieu of tithes in the Township of Chelford in the Parish of Prestbury in the County of Chester was on the first day of January in the year one thousand eight hundred and forty eight confirmed by the Tithe Commissioners for England and Wales of which award with the schedule therein comprised the following is a copy.

To all men to whom these present shall come I, John Job Rawlinson of Graythwaite in the County of Lancaster Barrister at Law, send greetings.

Whereas I have been duly appointed and sworn as Assistant Tithe Commissioner according to the provisions of the Act for the commutation of Tithes in England and Wales and have also duly been appointed as such Assistant Commissioner to ascertain and award the sums to be paid by way of rent charge instead of the tithes of the Township of Chelford in the Parish of Prestbury and County of Chester.

And Whereas I have held divers meetings for that purpose in the said Parish and near to the said Township of which meetings due notice was given for the information of the Landowners and Tithe owners of the said Township.

And Whereas I have fully considered all the allegation and proofs handed to me at the said meetings by all parties interested and have myself made all enquiries concerning the premises which appeared to be necessary.

And Whereas I find that the Glebe Lands of the Incumbent Curate of Chelford Chapel situate within the said Township and containing by estimation eleven acres and two roods are by prescription or other lawful means absolutely exempt from all Tithes whether the same be in the occupation of such Curate himself or not.

And that all the Tithes arising or accruing upon in respect of all the residue of the Lands of the said Township except a certain Farm and Lands thereof of which (*name not stated*) Furnival of the Town of Ashby de la Zouch in the County of Leicester Spinster is the owner and George Beech and William Lockett are the occupiers have been absolutely merged and extinguished in the Freehold and Inheritance of the Land from which the same arose and were issuing.

And that the said Lands of the said (*name not stated*) Furnival are subject to payment of all manner of Tithes in kind and contain by estimation one hundred and seventeen acres of which thirty acres are cultivated as arable land and all the rest is meadow or pasture.

And Whereas I find that John Dixon of Astle in the said county of Chester Esquire is Impropriator of all the Tithes arising or accruing upon or in respect of all the Lands of the said Township which remain subject to payment of Tithes.

And Whereas I have estimated the clear annual value of the Tithes of the said Township in the manner directed by the said Act for the Commutation of Tithes in England and Wales.

Now know ye that I the said John Job Rawlinson in the exercise of all the powers vested in me as such Assistant Commissioner as aforesaid do make this my Award of and concerning the premises that is to say

I Award that the annual sum of Eighteen pounds by way of rent charge subject to the provisions of the said Act shall be paid to the said John Dixon his heirs and assigns instead of all the Tithes arising or accruing upon or in respect of all the lands of the said Township which remain subject to the payment of tithes.

The aforegoing rent charge to be in lieu not only of all Tithes payable in kind but also in lieu of all moderate composition real and prescriptive and customary payments if any for Tithes payable in respect of all or any lands of the said Township of Chelford which are subject to payment of Tithes or in respect of the produce.

In Testimony whereof I have hereunto set my hand this eighteenth day of December in the year of our Lord one thousand eight hundred and forty seven.

        Signed

            J J Rawlinson

Now I Thomas Proudman of Sandbach in the County of Chester Attorneys clerk having been duly appointed valuer to apportion the total sum awarded to be paid by way of rent charge in lieu of Tithes amongst the several Lands of the said Township of Chelford do hereby apportion the rent charge as follows.

      Gross rent charge payable to the Tithe owner in lieu of Tithes for the Township of Chelford in the Parish of Prestbury in the County of Chester Eighteen Pounds.

Value in Imperial Bushels and decimal parts of an Imperial Bushel of wheat, barley and oats viz.

	Price per Bushel	Bushels and decimal parts
Wheat	7 0¼	17-09198
Barley	3 11½	30-31379
Oats	2 9	43-63036

LANDOWNER	OCCUPIER	NO. on Plan	DESCRIPTION	QTY Statute Measure A R P	Payable to Impropriator £ s d
Miss Frances Furnival	William Lockett	1	Mr Brookes part of house and Garden	1 - 37	4 10
" "	" "	2	Tenants part of house and garden and outbuildings	3 11	3 3
" "	" "	8	Part of Gibb Croft	3 3 1	15 2
" "	" "	8a	Part of Gibb Croft	4 - 23	16 9
				9 3 35	2 - -
" "	George Beech	3	Barn Croft	3 1 4	10 1
" "	" "	4	Near Dale Field	10 - -	1 10 3
" "	" "	5	Far Dale Field	9 2 6	1 9 3
" "	" "	6	Higher Fulshaw meadow 7.0.0 Gravel and other pits 0.3.18	7 3 18	1 2 2
" "	" "	7	Lower Fulshaw meadow	7 1 12	1 2 10
" "	" "	9	Great Creek Moss	13 3 -	2 2 3
" "	" "	10	Wheat on Gorsty Moss 7.0.14 Pit on Gorsty Moss 0.1.0	7 1 14	1 2 6
" "	" "	11	Little Creek Moss and Furlong	9 2 20	1 9 6
" "	" "	12	Hade or Hedge Meadow	2 - 13	6 5
" "	" "	13	Cross Croft	1 - 20	3 5
" "	" "	14	Town Field	5 2 15	19 2
" "	" "	15	Mere Clough	4 2 6	13 11
" "	" "	16	New Hobbarding	3 - 39	9 11
" "	" "	17	Hobbarding Meadow	2 - 31	6 9

LANDOWNER	OCCUPIER	NO. on Plan	DESCRIPTION		QTY IN Statute Measure			Payable to Impropriator		
					A	R	P	£	s	d
Miss Frances Furnival	George Beech	18	Lower Hobbarding 3 2 0 Pits - 1 20	}	3	3	20		11	11
" "	"	19	Horse Hobbarding		4	1	11		13	3
" "	"	20	Intake		5	-	5		15	5
" "	"	21	Allotment on Chelford Heath Arable 1 2 28 Pitts 1 3 25	}	3	2	13		11	-
		22	Share of occupation Lanes		-	2	33	-	-	-
					105	-	-	16	-	-
			Green and Waste		3	3	27			

WMP note   The apportionment map (see next page) was based on an earlier map of 1789 and therefore may not be completely accurate at the time of the Tithe Award.

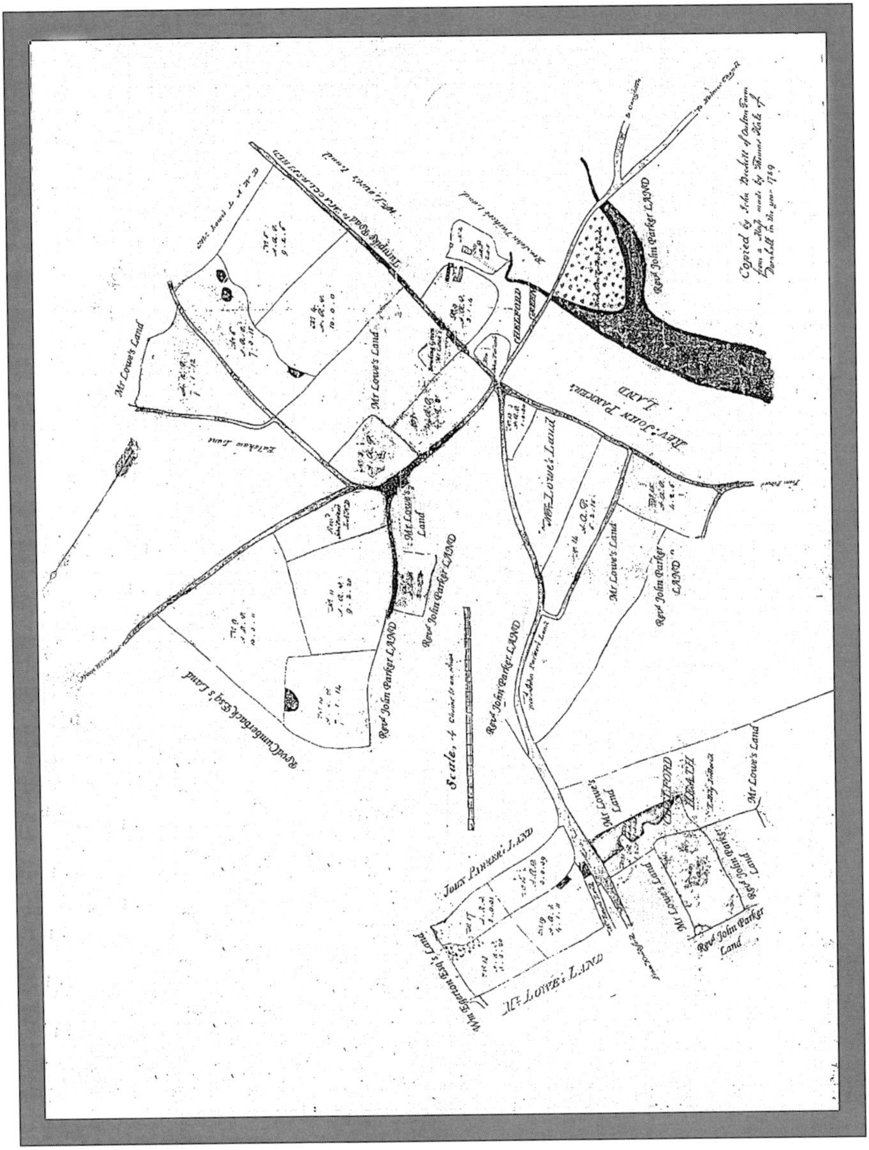
Mr Lowe's Land
Revd John Parker LAND
Rev. John Parker's LAND
Revd Cumberbach Esq's Land
John Parker's LAND
Mr Lowe's LAND
HEATH

SOLDIERS WHO DIED IN THE GREAT WAR
CHELFORD, SNELSON, LOWER WITHINGTON AND OLD WITHINGTON

The list below includes soldiers who were born and/or resided in Chelford, Snelson, Lower Withington and Old Withington.

       b = born   e = enlisted   r = residence

ALLAN   William Peter, b. Chelford, Cheshire, e. Keighley, Yorks, r. Patricroft, Lancs, 16042, PRIVATE, killed in action, France & Flanders, 29/07/16, Duke of Wellington's (West Riding Regiment), 10th Battalion.

ANTROBUS   William, b. Chelford, Cheshire, e. Manchester, r. Wilmslow, Cheshire, 28244, PRIVATE, Died of wounds, France & Flanders, 28/04/17, Royal Scots Fusiliers, 1st Battalion.

BINNERSLEY   Thomas William, e. Congleton, Cheshire, r. Lower Withington, Cheshire, 37347, PRIVATE, Killed in action, France & Flanders, 10/01/17, FORMERLY 4152, CHESHIRE REGT., Lancashire Fusiliers, 9th Battalion.

BLACKHURST   Frank, b. Lower Withington, Cheshire, e. Macclesfield, Cheshire, 18003, PRIVATE, Killed in action, France & Flanders, 07/06/17, Cheshire Regiment, 10th Battalion.

BLACKHURST   Fred, b. Lower Withington, Chelford, Cheshire, e. Macclesfield, Cheshire, 18002, PRIVATE, Killed in action, France & Flanders, 04/10/17, Cheshire Regiment, 1st Battalion.

BOON   Richard, b. Chelford, Cheshire, e. Macclesfield Cheshire, 18287, PRIVATE, Killed in action, France & Flanders, 24/05/15, Cheshire Regiment, 2nd Battalion.

BOWERS   William, e. Manchester, r. Chelford, Cheshire, 205417, PRIVATE, Killed in action, France & Flanders, 22/04/18, FORMERLY 251373, MANCHESTER REGIMENT, Sherwood Foresters (Nottinghamshire and Derbyshire Regiment), 1st Battalion.

BRADLEY   Nathan, b. Siddington, Cheshire, e. Wilmslow, Cheshire, r. Chelford, Cheshire, 277624 PRIVATE, Killed in action, France & Flanders, 30/05/17, Manchester Regiment, 2/7th Battalion.

CALLWOOD   Herbert, b. Chelford, Cheshire, e. Knutsford, Cheshire, r. Chelford, 31509, PRIVATE, Killed in action, France & Flanders, 18/02/17, FORMERLY 952, CHESHIRE, YEO., Prince of Wales's Volunteers (South Lancashire Regiment), 2nd Battalion.

CARTWRIGHT Walter, b. Old Withington, Cheshire, e. Manchester, 25120, GDSN., Died of wounds, France & Flanders, 26/09/16, Grenadier Guards, 4th Battalion.

EDEN   George, b. Chelford, Cheshire, e. Manchester, Lancs., r. Manchester, 5966, SERGT., Killed in action, France & Flanders, 28/09/15, Queen's Own Cameron Highlanders, 1st Battalion.

GREENWOOD   Wilfred, b. Dewsbury, Yorks., e. Manchester, r. Chelford, Cheshire, B/201475, RIFLEMAN, Killed in Action, France & Flanders, 30/10/17, FORMERLY, M/2/103435, R.A.S.C., Rifle Brigade (The Prince Consort's Own), 1/28th Regiment.

HARROP   William, b. Chelford, Cheshire, e. Altrincham, r. Hale, 202143, PRIVATE, Died of wounds, France & Flanders, 24/10/18, Cheshire Regiment, 1st Battalion.

HATTON   William, b. Nether Alderley, Cheshire, e. Chester, r. Chelford Cheshire, 31050, PRIVATE, Killed in action, France & Flanders, 10/04/18, FORMERLY 36845, CHESHIRE REGT., Prince of Wales's Volunteers (South Lancashire Regiment), 2nd Battalion.

HULSE   John, b. Stoke, Staffs, e. Leeds, r. Chelford, Cheshire, 4885, RIFLEMAN, Died of wounds, France & Flanders, 10/11/14, King's Royal Rifle Corps, 1st Battalion.

MORRIS   Thomas James, b. Chelford, Cheshire, e. Macclesfield, r. Crewe, 203116, PRIVATE, Died, Egypt, 03/11/18, FORMERLY 3799, 7TH CHES. REGT., Welsh Regiment, 4/5th Battalion.

MOSS   Fred, b. Chelford, Cheshire, e. Bury, Lancs, 1798, PRIVATE, Died of wounds, France & Flanders, 08/08/16, Lancashire Fusiliers, 2/5th Battalion.

MOSTON   Leonard, b. Wimperley? (Timperley?), Cheshire, e. Knutsford, Cheshire, r. Chelford, Cheshire, 6670, PRIVATE, Died, Solonika,

	29/09/18, FORMERLY, 15904, CHES. REGT., Army Cycle Corps.
NORBURY	Edwin, b. Chelford, Cheshire, e. Stockport, Cheshire, 45001, PRIVATE, Killed in action, France & Flanders, 13/07/17, FORMERLY, 422. C.C., NORTHUMBERLAND FUSILIERS, 19th Battalion (Tyneside Pioneers).
POPE	Walter, b. Stockport, Cheshire, e. Manchester, r. Chelford, Cheshire, 2119, L/CPL, Killed in action, Gallipoli, 04/06/15, Manchester Regiment, 1/7th Battalion.
POTTS	Frederick, b. Chelford, Cheshire, e. Manchester, 27201, PRIVATE, Died of wounds, Home, 17/05/17, Royal Scots (Lothian Regiment), 12th Battalion.
SHORE	Thomas, b. Snelson, Chelford, Cheshire, e. Wilmslow, Cheshire, 49628, PRIVATE Died of wounds, France & Flanders, 02/10/18, Royal Inniskilling Fusiliers, 1st Battalion, FORMERLY 28000, SOUTH LANC. REGT.
SLATER	Sam, b. Lower Withington, Cheshire, e. Northwich, r. Lower Withington, T4/090358, DVR., Killed in action, France & Flanders, 29/04/18, Royal Army Service Corps.
STREET	Abraham, b. Chelford, Cheshire, e. Wilmslow, Cheshire, 36183, PRIVATE, Died, Home, 06/05/16, Cheshire Regiment, 14th Battalion.
TOMLINSON	William Henry, b. Chelford, Cheshire, e. Stockport, 38661, PRIVATE, Died of wounds, France & Flanders, 28/05/18, King's Own (Royal Lancaster Regiment), 2/5th Battalion.
VENABLES	John, b. Chelford, Cheshire, e. Manchester, r. Chelford, 24529, PRIVATE, Died of wounds, France & Flanders, 18/10/18, FORMERLY 37308, WELSH REGT., Machine Gun Corps, (Infantry).
VENABLES	William, b. Chelford, Cheshire, e. Stockport, Cheshire, 15603, PRIVATE, Killed in action, France & Flanders, 09/07/16, FORMERLY 17380, CHES. REGT., Prince of Wales's Volunteers (South Lancashire Regiment), 8th Battalion.

WOOD   George, b. Lower Withington, Cheshire, e Siddington, Cheshire, 33190, PRIVATE, Died, Mesopotamia, 29/06/17, Cheshire Regiment, 8th Battalion.

WYATT   John, e. Marylebone, Middlesex, r. Chelford, Cheshire, 72910, PRIVATE, Died of wounds, France & Flanders, 29/06/18, FORMERLY 354670, LONDON REGT., Sherwood Foresters (Nottinghamshire and Derbyshire Regiment), 2nd Battalion.

In addition to the above soldiers the following officers died

2/Lt, Geoffrey Christian Lansdale WALSH – Cheshire Regiment, Killed in action 22/06/17.

The above information has been extracted from the CD ROM Soldiers Died in the Great War and has been reproduced by permission from The Naval and Military Press Limited.

Authors note: - There appears to be a number of instances above where a change of Regiment occurred. It was a practice during the First World War for officers and presumably soldiers also, to change regiment to a regiment serving at the front. This may explain certain changes shown in the records.

Additional information can be obtained through the internet visiting http://yard.ccta.gov.uk.

For example the following information was extracted for Samuel Slater born Lower Withington, Cheshire, enlisted Manchester and resided Lower Withington, died 29th April 1918.

In Memory of
S SLATER
Driver T4/090358
19th Reserve Park, Army Service Corps
who died on
Monday, 29th April 1918.

Commemorative Information

Cemetery:	GODEWAERSVELDE BRITISH CEMETERY, Nord, France
Grave Reference/ Panel Number:	I. S. 7.
Location:	Godewaersvelde is a village near the Belgian border, about 16 kilometres south-west of Ieper (in Belgium), and is half-way between Poperinge (in Belgium) and Hazebrouck (in France). The British Cemetery is a little east of the village.
Historical Information:	The British Cemetery was begun in July 1917, between the Battle of Messines and the Battles of Ypres, when three Casualty Clearing Stations were moved to Godewaersvelde. The 37th and the 41st buried in it until November 1917, and the 11th until April, 1918; and from April to August, 1918, during the German Offensive in Flanders, Field Ambulance and fighting units carried on the burials. A considerable French Plot was made on the terrace at the higher end of the Cemetery in May and June, 1918, but the graves were removed after the Armistice. Five graves of soldiers of the 110th Brigade, Royal Field Artillery, in Plot II, Row AA, were brought in from a point nearer the Mont des Cats. There are now over 900, 1914-18 war casualties commemorated in this site. The cemetery covers an area of 2,644 square metres and is enclosed by a brick wall. The Cross and the War Stone are on a grass terrace on the South-Western side. In May 1953 the graves in Godewaersvelde Churchyard (an airman, a Canadian and two unknown Indian soldiers) were concentrated into this Cemetery.

In Memory of
Driver S SLATER
19th Reserve Park, Army Service Corps
who died on Monday, 29th April 1918.

Remembered with honour
GODEWAERSVELDE BRITISH CEMETERY, Nord, France.

In the perpetual care of
the Commonwealth War Graves Commission

Commemorative Medallion presented to the family of Samuel Slater

POPULATION STUDY – CHELFORD AND DISTRICT

Prior to the implementation of formal census recording in the 19th century, calculating the population of towns and villages was a somewhat 'hit and miss' exercise. The very early records such as the Domesday Survey of 1086 and the Hundred Rolls were not census returns as we know them today and dealt mainly with landowners. The medieval records such as Poll Tax and Hearth Tax and the later Window Tax and Land Tax returns are valuable sources of information but only list the main person in the family liable for tax. In any case, the taxation system was so abused by the population that the figures should only be used as rough estimates. Similarly the Muster Rolls compiled at various times of national crisis only listed men available to fight in the event of a war. They were totally inaccurate relative to population calculation for specific villages due to omissions and the common practice of those eligible for service paying other members of the population to carry out their military duty.

There are, however, a number of local population studies instigated mainly by local vicars or landowners. These listings were usually carried out by the village worthies or church officials. If these records have survived they are usually found in or with the Parish Registers. As far as can be established there are no such records for Chelford and district, although there is an analysis of the christenings in Chelford church from 1720 to 1820 listing the number of males and females christened both in wedlock or illegitimate (see later). The list was probably drawn up by the Rev. Thomas Mawdesley who was the incumbent of St John the Evangelist Church, Chelford at that time.

Two major factors, which have affected the development of the village of Chelford, are the building of the railway in the early 1840's and the Seddon housing estate towards the end of the 20th century; otherwise the population of the district has remained constant. The 1841 census shows an increase reflecting the number of workers who moved into the district at that time to construct the railway. The railway workers appear in the census in groups, indicating that they probably lived on farms rather than in one central camp.

The 1871 Census returns contain information describing each village and covering the area of each census.

- CHELFORD -   Name of Enumerator – Mr Nehemiah Thornley

The whole of the Township of Chelford including Astle Hall and Park, the Vicarage and Chapel, Manor House and Farm, Public House, Smithy and a School well attended. There is a first class station on the L + NW Railway, the Dixon Arms being near and several good cottages occupied by the Railway Officials and Coal Agent. The boundary adjoins Marthall in the Bucklow Hundred on the North side and Nether Alderley on the South. The Macclesfield and Knutsford Turnpike Road goes through the Township.

- SNELSON -   Name of Enumerator – Mr Nehemiah Thornley

The whole of the Township of Snelson in the Parish of Rostherne (Bucklow Hundred) including the residences of several gentlemen in business. The farms are scattered over the township. The L + NW Railway passes through, the Chelford station being near. The boundary is direct from Peover to Nether Alderley.

- LOWER WITHINGTON -   Name of Enumerator – Mr John Hurstfield

The whole of the Township of Lower Withington.

- OLD WITHINGTON -   Name of Enumerator – Mr Edwin Jepson

The whole of the Township of Old Withington including Withington Hall, Piggot's Hill Farm on the way to Siddington, Lapwing Hall Farm and a Smithy near the Hall. The Boundary adjoining Siddington to the South East and Lower Withington and Chelford to the North. The Manchester and Wilmslow and Congleton Turnpike Road passes through the Township.

CHRISTENINGS IN CHELFORD CHURCH FROM 1720 TO 1820

Years	M	F	Illegitimate M	Illegitimate F	Total
1720-1729	41	55	5	2	103
1730-1739	73	76	3	1	153
1740-1749	62	80	7	4	153
1750-1759	90	81	6	7	184
1760-1769	94	79	4	5	182
1770-1779	53	52	-	3	108
1780-1789	83	61	3	3	150
1790-1799	78	98	7	3	186
1800-1809	107	108	13	7	235
1810-1819	159	123	1	7	290
	840	813	49	42	1744

< 1653 >   < 91 >

< 1744 >

5.5% were illegitimate in line with the National figure of 5 to 7% for this period.

Source of reference p182/15/1 Cheshire County Record Office

Using estimates from Hearth Tax returns for 1664[1], the census returns for the 19th century, information from the Office of National Statistics and the Parish Fact File for the Borough of Macclesfield, the following chart showing the number of people resident can be drawn up.

	Chelford	Old Withington	Lower Withington	Snelson	Total
1664[1]	250	295	295	45	885
1811	188	178	584	126	1076
1821	184[2]	164	615	137	1100
1831	186	191	584	136	1097
1841	201	192	780[3]	199	1372[4]
1851	260[5]	189	570	169	1188
1861	241	170	578	158	1147
1871	273	161	544	159	1137
1881	313	155	576	120	1164
1891	341	129	551	185	1206[6]
1901	374	121	578	170	1243
1911	384	148	533	201	1266
1921	355	136	495	187	1173
1931	341	125	531	200	1197
1951	392	-[7]	661	160	1213
1961	437	-	590	184	1211
1971	431	-	507	154	1092
1981	532	-	526	142	1200
1991	1246[8]	-	489	151	1886

- Notes relative to Population Table previous page –

1. *4.5 people per household is the accepted figure for mid 17th century though I consider this figure to be somewhat high. The figures shown are therefore to be taken as estimates only.*

2. *Estimated by author.*

3. *The 1841 Census for Lower Withington includes a Police Officer, Thomas Hulse, age 26, born in Cheshire. However, neither Thomas Hulse nor any other Police Officer is recorded in the 1851 Census. The Cheshire Police was not formed until 1856 and prior to that date the organisation of the Police Force was on an 'ad hoc' basis (Chelford had a Policeman in 1851). Perhaps the Policeman in Lower Withington in 1841 was required to control the large number of Railway Workers in the village at that time.*

   From 1851, Chelford had a regular Policeman and as no reference is made to a Policeman in any of the later Lower Withington census returns for the second half of the 19th century, presumably the Chelford Policeman also had a responsibility for adjoining villages.

4. *Included in this figure were 81 persons classified as Railway Labourers or Excavators, of these 16 were in Chelford, 2 in Old Withington, 34 in Lower Withington and 29 in Snelson, all presumably working on the construction of the railway throughout the district. The census for Lower Withington refers to Excavators as well as Railway Labourers, probably when the enumerator changed the occupational description and not because there was an occupational difference. A number of Excavators/Railway Labourers, particularly those resident in Lower Withington, had their families with them. The Snelson record also shows Thomas Collins, age 45, Railway Contractor. Perhaps he was in charge of the construction.*

5. *Sharp increase in Railway Workers living in new property built near Chelford Station.*

6. *By analysing the 1891 Census returns in relation to the number of households the following comparison can be shown.*

	Population	No. of Households	No of Persons Per household
Chelford	341	63	5.4
Old Withington	129	25	5.2
Lower Withington	551	116	4.7
Snelson	_185_	_41_	_4.5_
Total	1206	245	4.9

7. From 1951 Old Withington and Lower Withington were amalgamated as Withington. From 1981 the designation became Lower Withington in Macclesfield County District.

8. Sharp increase as a result of the Dixon Drive development.

By analysing the 1881 Census it is possible to establish the names of people born in Chelford who moved away and by 1881 were living elsewhere.

For example, the list below[α] shows people born in Chelford who by 1881 were resident in Staffordshire.

Name	Relation To head	Occupation	Marital State	Age	Place of residence Census Date
Eliz S Bagnall	Step-dau	Scholar	U	8	Russell St., Castle Church
(Head of house = Thomas Barratt, Railway Engine Driver)					
Wm C Stanley	Servant	Drapers' Porter	U	22	Greengate Street Stafford St Mary
(Head of house = Sarah A Brookfield Draper)					
John Cooks	Head	Coal Miner	M	38	Wood Street, Audley
(Married to Jane born Haslington)					
Mary Ann Wall	Wife	Wife	M	38	Red Street, Crown Inn, Audley
(Head of House = William Wall, Innkeeper)					
Thomas Slack	Head	Labourer	M	58	Near St Lukes Church, Mow Cop
(Married to Ann = born Mow Cop)					
Victoria Rice	Dau	Scholar	U	13	Sheppard Street, Stoke

α   Taken from W K Plant's private papers.

(Head of house = Alice Mary Rice, wife of Railway Agent)						
Kate M Harden	Dau	-	U	10	Burton Road, Streathay	
(Head of house = Wm Hamden (Harden), Retired Railway Guard						
Grace Leigh Bennett	Niece	Wife of Rector of Thyrburgh	M	32	Rectory, Hamstall, Ridware	
(Head of house = Humberston Shepwith, Rector of Hamstall Ridware)						
Margaret McGrath	Dau	Scholar	-	3	Rookery Lane, Aldridge	
(Head of house = Thomas McGrath, Agricultural Labourer age 49)						
(Head of house = Thomas McGrath, Agricultural Labourer age 25)						
note – Two head of house shown both Thomas McGrath – possibly father and son.						
Jesse Wright	Head	Coachman	M	42	New Road, Buddulph	

(Married to Eliza, born Biddulph)

Likewise a total of 78 persons born in Chelford had moved to Lancashire by 1881, presumably in a number of cases to find suitable employment, and were shown in the census of that year. A further study would be required to establish why this movement took place pre 1881. Very little migration took place from Chelford to counties other than Staffordshire and Lancashire.

The 1881 Census also shows that 135 persons born in Chelford had moved to other area of Cheshire, the majority within a ten-mile radius of Chelford. The complete list is as follows.

Name	Age	Place resident on day of Census	Name	Age	Place resident on day of Census
Eliza Baguley	63	Bollin Fee	Sarah Barley	22	Stockport
Henry Beeston	34	Poynton	Henry Bell	7	Snelson
Wm H Bentley	6	Blackden	Randle Blackshaw	67	Kermincham
Betty Blackshaw	21	Allostock	Wm Bloor	42	Mottram St Andrew
Joseph Bloor	16	Mottram St Andrew	Annie Bloor	14	Mottram St Andrew
Ann Booth	73	Romiley	Olive Bostock	72	Sandbach
James Bracegirdle	23	Macclesfield	Sarah Bradbury	56	Tytherington

Name	Age	Place resident on day of Census	Name	Age	Place resident on day of Census
William H Bradbury	28	Chorley in Macclesfield	Edward Broadhurst	78	Birkenhead
John Broadhurst	69	Altrincham	Edward Broadhurst	63	Bollin Fee
Joseph Broadhurst	60	Pownall Fee	Richard Broadhurst	55	Snelson
Sarah Brocklehurst	62	Birtles	Joseph Brookes	17	Old Withington Hall
Elizabeth E Buckley	25	Nether Alderley	Elizabeth Burgess	28	Chorley in Macclesfield
Charles Burgess	17	Henbury	William H Burgess	8	Nether Alderley
Margaret Callwood	38	Altrincham	Ann Casey	79	Cheadle
Margaret Clarke	5	Snelson	Lily J Clarke	3	Snelson
William Cooper	81	Macclesfield	Edwin Cooper	85	Macclesfield
Charles Coops	76	Snelson	George Coops	71	Toft
Ann Coppack	54	Chester	James Dale	23	Nether Alderley
Sarah E Davies	15	Snelson	Sarah Dean	83	Macclesfield
Eliz Debman	48	Dunham Hall	Martha Drinkwater	49	Nether Knutsford
Leigh Eden	14	Nether Alderley	George Foden	44	Macclesfield
John Ford	63	Great Warford	Mary Ford	50	Snelson
Thomas Ford	47	Fulshaw	Joseph Ford	40	Rudheath
Edwin Ford	28	Snelson	Mary E Ford	17	Snelson
May Ford	5	Snelson	John Forrest	75	Great Warford
Maria Foster	29	Latchford	Ada Hale	13	Witton
Henry H Halford	32	Birkenhead	Ann Hankey	25	Nether Knutsford
Ann Harrison	68	Castle	George S Helling	18	Walgherton
Mary Henshaw	75	Fulshaw	Daniel Henshaw	65	Stockport
Eliz Henshaw	64	Handforth	Mary A Henshall	27	Macclesfield
Alfred Holding	12	Lower Withington	Wm Holt	36	Henbury
Mary Ann Hope	27	Ollerton	Ellen Hope	12	Handforth

338

Name	Age	Place resident on day of Census	Name	Age	Place resident on day of Census
Isabella Howarth	17	Macclesfield	Edith Hughes	23	Runcorn
Thomas Jennings	71	Macclesfield	Fanny Jennings	24	Great Warford
Eliza Jennings	21	Great Warford	Mary Ann Knight	32	Poynton
Mary Barton Leech	64	Nether Peover	Wm T Lesther	50	Witton
John Lockett	48	Stockport	Mgt Loundes	23	Stockport
Alice M Massey	4	Peover Superior	Arthur Wm McConnel	16	Church Hulme
Wm Ashton McConnel	14	Church Hulme	Ethel Alice McConnel	12	Church Hulme
Katharine L McConnel	10	Church Hulme	Elenor Georgina McConnel	7	Church Hulme
Thomas Mellor	57	Willaston	Wm Mellor	42	Fulshaw
Samuel Mellor	39	Pownall Fee	George Mellor	35	Stockport
John Mellor	28	Bradwell	James Moor	29	Ollerton
Jassey Moore	3	Peover Superior	Hannah Mullard	27	Stockport
Wm Nixon	15	Marton	Wm Nixon	14	Macclesfield
Eliz Nixon	9	Macclesfield	Bertha Norbury	10	Ashley
Walter Norbury	6	Ashley	Eliz C Norbury	4	Ashley
Frederick Oldham	2	Newton in Ashton Under Lyne	Frances Ann Peers	9	Mere
John W Peers	8	Mere	Eliz Q Peers	3	Mere
Betty Perrin	72	Timperley	Jessie Phillip	17	Macclesfield
Frank Phillips	14	Wincle	Jane Potts	57	Adlington
Henry M Rackham	26	Butley	Joseph Roberts	40	Nether Alderley
Sarah Ann Roberts	29	Chorley in Macclesfield	Mary Spooner	51	Macclesfield
Jane Steel	45	Marthall	John Steel	16	Marthall
Isabella Steel	6	Marthall	George Wm Steel	5	Marthall
Arthur Steel	25	Over Knutsford	Emelia J Steel	21	Chorley Hall

Name	Age	Place resident on day of Census	Name	Age	Place resident on day of Census
Wm Steel	19	Old Withington Hall	Harriet Steel	18	Gawsworth
Sarah Stelfox	53	Lymm	Jane Street	55	Peover Superior
Mary Ellen Tomlinson	1	Snelson	Betty Torkington	76	Poynton
Rebecca Unwin	65	Sutton	Edwin Walker	47	Stockport
Amelia Warburton	30	Monks Coppenhall	Ann Waters	58	Macclesfield
Eliz Whittaker	70	Capesthorne	Amelia Whittaker	23	Hale
Alex Wilson	12	Nether Alderley	Isaac Witch	39	Nether Knutsford
Sarah Wood	44	Adlington	Hannah Wood	37	Bollin Fee
Ann Worthington	46	Northenden	Charles Worthington	40	Cheadle
Annie Worthington	22	Over Alderley	Cath Wragg	63	Peover Superior
Hannah Wragg	37	Sutton	Joseph Wright	30	Sutton
Wm Wright	27	Sutton			

AND FINALLY

THE MYSTERIOUS TUNNELS

Whilst researching this book a number of villagers have mentioned a supposed tunnel between Chelford Church and the nearby Manor House, dating back to the 13th Century when Chelford village, the mill, the landed property and rents of Asthull and Wythington were given by Robert de Worth to the monks of Chester.

Near the Church, in the grounds of the Manor House, was a tithe barn and it is probable that this barn was used to receive and store the tithes paid in produce.

It is said that the Manor House was once a monastery and that a tunnel led from the house to the church, so that the monks had a quick and easy access for prayers. The farm to the east of the Manor House is still called Abbey Farm.

However, as nearly every village has similar stories and, considering that the land between the Manor House and the church would have been boggy and not suitable for the digging of tunnels, the story was discounted.

That was until Stephen Mills, together with others when installing a new oil tank for the church, discovered evidence of not one possible tunnel but two, one beneath the present vestry and the other in the form of seven arches in the south side of the Church, constructed in Georgian style brick with access underneath the font.

So the question is, what, when and why were these tunnels constructed?

Were they there when the church was rebuilt in 1776 and were they part of the original church?

Were they part of the new Georgian church and subsequently lost by building extensions when the tower and spire at the west end were added in 1840?

Were they for drainage purposes?

Is there any biblical significance in seven arches?

If any readers have any suggestions please contact one of the authors of this book.

FURTHER READING – CHELFORD

Books

ANON

    Chelford Parish Hall Souvenir and Quotation Book
        Published by W Keith Plant 22 Chapel Croft, Chelford
    Reproduction of Quotations submitted by the then villagers of Chelford on the occasion of the opening of Chelford Parish Hall, 30 July 1908.

CHESHIRE FEDERATION OF WOMEN'S INSTITUTES

    The Cheshire Village Book
        Countryside Books, Newbury & CFWI, Chester 1990
    Snippets of history and reminiscence from Chelford on p.55-56

COMBER, WINIFRED M; GIBSON, Lesley & HAWORTH, Dorothy (Editors)

    Cheshire Village Memories II
        Cheshire Federation of Women's Institutes, 1961
    Similar to the preceding work but contains information not found in it. Chelford is covered on p.38-40

DEPARTMENT OF THE ENVIRONMENT

    List of Buildings of Special Architectural or Historic Interest.
        Borough of Macclesfield, Cheshire. (Parishes of Chelford... Withington). DOE, 1984
    Chelford is covered on p.1-5. Gives approximate date, architect where known, and features of merit.

DODGSON, J McN

    The Place-Names of Cheshire. Part I:
    Macclesfield Hundred
        Cambridge University Press, 1970
    Chelford is covered on p.75-77. Useful for origins of names of places, fields, streets etc. For more detailed study, needs to be used in conjunction with Part V (place-name elements).

EARWAKER. J P

East Cheshire: Past and Present. Volume II
Author, 1880
Account of Chelford on p.360-370.

PLANT W KEITH + MAVIS PLANT + ROGER ROYCROFT + JULIA SLATER

Chelford A Cheshire Village
Published by the Authors 1999
325p of information, historical memories etc., including details of past and present activities in the village. Produced to commemorate the Millennium, the 225th anniversary of the rebuilding of the village church and the retirement of the then (Rev. John Ellis) Vicar of St John the Evangelist Church, Chelford for 18 years.

PLANT W KEITH + MAVIS PLANT

Chelford Evacuees Reunion Saturday 15 July 2000
Published by the Authors 2000
The story of Second World War Evacuees from Gorton, Manchester and East London, including memories of Chelford by the evacuees and an edited version of Chelford School Log Book during the war years.

PLANT, W KEITH

Chelford: 19th Century. A Demographic and Historical Study.
W Keith Plant, 22 Chapel Croft, Chelford, near Macclesfield, SK11 9SU, 1995
Statistical information from censuses, tithe apportionments and trade directories, plus details of specific areas of the village and the families resident there during the period.

ROYCROFT, ROGER

Reflections upon the Chelford Railway Disaster of 22nd December 1894.
1994

Extremely detailed account of the accident, inquest, inquiry and final report. Includes details of killed and known injured.

Articles

ANON

"The Homes of Cheshire – 28. The Manor House, Chelford"
Cheshire Life, August 1952, p.18-20 (Part I);
September 1952, p.21-23 (Part II)
History of the building, plus description of interior, barn and gardens.

"Tales from an Edwardian Lady's Garden"
Cheshire Life, December 1985, p.43
Brief biography of Frances Eliza Crompton, writer of books for children. She was born at Butley and resided at Chelford.

"Chelford Evacuees"
Living Edge, September 2000, p32.
Story of Chelford Evacuees Reunion including picture of evacuees.

BELL, T HEDLEY

"Mere Water: Farmwood Pool, Chelford"
Cheshire Life, July 1977 p.42-43
The pool was formed as a result of sand extraction. The article describes birds and other wildlife of the area, turned into a nature reserve by its owner, Eric Crosby.

BRACK, ALAN

"Chelford Chronicle"
Cheshire Life, January 2000 – p117-121.
Review of Publication 'Chelford – A Cheshire Village'
Including pictures of village.

KENNETT, CECIL

"The Charm of Chelford"
Cheshire Life, May 1965, p.61, 63
Light-hearted view of the paradox that, although Chelford figures prominently on signposts, it is surprisingly difficult to find.

LONGDEN, GEORGE

"Sporting Chelford"
Living Edge, April 2000, p61.
Some notable events in the Life of a Cheshire Village including a review of 'Chelford – A Cheshire Village'.

NILAND, KIRSTIE

"To Market to Market"
Cheshire Life, November 1997 – p60-63.
Reflections on Chelford and it's activities and including review of 'Reflections Upon The Chelford Railway Disaster' by Roger Roycroft.

O'NEILL, PATRICK

"To Market, To Market"
Cheshire Life, July 1995, p.36-36
A look at Chelford Market, the biggest market for hay, straw and calves in the country.

SHARPLEY, ROBIN

"Turn Off and Tarry: Chelford"
Cheshire Life, November 1975, p.80-81, 83-84
Profile of the village, concentrating on the Manor House, other buildings, and the market.

SKINNER, TONY

"First Class Service"
Cheshire Life, March 1995, p.150-151
Ruth and Bernard Annikin, who run the post office and general stores at Chelford.

STEAD, ROBERT

"Lawn Order"
Cheshire Link, July 1989, p.36-41
The garden at Astle Farm, which at the time of writing held the Cheshire County Farm Gardens championship.

WALSH, AUDREY CECIL & BRILL, BARBARA

    "Relatively Speaking"
        Cheshire Life, January 1986, p.33
    Miss Walsh recounts memories of her mother, children's writer, Frances Eliza Crompton, who lived at Larchwood, Chelford.

WRIGHT, BEN

    "Breeding in Cheshire"
        Cheshire Life, May 1963, p.60-61,63
    Visit to Mr Blair Gething of Chelford, breeder of racing pigeons.

YARWOOD, DEREK

    "Sand Storm"
        Cheshire Life, December 1988, p.88-91
    Fight by residents of Chelford and neighbouring villages to prevent the granting of planning permission for further sand extraction in the area.

18th Century Dovecote on Withington Hall Estate now used as boiler house.